BALLYHOO!

BALLYHOO!

The Roughhousers,
Con Artists, and
Wildmen
Who Invented
Professional Wrestling

Jon Langmead

UNIVERSITY OF MISSOURI PRESS
Columbia

Copyright © 2023 by
The Curators of the University of Missouri
University of Missouri Press, Columbia, Missouri 65211
Printed and bound in the United States of America
All rights reserved. First printing, 2023.

Library of Congress Cataloging-in-Publication Data

Names: Langmead, Jon, 1975- author.
Title: Ballyhoo! : the roughhousers, con artists, and wildmen who invented
    professional wrestling / Jon Langmead.
Description: Columbia : University of Missouri Press, [2023] | Series:
    Sports and American culture / Adam Criblez, series editor | Includes
    bibliographical references and index.
Identifiers: LCCN 2023024871 (print) | LCCN 2023024872 (ebook) | ISBN
    9780826222992 (hardcover) | ISBN 9780826274953 (ebook)
Subjects: LCSH: Wrestling--United States--History. | Wrestling--Social
    aspects--United States. | Wrestlers--Social conditions--United States.
Classification: LCC GV1198.12 .L36 2023 (print) | LCC GV1198.12 (ebook) |
    DDC 796.8120973--dc23/eng/20230705
LC record available at https://lccn.loc.gov/2023024871
LC ebook record available at https://lccn.loc.gov/2023024872

♾™ This paper meets the requirements of the
American National Standard for Permanence of Paper
for Printed Library Materials, Z39.48, 1984.

Typefaces: Minion and Impact

SPORTS AND AMERICAN CULTURE
ADAM CRIBLEZ, SERIES EDITOR

This series explores the cultural dynamic between competitive athletics and society, the many ways in which sports shape the lives of Americans, in the United States and Latin America, from a historical and contemporary perspective. While international in scope, the series includes titles of regional interest to Missouri and the Midwest. Topics in the series range from studies of a single game, event, or season to histories of teams and programs, as well as biographical narratives of athletes, coaches, owners, journalists, and broadcasters.

For Steve Yohe.

"I have never seen an audience that didn't get a bigger kick out of being present at a battle that is obviously a fake, than out of a dozen honest endeavors."

—Paul Gallico, 1933

"You can't expose anything nowadays. Rather, I mean you can expose and expose and what does it get you?

—Jack Curley, 1931

Contents

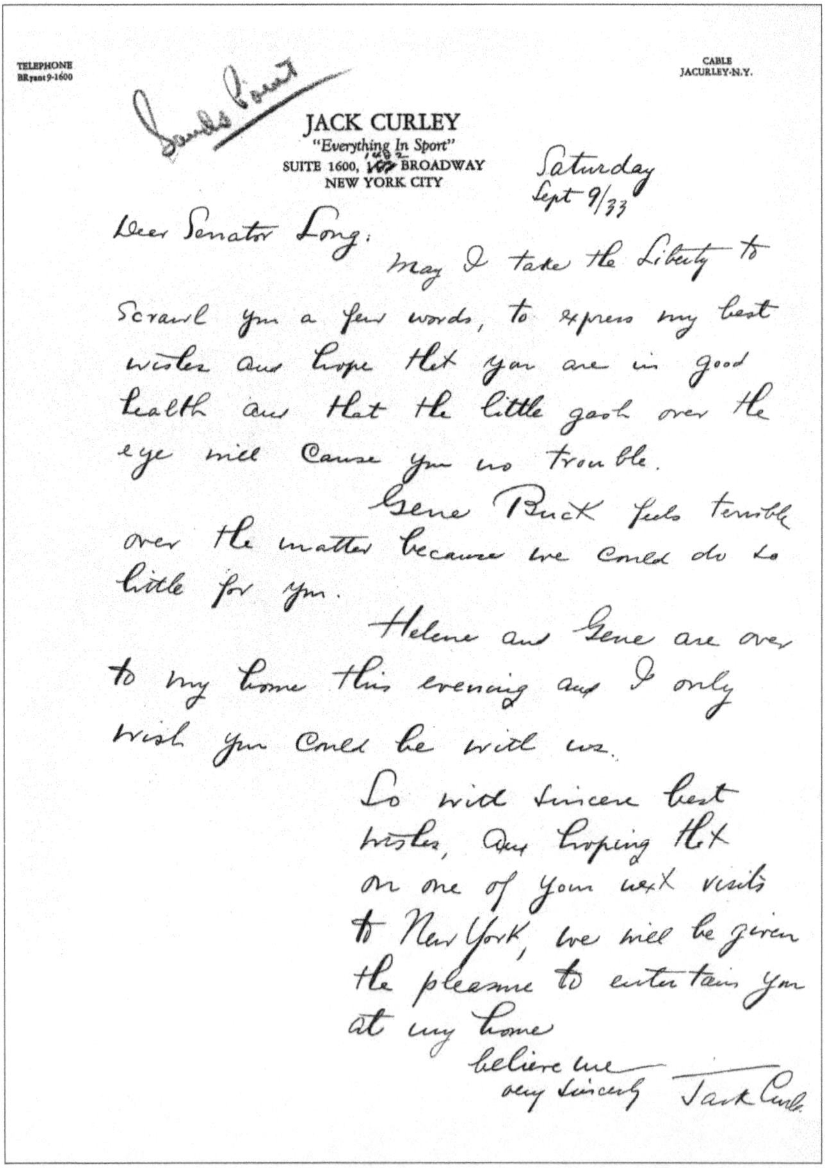

TELEPHONE
BRyant 9-1600

CABLE
JACURLEY-N.Y.

Sands Point

JACK CURLEY
"Everything In Sport"
SUITE 1600, 1482 BROADWAY
NEW YORK CITY

Saturday
Sept 9/33

Dear Senator Long:

May I take the Liberty to scrawl you a few words, to express my best wishes and hope that you are in good health and that the little gash over the eye will cause you no trouble.

Gene Buck feels terrible over the matter because we could do so little for you.

Helene and Gene are over to my home this evening and I only wish you could be with us.

So with sincere best wishes, and hoping that on one of your next visits to New York, we will be given the pleasure to entertain you at my home

believe me
very sincerely Jack Curley

FIGURE 1. Letter from Jack Curley to Huey Long, September 9, 1933. Courtesy of the History Center, Port Washington Public Library, Port Washington, New York.

Prologue

The Kingfish Takes a Powder

IT WAS ALMOST midnight on Saturday, August 26, 1933, when Louisiana Senator Huey P. Long stumbled out of the washroom of the Sands Point Bath and Tennis Club, well past the number of Sazeracs he normally let himself drink and deep into a night he was already going to regret. He was bleeding from his forehead and looking to make a quick exit.

Called the "Kingfish" for his breezy blend of a conman's silver tongue and a dictator's iron fist, Long was a political force either on the rise or in decline, depending on the angle from which he was being observed. Equipped with a quick wit and a booming voice, in just fifteen years, he'd risen from serving as a member of Louisiana's Railroad Commission to being elected as one of its United States senators. Famous for his loud promises to smash the corruption choking America, he was eyeing a challenge to Franklin Roosevelt for the Democratic Presidential nomination in 1936. But throughout his career, accusations of staggering graft, abuses of power, and voting fraud had trailed him. A scandal at a high-priced weekend party in one of the wealthiest parts of New York was the last thing he needed.

The Sands Point Bath and Tennis Club was located in Great Neck, an exclusive neighborhood on the tip of the Port Washington peninsula, home to mansions owned by Guggenheims, Vanderbilts, and Goulds. Overlooking Manhasset Bay from three sides and lounging across several acres of what came to be called "The Gold Coast," it featured a saltwater pool, bathing cabanas, and separate landings for yachts and seaplanes. Long had gone to Great Neck to visit his friend Gene Buck, the wildly successful songwriter and longtime producer of the Ziegfeld Follies. One of Buck's songs, "That Shakespearian Rag," had been referenced a decade earlier by T. S. Eliot in *The Waste Land*. Buck was one of the most prominent members of what writer Judith Goldstein called Great Neck's "potent mix of merchant princes, robber barons, artists, writers, Broadway moguls, actors, actresses, and journalists," which had also included, at different times, Ring Lardner, Lillian Russell, Groucho Marx, Basil Rathbone, and Eddie Cantor.[1] F. Scott Fitzgerald had moved there in 1922 and used it as his setting for *The Great Gatsby*. "[Great Neck]," he wrote, "is one of those little towns springing up on all sides of New York which are built especially for those who have made money suddenly but have never had money before."[2]

Leery of the enemies he imagined gathering all around him, Long normally traveled with bodyguards. For his trip to Great Neck, though, he had decided to leave them back in Manhattan. The evening started with drinks at Buck's estate. Prohibition was in its last days but was still the law of the land, though you'd have never known it by visiting Great Neck, where all-night, booze-soaked parties were far from uncommon. Egged on by one of Buck's guests, Long demonstrated how to make Sazeracs, a potent rye whiskey and absinthe cocktail popular in New Orleans. While he tended to be cautious about drinking in public, out among Great Neck's rolling hills and saltwater breezes, he made an exception and finished off several himself.[3]

Upon arriving at Sands Point, he posed for a photograph with Buck and his friends. From there, they hurried to their seats for the floor show. After dinner, Long made his way into the crowd to mingle among the more than six hundred guests. Intoxicated and riding high, he wheeled around the room, loudly insulting the partygoers, the staff, and the musicians. Stories would later circulate that he went behind the bar to show the bartender how to fix a drink and that he'd gone from table to table, eating sticks of buttered asparagus off people's plates. It was said that after taking food from one woman, he told her, "I'll eat this for you. You're too fat already."[4]

He returned to Buck's table around 11 p.m., looking for the restroom. He probably thought his evening was winding down. Had things ended there, his performance would have passed without a mention other than whispered comments from horrified guests about the boorish interloper from Louisiana. Instead, it was just the middle of what would become a very bad night for him.

Long stayed in the restroom for close to thirty minutes. When he came out, he was holding a napkin over his swiftly swelling left eye and bleeding from his forehead. Taking a hold of Buck, he said, "Gene, let's get out of here. I'm on the spot."[5]

In a panic, Buck grabbed his friend and fellow Great Neck resident Jack Curley, a reliably sober fifty-seven-year-old sports promoter with thin white hair, bulbous eyes, lips like a grouper, and a wide, red face that looked, as one reporter noted, "as if it were being constantly pressed against an invisible pane of glass."[6] Buck pulled him into the front room. "My God, Jack," he said. "Huey has been socked!"[7]

During a late-night emergency, there were few people more useful than Jack Curley. He'd been managing emergencies his whole life and had yet to let one get the better of him. A well-known figure in American entertainment since the turn of the century, by 1933, Curley's name had become synonymous with professional wrestling. The monthly wrestling shows he presented at Manhattan's Madison Square Garden drew sizable audiences, and on any night of the week, you could find his athletes working arenas all along the East Coast. How honest any of it was, though, was anyone's guess.

Curley hurried Long back into the restroom, washed the blood off his face, and gave him a cold towel to try to stop his eye from swelling. He then ushered Long and Buck into his car and drove into town to find a doctor. When they couldn't turn one up, Curley and Buck packed Long into a taxi and sent him back to Manhattan. "You should have heard him whining and blubbering like a kid," Curley would later say. "Why, he was scared stiff even after Gene Buck and I got him away."[8]

Long rushed out of New York the next day on a train to Wisconsin. He never made a formal complaint related to whatever had happened to him. Word of it, he naively hoped, would stay at Sands Point.

Unflattering stories about the evening began seeping into newspapers by Monday. "I'll not discuss what happened on Long Island," an edgy Long told the reporters who lobbed questions at him as he stepped off the train in Milwaukee. "I won't even say I was there recently or that I came here directly from there."[9] Next, he issued a formal statement to the Associated Press: "I have been repeatedly threatened," he hinted darkly. "Any number of warnings have been given, even by column writers, that such a thing would happen to me sooner or later. I was lucky to have escaped with such trivial injury and am grateful." Three or four men had attacked him from behind, he claimed. Though he was uncertain as to just how many assailants there had been, he was sure that one had come at him with something sharp while another blocked the door. "I ducked just so that it grazed my forehead," he said. "I stumbled low through him and managed to wriggle clear."[10]

That evening, he gave a fiery speech to the Veterans of Foreign Wars convention, railing against Wall Street, the administration of President Roosevelt, and the press. Reporters, he told the crowd, were "skunks in the woods." Anyone believing what they read in newspapers, he said, "should be bored with a hollow horn." When photographers tried taking his picture in the hopes of snapping an exclusive shot of the Senator's bruised profile, Long told his bodyguards, "Bust 'em up, boys." They responded by attacking an Associated Press photographer and smashing his camera.[11]

Long's alleged attackers were never located. In a version of the story he later circulated, Long pegged his assailant as a blackjack-wielding representative of the J. P. Morgan banking house, against which he had recently taken a powerful stand. Blame soon shifted onto multiple partygoers, including a New York attorney, the chief of the Port Washington police department, and a pilot and oil executive named Alford J. Williams, who had drawn particular suspicion when he was spotted with a swollen right hand daubed in iodine. When New Orleans Mayor T. S. Walmsley was asked for his take on the incident, he'd replied, "Huey's enemies will believe the story published generally in the newspapers. His friends will believe the senator's version."[12]

The truth of the incident is likely rather pitiful. The explanation offered by reporters that stuck was that Long had been punched after coming up from behind a man using the urinal and attempting unsuccessfully to urinate between his legs. Long is thought to have only discussed the evening with one of his closest friends, his bodyguard Murphy Roden. "It was an accident," Roden later said. "He just swung it too far and hit the fellow's shoe, and he socked him."[13]

Long had made a career of being coarse and ill-mannered to reporters and other politicians. The Sands Point mess, though, was something different, and it stuck to him. Thumbing your nose at stuffed shirts in the Senate was one thing, but many of his supporters back in rural Louisiana questioned just what Long had been doing out on Long Island mixing with East Coast elites in the first place. Almost two months after the incident, while being heckled during a speech at the Louisiana State Fair, Long yelled, "Come down here out of that there grandstand, and I'll man-to-man it with you. And I won't have five or six men jump on you like they did to me at Sands Point!"[14]

The debacle helped to derail Long's plans for mounting a run at the Presidency. He was shot and killed in Baton Rouge on September 10, 1935, by the son-in-law of one of his political opponents. Long's command of his most loyal supporters in the state was so strong that even years after his death, schoolchildren in the northern part of Louisiana believed he was alive and had, in fact, been elected President.[15]

For Jack Curley, the Sands Point party had been a rare night off during what would turn out to be one of the most successful stretches of his career. Two weeks after his unexpected run-in with Long, he'd written him to invite him to dinner at his Great Neck home. "Hope that you are in good health and that the little gash over the eye will cause you no trouble," Curley wrote. "Gene Buck feels terrible over the matter, because we could do so little for you."[16] Curley had been on record all along saying that he thought Long's stories about the evening were bunk. Still, a part of him must have smiled when he heard of Long's vigorous defense of them.

Curley was himself skilled at dropping provocative semi-truths as a means to deflect hard questions. In professional wrestling, where he made his money, the truth came into play only when it could no longer be dodged. Even then, it hardly mattered all that much. No matter what anyone said or wrote, it was always better to stick to the contention that everything was on the up and up. Should that fail, change the story. If spectators, reporters, or even government officials thought a match looked off, blame an injury or an illness. Then, offer to settle the matter with a rematch, with ticket prices doubled.

Jack Curley didn't singlehandedly create professional wrestling. It would ultimately take a network of loosely connected showmen, far-seeing businessmen, hucksters, grifters, carnies, and some genuinely tough, gifted athletes to do so—one-time fixtures of sports pages like "Strangler" Ed Lewis, Billy Sandow, "Dynamite" Gus Sonnenberg, Toots Mondt, Jack Pfefer, and "The Golden Greek" Jim Londos. Curley did, however, lead the way in changing it from a laborious test of endurance for athletes and audiences alike into a sleek, modern, stadium-filling spectacle and staple of American popular entertainment. "The story of his career," wrote *Ring* magazine founder and sports historian Nat Fleischer, "is the story of the rise of boxing and wrestling in America from infancy to gigantic commercial enterprises."[17]

The son of Alsatian immigrants who had fled Europe in fear for their lives, Curley won and lost several fortunes, was accused of rigging championships in three sports, and had been close at different points in his life with opera singer Enrico Caruso ("One of the finest, gayest characters I have ever known."),[18] the British-suffragist Emmeline Pankhurst ("I'll always believe she was the most remarkable woman I ever knew."), Democratic-presidential nominee William Jennings Bryan ("I could sit and listen to him talk by the hour."),[19] and the socialist union-organizer Eugene Debs ("A lovable man and a great American.").[20] He collected antiques. He vigorously supported the New Deal. He may or may not have been a pallbearer at the funeral of President Theodore Roosevelt.[21] "He was interested in a thousand things," wrote *Esquire*'s Curt Riess. "There was only one thing he could never get excited about, and that was whether people thought his wrestling bouts were faked or on the level."[22]

For serious-minded sportswriters and fans, the problem with professional wrestling had always been that too often the matches were disgraceful, bald-faced put-ons.[23] Few people with more than a passing interest in sports could take it seriously. For Curley, the question of the competitors' sincerity was a red herring. The real problem with professional wrestling, as he saw it, was that, too often, the matches were bores. If he could guarantee them to be exciting and the contestants compelling, he knew that people would pay to watch. He would let the audience sort it out for themselves just how much it mattered whether they could believe that the whole thing was honest.

Wrestlers made their living in a world that was somehow real and utter fiction at the exact same time. The line separating the two was always shifting, and the trick was to make sure that the audience could never grow comfortable with just where it was resting. Legitimate matches were often derided as fakes, while matches that were thoroughly cooked were often taken for honest and drew the loudest cheers.[24] "Probably half the folk who attend the Curley carnivals are hep to the hooligans who entertain them," wrote reporter Jack Miley in 1936. "The other fifty percent of the spectators are equally certain they are witnessing the genuine article. That has been the secret of Curley's success. He satisfies the scoffers and the believers, too. He has made rassling a state of mind."[25]

Jack Curley's job was to keep people guessing at what they'd just seen with their own eyes. It wasn't exactly the job he'd wanted, but it was the one he'd landed in, and he did it masterfully. "[He] is in one respect a greater showman than Barnum," wrote Alva Johnston in a remarkable 10,000-word profile of Curley that ran across three issues of the *New Yorker* in the summer of 1934. "Barnum preyed on the credulity of the public; Curley profits from its incredulity. . . . [Wrestling fans] are the most skeptical men on Earth. The true wrestling-fancier would not believe his own deathbed confession."[26]

Curley was known to be somewhat coy with his audiences. He profited off their naivety or their cynicism equally. "Many persons have such a horror of being taken in," Barnum himself once wrote, "that they believe themselves to be a sham, and in this way are continually humbugging themselves."[27] Curley was America's baron of professional wrestling for more than twenty years. Had he not happened into it while just a teenager in Chicago, it's very likely the sport would not have survived its first flush of large-scale national success at the beginning of the 1900s. But even when his audiences dwindled down to almost zero, he provided them with a show. It was what he lived for, and he always found a way to keep the show going.

BALLYHOO!

PART I

The Sporting Whirl
1874–1917

FIGURE 2. Jack Curley. From the author's personal collection.

CHAPTER 1

The Glamour of the Streets
and the Life That Seethed About Them

WHAT JACK CURLEY remembered most from his childhood were the ships—square-riggers with their bowsprits jutting over the wharfs along San Francisco's shoreline. They beckoned him out into a world humming with possibility and a thousand different things to get excited over. San Francisco's wharfs were alive then. Merchants, fishermen, and three-card monte dealers haunted the boards; steamers and sailing ships waited in deep water while flat-bottomed lighters and row boats carried people to shore. Reflecting on his colorful childhood almost thirty years later, Curley could still see the horsecars struggling up the city's endless hills, the glow of the gas light, and the bare-knuckled boxers who punched each other bloody in the city's tiny fight clubs. He remembered, too, "sailors, drifters, smartly dressed swells. . . . This was the background of my formative years, the years that gave me my first glimpse of the sporting whirl and decided me on the career that has carried me to all parts of the globe, not only to see sporting history in the making over a span of two generations but to contribute something to the making of it."[1]

From the very beginning, his was a world in motion. Jack Curley was born in San Francisco on the Fourth of July in 1876. There were no announcements of his birth in local newspapers, and there is no surviving paperwork to document it since the majority of the city's records were destroyed in the fire that engulfed it immediately after the Great Earthquake of 1906. In fact, the earliest-known articles written about Curley have him as being from either St. Louis, New York, or Strasbourg.[2] It's impossible to know which of these are mistakes of reporting and which are the result of Curley having shuffled the details of his background to suit a specific need. That he was a born exaggerator unencumbered by any notion of sticking to strict facts when recounting the events of his life only complicates matters further. Still, in his later years, when discussing his life for features that would run in the *New Yorker*, the *Ring*, and other prominent newspapers and magazines, he uniformly stuck to San Francisco as his birthplace, so we'll take him at his word. In the end, he was from anywhere and everywhere. The vagaries surrounding his birth and his hearty embrace of the American ideal of self-reinvention befit the life he would go on to live.

San Francisco marked the 1876 centennial in a grand manner. Civic leaders staged a three-day celebration, shuttering businesses and draping the city in flags and bunting. They were commemorating not just the founding of the United States but their own improbable growth. Only decades prior, the Gold Rush of 1849 transformed San Francisco into one of the major cities of the West, its population exploding from around 35,000 residents in 1852 to more than half a million by 1870.

The day started foggy but cleared early as almost 400,000 people packed into the city to watch re-enactments of Revolutionary War battles and a procession of civic leaders and military detachments wind down Market Street, the city's main thoroughfare. As a nighttime parade crossed between Fourth and Fifth Streets, Father Joseph Neri, a Jesuit priest and professor of natural sciences at the city's St. Ignatius College, flipped a switch to illuminate a series of lights, lamps, and reflectors strung from the roof of the college's three-story building. Neri's miraculous invention cast a stream of soft light on the people below.[3]

Somewhere amid all that reverie, Jacques Armand Schuel was born. The name Jack Curley would come later, when he was a teenager working for criminals and running with lowlifes in Chicago. The story he most commonly told about his family was that his father, Henri, had fled the family home in Strasbourg in 1871 at the end of the Franco–Prussian War, fearing reprisals from the newly installed government. After landing in New York, Henri and his wife, whose name is not known, made their way west to California, where Jack was born. Miserable with their living conditions in San Francisco and aching for the old world they'd left behind, the family moved Jack and his siblings back to Europe when he was only four years old. His mother took the children home to her native Alsace. Henri, still wary of returning to the region, went to live in Paris.

In Alsace, Jack shuffled between living with his two tough, demanding, and abusive uncles. He would later cite the experience as the source of his fierce work ethic and his habit of responding whenever he was called. He developed a lifelong aversion to alcohol there, too, after his younger brother died from accidentally ingesting a fatal amount of *kirschwasser.* "That seared me onto the wagon," he would remember.[4] In 1888, Henri brought the family back to San Francisco and found work with the Geary Street Railroad company, one of the eight cable car companies operating the six hundred cable cars that ran on more than a hundred miles of single cable track laid around the city.[5]

Unusually large for his age, Jack turned his attention to boxing. San Francisco in the early 1900s was a hotbed for the sport—men in the city outnumbered women by better than two-to-one, and there were large ethnic conclaves whose residents were willing to spend their disposable income betting on the fighters who shared their heritage. Taken with the sport, young Jack scrapped his plans to attend business school. "[I was] caught," he would later remember, "by the glamour of the streets and the life that seethed about them." He went to work as a copyboy with the *San Francisco Chronicle* and, happy to work all hours, was soon promoted and sent out into the city as a police reporter and to cover late-breaking emergencies. His career at the *Chronicle* came to a sudden and embarrassing stop when the paper's city editor fired him for turning in a fabricated story that Jack claimed a more senior reporter had handed off to him.[6]

He next found work at a Market Street saloon owned by boxer George LaBlanche. LaBlanche was a fast, tough, hard-drinking scrapper from Canada with closely cropped hair, a handlebar mustache, and an uneven reputation when it came to winning fights. Jack was enthralled with his new boss, having developed what he described as tremendous admiration for him after witnessing his most famous bout on August 27, 1889. Jack had skipped school that day so he could arrive early and secure a spot outside the California Athletic Club to watch the fight. He climbed to the roof of a neighboring church and followed the action as best he could through the club's windows. Down in the street below, a crowd of men who hadn't been able to find a spot among the hundreds packed inside waited for updates to be passed out from those who had.[7]

LaBlanche's opponent, Jack Dempsey, was boxing's twenty-six-year-old undefeated middleweight champion. Unusually fresh-faced and well-spoken, Dempsey had been dubbed "The Nonpareil" by fans and writers. Few granted LaBlanche much of a chance of winning, and by the fight's twenty-sixth round, Dempsey had things well in hand. Blasted by heavy blows to his ribs and neck, LaBlanche retreated to a corner of the ring, forcing the referee to call for a break. When Dempsey stepped back, his hands held low at his waist, LaBlanche closed his eyes, planted his left foot, and spun clockwise on his heel. The back of his right hand, jutting out like a stick, clobbered Dempsey in the jaw. Dempsey collapsed face-first in the ring, breaking his nose when he hit the mat. Some attendees would later comment that he fell like a man who had been struck by a hammer.[8]

LaBlanche collected up his winnings and walked out into the downtown San Francisco night. The punch that LaBlanche used to get the win, typically called a pivot punch, was a mostly novel one for boxing. Some states had already outlawed it, but California had not. The fight's referee let it slide. The win made LaBlanche so notorious that boxing historians still refer to pivot punches as the "LaBlanche swing." Young Jack never forgot the fight or sitting in the late August night watching it. "I had given no heed to the illegality of the blow and was impressed only with the fact that [LaBlanche] had knocked out the great Dempsey," he later wrote.[9] The crowds, the competition, and the clamor of the show had sunk their hooks into him. Driving a cable car like his father was not going to be an option.

When stories of the wonders being prepared for the 1893 Chicago World's Fair reached San Francisco, Jack couldn't resist the urge to see them for himself. Still just a teenager, he and a friend boarded a train out of San Francisco, seeking, as he would later write, adventure and fortune. Their money lasted them only as far as Sacramento, where they were thrown off the train. They worked odd jobs and rode freight cars the rest of the way, losing each other in Salt Lake City. Upon finally arriving in Chicago, Jack was home. "Chicago during the fair was a boomtown for youthful adventurers like myself," he later wrote. "Work was plentiful; fun was to be had cheaply. I slipped easily from job to job, saw the fair exactly twice, made friends among the sporting fraternity, and thoroughly enjoyed myself."[10]

He befriended George Siler, a respected referee and sports editor for the *Chicago Globe*. "He took me to the Fitzsimmons–Corbett and

Fitzsimmons–Maher fights where I got my first great thrills," Jack later wrote, "and I've been getting them ever since."[11] Siler helped him find work with boxer Alex Greggains, who took Jack on as one of his seconds for an eventful fight in Roby, Indiana, that settled his intent to pursue a future in show business. According to Jack (though his version of what occurred appears, unsurprisingly, to be an exaggeration), the Indiana state militia patrolled the area around the arena on the evening of the fight and harassed fans who tried to attend. With only a sparse crowd inside, the bout went ahead as planned. As the match built to a furious peak, the wooden arena caught fire. Greggains was arrested in the panic and confusion that followed while both Jack and Greggains's opponent managed to slip away. "Naturally, after all that excitement, no ordinary job would have suited a youngster like me," he later wrote.[12]

When work from the fair dried up after its closing, Jack found himself among the thousands of men forced to sleep in the city's parks and streets. Drifting in and out of desperation, he took odd reporting jobs at local papers and began waiting tables at the city's sixteen-story Great Northern Hotel. Near the end of 1903, he met boxing promoter P. J. "Paddy" Carroll. Carroll was the most consequential connection Jack had made in Chicago yet. In Carroll's slippery, extravagant world, the men dressed slick in tight-fitting suits with diamond-studded rings and stickpins. When in public, they moved slow down the street so people could take notice. Clothing, jewelry, sex, and money were king, and though still largely just a hanger-on, Jack would soon be dressing in sharp three-piece suits, keeping a flower in his lapel, and wearing his top hat at a rakish tilt.

Carroll put him to work attending to boxers and handling errands at Chicago's Pelican Athletic Club. Still only in his late teens, Jack was an ideal assistant, eager to work and bulky and intimidating enough to keep trouble at arm's length. Working at the Pelican would turn out to be the ideal training ground for him. "Carroll had no small measure of ability as a promoter, but he was lazy, and as time wore on, he left many of the details of the management of the club to me," he wrote. "I learned a great deal about the business to which I was to devote my life. I made matches, handled all arrangements with the fighters and their managers, got out what little publicity we could command and virtually staged the shows."[13] His name, too, would change. "Jacques," he was told, was too

French, "Schuel" too Jewish. His new name would be Jack Curley, the surname taken from the blond ringlets of hair that crowned his head.[14]

In addition to organizing fights, Curley participated in several himself—a decision that resulted in some hard-hitting defeats. The last punch he took in the ring was from a boxer named Bob Long, who landed a right hand behind Curley's ear. "Sometimes I think I can feel it yet," Curley later wrote.[15] He quickly deduced, too, that when it came to payouts for a night of boxing, the boxer himself tended to take home the smallest share. It was often the fight's promoter, it seemed, who took the largest cut. Still, fight promotion was a precarious way to earn a living, given the state of boxing at the time. Boxing matches at the end of the nineteenth century were scattershot undertakings. Prizefighting was popular but largely illegal across the country. Held under London Prize Ring rules, professional fights were long, brutal, bare-knuckle affairs. And besides being plainly violent, fights could be blatantly crooked, with endings engineered to satisfy whichever gambler had applied the most muscle.

Even high-profile fights held in major cities sometimes ended with police action instead of knockouts. When heavyweight champion John L. Sullivan took on Paddy Ryan in 1885 in front of a crowd of 10,000 people at Madison Square Garden, police called the match off in the first round when they deemed that the action had grown too intense.[16] More typically, fights were covert affairs held in backrooms, horse stables, or on barges parked offshore. The 1896 heavyweight championship fight between Peter Maher and Bob Fitzsimmons was fought on a sandbar just outside Langtry, Texas, to circumvent the state's ban on prizefights. Anywhere, it seemed, could host a boxing match as long as it was far enough out of the way to avoid attracting the local police. "I remember a fight I promoted in an old distillery in Iowa City, Iowa," Curley later wrote. "The ring consisted of four men holding up a rope. If one of them had fallen down, the whole ring would have gone down. And they were the light too. Each one of them held a gasoline torch!"[17]

For spectators, simply getting to the fights often posed a challenge. Ticket holders would often be required to meet and board dedicated train cars to travel to the fight location, usually with no idea of exactly where they were headed. "We had a horrible time getting to the scene of the fight," remembered an attendee to the Jake Kilrain and John L. Sullivan heavyweight championship fight of 1889. "We were packed in like a lot of hogs. No one knew where they were going. The railroad tickets simply said, 'To Destination' and 'From Destination'."[18]

As a result, fight promotion was not a business for the faint of heart. To those trying to pull the fights off, boxing seemed to exist solely on the whim of elected officials and police, many of whom, when they weren't busy arresting fighters, might be found seated ringside. More often than not, saloons were where boxing business was conducted, plans were hatched, and deals were brokered. "Years ago, all the big matches were made in the saloons," Charley Rose, a turn-of-the-century manager and promoter, would write years later.[19] Successful promoters had to negotiate a tangle of local legislation, not to mention mobsters and politicians looking to be cut in on receipts. And with boxing illegal in most cities, deciding just how much attention to draw to a fight was never easy. Too little promotion and your fight would draw crickets. Too much and you risked drawing law enforcement. What promotion could be done was usually little more than well-placed gossip. These whisper campaigns themselves required delicacy. If word leaked to the wrong ears, months of work could disappear overnight and leave a promoter either scrambling to find an alternative location to host their fight or facing massive losses.[20]

Professional wrestling, Curley would soon discover, was unregulated for the most part. Though far less prestigious than boxing, wrestling matches were much easier to organize and could be held with little concern over interference. Curley later claimed to have put on his first professional wrestling match when he was just sixteen or seventeen, sometime in 1893, not long after he first arrived in Chicago. Little information is available on it, but the match was said to have been staged in a tavern on the city's north side. In it, Curley matched a local wrestler named Rooney against an athlete from Africa who was passing through the city as part of a traveling variety show. Wrestling must have presented an intriguing sideline for him. Though he didn't know it at the time, it would turn out to be an ideal fit.[21]

Organized, professional sports were just taking shape in the late nineteenth century. "At that time," Curley later wrote, "bi-league baseball was drawing a few meager thousands into ramshackle wooden stands, and football was drawing practically nobody but the student rooters. Golf was an unknown game as far as the general public was concerned, and horse racing was only a hobby. Tennis was a 'sissy game.' Sport was then just sport—nobody thought of it as a business."[22]

The first avowed professional baseball team, the Cincinnati Red Stockings, appeared in 1869. The first professional football teams and professional basketball league formed in the late 1890s. Professional athletes were looked at with skepticism from the very beginning. They were greedy and ignorant, it was said, little more than mercenaries and hirelings, not to mention easy and often ready prey for gamblers and criminals eager to influence the outcome of a game.[23] Amateur athletic clubs formed in response, elite organizations purportedly dedicated to preserving the love of sport and fair competition, unsullied by the pay-to-play ethos of the professionals. That a dedication to amateurism was a luxury all but reserved for the wealthy did not prevent it from being used as a cudgel against those promoting sports as commercial entertainment. From the very beginning, Jack Curley was steadfastly on the side of the professionals.

By 1903, he was busy putting on events where he could, covering sports for Chicago's *Inter Ocean* newspaper, and managing boxer George Gardiner when he received an offer to go to work for mobster, politician, and all-around purveyor of vice Andy Craig. Craig had built a fortune fencing stolen goods, posting bail for the pickpockets and thieves who collected around him, and running a chain of saloons that included the notorious Tivoli resort. "Craig is the worst offender on the street and shows more boldness in one hour than the rest of the owners of places of that character allow to crop out in a single day," said the city's police chief, George Shippy.[24] Turn of the century Chicago was a swarm of fixers, grifters, and conmen, and given Curley's close working relationship with Craig, it's impossible to imagine that he did not gain first-hand knowledge of the inner workings of many of the scams, big and small, being run throughout the city at the time.

Craig's proposition was to allow himself to be referred to as Gardiner's manager instead of Curley. Curley would keep his usual cut of Gardiner's earnings (typically around $400 per fight) and advise Craig when the odds on Gardiner were favorable enough for Craig to bet. Craig would get the notoriety of having a hand in the fight game, and Curley would get a cut of Craig's gambling earnings. "Those were the days when the only money to amount to anything in any line of sport was collected by gamblers," Curley later wrote. "I knew Craig was wealthy and would bet freely. I realized it was an opportunity for me to cut in on some really big money for the first time in my life."[25]

The relationship paid dividends for both men. At a fight in Louisville, Craig covered $45,000 in bets on Gardiner. When Gardiner won, Curley cleared $800 for his work arranging the fight and $20,000 for his gambling advice to Craig. "I think we laughed all the way back to Chicago," Curley remembered of the day.[26] As a principal part of Craig's circle, Curley traveled in style. As Curley was sure to be sober at all hours, Craig took to trusting him with his swollen bankroll on evenings when he was too drunk to trust himself with it. A grateful Craig also purchased Curley a Pope-Toledo automobile and installed an ex-boxer to be his chauffeur. Cars were still considered not just luxurious novelties but often dangerous and undependable to boot. "[I] was the envy of my less fortunate friends as I rolled about town," Curley later wrote, "secretly hoping the contraption wouldn't break down that the urchins in the street might assail my ears with 'Get a horse!'"[27]

The ride ended in November 1903, when Gardiner lost a heartbreaking fight to Bob Fitzsimmons, a former heavyweight champion. Curley had been convinced that Fitzsimmons was well past his prime and that while his name would prove a hefty draw, Gardiner would handily defeat him. Curley was surprised to discover that, more than anything, the specter of Fitzsimmons's reputation served only to unnerve Gardiner. "The fight game is a very funny one. It is full of breaks, and you can never tell if they will be for or against you," Curley wrote. "The great name of Fitzsimmons, on which I had banked only as an adornment for [Gardiner's] record of victories, had a dismaying effect on him. Courageous in every previous fight he had had, he was frightened half to death." Gardiner lost the fight in twenty rounds and was never the same.[28]

In December 1903, the Tivoli was ordered closed by Chicago Mayor Carter Harrison after a city committee labeled it a "resort of disreputable persons, pickpockets, thieves, women, confidence men, and lawbreakers generally."[29] Curley had cut his teeth there, but it was time for him to move on. He opened his own saloon, where he hosted fights and served free lunches to attract midday clientele who could be plied with beer once seated at the bar. In September 1905 while on his way to visit his son at work, Curley's father, Henri, passed away quietly while riding on a Chicago streetcar.[30] His death left Curley with no known family in America. Having just turned twenty-nine, he would spend the next decade traveling the country and, soon, the world.

He skirted the law and good taste everywhere he went. In Butte, Montana, he staged what was advertised to locals as the "First Bullfight in America," an event that drew an angry response from the state's government and an even angrier one from the crowd of enraged miners who Curley claimed tore apart his 15,000-seat pinewood arena when the sleepy bull could not be stimulated into action. "A promoter's first thought is to protect the money," Curley wrote of the situation. "I grabbed the receipts and beat it back to town, in peril of my life."[31]

In Davenport, Iowa, a bout he staged between boxers Kid Herman and Packy McFarland drew an armed response from the state militia. The militia's commanding officer, anxious over a point of law and hesitant to stop the fight before he could clarify it, had wired the governor for direction. Waiting outside, Curley intercepted the Western Union boy carrying the governor's reply, promising him that he would deliver it. With the militia lined up just feet from the ring and waiting on information that Curley made sure would arrive too late, the boxers punched their way to a fifteen-round no-decision.[32]

In Chicago, he claimed to have helped invent the one-piece bathing suit popularized by swimmer and diver Annette Kellerman. Though undoubtedly an exaggeration, his story was that while managing Kellerman during her appearances in the city, likely in 1907, he stitched a piece of fabric between the two parts of her bathing suit to keep the upper half from climbing up each time she hit the water. "It struck us as a good idea at the time, but nothing was immediately done," Curley later wrote. "Not long afterward, the Annette Kellerman bathing suit came on the market. It was all in one piece, the start of the revolution in women's beach costuming—and the outgrowth of just a few stitches."[33]

By 1909, Curley had tried his hand at staging almost anything that he thought he could convince people to pay an admission fee to see. He'd also established himself more firmly in the business of professional wrestling, having promoted major matches in Chicago and Kansas City. Promoter is a strange, moving target of a job title but one that fit him perfectly. A promoter's business, Curley later said, was to "see how much they will give you to bring an attraction to a town, and, if that doesn't work, you see how much you have to pay them to let you do it."[34] It was as simple and as difficult as convincing people to pay for a ticket to see a show. You had to give them what you already knew they wanted and sell them on the new things they would come to demand. As large as the athletes he often worked with, Curley combined his physical size with a warm and gregarious manner. He committed himself to making sure that the talent arrived on time and as advertised, that the show went ahead as scheduled, and that a paying audience turned up to watch it. The *New Yorker*'s A.J. Liebling would later describe him as the "walking embodiment of the popular conception of a promoter."[35]

By the end of the first decade of the twentieth century, Curley had worked his way up from hopping freight cars and sleeping on park benches to associating with mobsters, professional athletes, and politicians. The responsibility of putting on a nonstop show brought with it a never-ending string of details and problems, but as chaos and emergencies collected around him one after another, he always kept his head about him. "Promoting," wrote the *New Yorker*'s Alva Johnston, "would be easy except for the emergencies. It is merely a matter of causing battlers to battle and of collecting the gate receipts, but somehow most promoters go broke or crazy or into hiding. It is the emergencies that get them."[36] By the start of 1909, Jack Curley's emergencies were just beginning.

FIGURE 3. Yusuf İsmail. Courtesy of the Albert Davis Collection, the H. J. Lutcher Stark Center for Physical Culture and Sports, the University of Texas at Austin.

CHAPTER 2

A Fake Verisimilitude

JACK CURLEY DIDN'T invent professional wrestling. No one person possibly could have. Though the incentives for competing and the specific rules of engagement have varied, traces of two athletes competing by using an agreed-upon catalog of holds can be found across the globe and throughout history. In America, Union soldiers returning home from the Civil War helped to spread a style called collar-and-elbow. This method of wrestling had been one of the most popular ways to pass time in camp. These matches had served, too, as a way to improve the skills they would need to rely on to stay alive should they lose their weapon in the heat of combat.[1]

Introduced by Irish immigrants to Vermont in the first half of the nineteenth century, collar-and-elbow matches commenced with contestants in a standing position, with one hand on their opponent's collarbone and one on their elbow. A fall was called when a wrestler was tripped, thrown, or otherwise knocked off their feet. As the sport's popularity grew, men were soon wrestling for exercise, competition, and fun in taverns and town halls, as well as at picnics, public meetings, and festivals.[2]

By the 1870s, a new style of wrestling, introduced to the country from Europe, had begun to overtake collar-and-elbow in popularity. Called Greco-Roman, it had been practiced in neither ancient Greece nor Rome.[3] The name lent it a certain panache and a sense of history, even though it wasn't all that old. In Greco-Roman matches, blocky, sweaty athletes used balance and raw power to try to force their opponent to the ground, where, unlike in collar-and-elbow matches, the grappling would continue. Once a wrestler was down, considerable time and energy were spent trying to turn them over onto their backs. A fall was declared when some combination of a wrestler's body parts—both shoulders and a hip, both hips and a shoulder—touched the mat at the same time. Contestants would rock from side to side to avoid being pinned or stretch their limbs out and lie flat on their stomachs, forcing their opponent to peel them up and turn them over. If a wrestler was in danger of being pinned, they used the tops of their heads and feet as bases to arch their backs up and off the mat. Falls in a Greco-Roman match could last a few minutes or several hours. It was grueling for the contestants but often ponderous for spectators, for once both men were off their feet, much of the maneuvering for position was obscured from the onlookers.

The limitations of the style, however, left a surprising amount of room for clever performers to convey suspense and uncertainty. The most popular wrestlers tried to vary the pacing of their matches. They learned to read a room. They would follow a long stretch spent on the mat with a series of dramatic throws and rapid-fire near-falls. They would lift their opponent off their feet and heave them about the ring. A fall that lasted minutes would be followed by one that lasted an hour. They became so adept at performing that they could stun an audience into a silence so deep that the only sound in the hall would be the heavy breathing of the wrestlers as they strained and struggled.

One of America's earliest-known professional Greco-Roman wrestlers was a French immigrant named Thiebaud Bauer. A born showman, Bauer had been a featured performer in wrestling shows at Paris's famed Moulin Rouge. He arrived in San Francisco in 1874, two years before Jack Curley was even born, sporting a thick handlebar mustache and a plan to market himself in his new country. A compelling mix of athlete and grifter, he declared himself the unbeaten champion wrestler of France. It was an unlikely claim, but who was in a position to refute it? "He is a fine-looking man and built like a gladiator," trumpeted the *San Francisco Chronicle* just months after Bauer's arrival in the city. "All the leading wrestlers of Europe have been laid on their backs by him."[4]

Bauer arranged a series of matches for himself against William Miller, an Australian immigrant running a school where he taught boxing and fencing to locals. Their first match, in November 1874, attracted just 200 spectators, but by the time they faced off again on May 28, 1875, the public had become so enthralled with the pair that the rush of people who tried to push their way through the doors of the city's grand Palace

Amphitheater to see them was so great that it caused the building's main stairway to give out.[5]

In post-Gold Rush San Francisco, gambling was so popular that the 1855 *Annals of San Francisco* declared it to be "the life and the soul of the place."[6] In hundreds of saloons, hotel bars, and public houses, roulette, faro, and monte were played throughout the day. One of the city's most popular forms of sports betting was invented in 1865 by Parisian bookmaker and founder of the Moulin Rouge, Pierre Oller. Called parimutuel betting, it allowed for the purchase of what were dubbed "pools."

Each pool sold represented a different possible outcome for a given contest. During the May 1875 match between Bauer and Miller, for example, one pool may have been for Bauer to win the match in straight falls. Another might have been for a particular fall not to exceed fifteen minutes. Still another may have been for the entire match to be over in less than an hour. Each pool came with different odds, and the odds at which a pool was sold could change throughout the course of a contest as a specific outcome became more or less likely. Since the entire amount wagered was divided among all purchasers of the winning pool, pool betting allowed for extraordinarily large payouts when a pool that had attracted only a few purchasers ended up winning. If one were fixing, say, a wrestling match, one would make sure that its outcome corresponded exactly to the pool likeliest to produce the biggest jackpot; at the same time, one would be sure that their friends understood exactly which pool to pour their money into.[7]

Bauer and Miller's match was intended for five falls. They split the evening's first four, and to most fans, the final one looked as if it could go to either man. The betting told a different story, though, as the odds for the fifth fall swung wildly in favor of Miller winning. As they began to sense a fix, the crowd became restless. "Don't do it. You will lose your money. It's a put-up thing," yelled a man standing near the ring to a spectator in the back trying to place a bet on Bauer. Another man, heavily invested in Bauer, yelled, "Let's declare it off. He has sold out the match." The air filled with catcalls and whistles. Spectators rushed into the ring, screaming wildly. Fearing a riot, Bauer and Miller tried to calm the crowd by declaring the whole match over. Miller shouted that he would fight anyone in the audience who claimed it had been fixed. When the police finally entered the ring, they ordered all the bets canceled. The evening, they announced, was through.[8]

Afterward, Miller blamed gamblers for creating the fiasco to disrupt the match after the odds had shifted away from their favor. Bauer claimed to have been confronted before the final fall by two men who threatened to shoot him if he lost. Reporters didn't buy it. The *San Francisco Chronicle* labeled the match "a job, a palpable job," and, in a lengthy expose, declared, "The public of San Francisco have been frightfully gulled. . . . [Wrestling], as practiced here, is a delusion and a snare."[9] Pro wrestling in the United States was off to a dubious start.

Following the match, Bauer and Miller left San Francisco and headed east. Bauer opened a saloon on Prince Street in Lower Manhattan, where he kept a group of trained bears he would wrestle with for the amusement of his customers. Miller went to work as the athletic director for the New York Police Athletic Club, a newly formed fundraising group for the widows and orphans of slain policemen. The group disbanded a little more than a year after Miller joined amid financial irregularities and negative press over a bloody fight between members that had spilled out of the club's gymnasium and onto 34th Street. One of the combatants was also one of the club's star attractions, a young officer from the 29th Precinct with a head of reddish curls and a sleek build named William Muldoon.[10]

Muldoon weighed more than 200 pounds and possessed a manicured physique that dazzled audiences. He would claim in his autobiography to have served in both the American Civil War and the Franco–Prussian War, though in truth he served in neither.[11] After moving to New York, he made a name for himself wrestling in his off-hours at Harry Hill's, the concert saloon at Houston and Mulberry Streets named for its English owner. Hill sanctioned boxing, wrestling, and theatrical variety shows on the saloon's main floor and gambling games in the basement. Hill's thrived from midnight to sunrise, mixing high-stakes gamblers, gawkers, prostitutes, roughnecks, tourists, politicians, and gangsters into a potent cocktail that Hill oversaw with sometimes brute force.[12]

Matches between trained wrestlers routinely went for at least an hour but frequently went much longer. Thiebaud Bauer and William Miller once wrestled a nine-hour match that ended at 5:40 a.m.[13] Miller and William Muldoon once wrestled until four in the morning, with neither man even winning a fall.[14] What's at once obvious yet mind-bending about these matches isn't necessarily the effort they involved but that they featured two bare-chested men in wool tights straining, sweating, and grimacing in front of hundreds—often thousands—of people for hours and hours. And in most cases, the outcome of all that struggle had already been agreed upon well in advance.

By January 19, 1880, when Muldoon wrestled against Bauer at Madison Square Garden, the newly christened open-air arena on the corner of 26th Street and Madison Avenue, for what the pair was calling the Greco-Roman World Championship, professional wrestling matches had already earned a suspect reputation in New York. Just two months prior, the *Brooklyn Daily Eagle* had even declared, "There cannot be the slightest doubt in the minds of any sporting man that there has scarcely been an honest wrestling match in the country in the last two or three years."[15]

Though newspapers were dismissing matches as humbugs and frauds, they could still draw crowds. Four thousand people turned out to see the 1880 Muldoon-Bauer match, and with Harry Hill himself acting as referee, the two men put on a stellar show. They split the match's two opening falls. In the third, after only three minutes, Bauer turned to face the audience, drew a breath, and grandly wiped the sweat from his brow. Muldoon came up from behind, grabbed hold of Bauer's wrist, and threw him over his head and down to the mat. Hopping on his stunned opponent, he forced his shoulders down for the win. Muldoon's friends rushed the ring, lifted him up onto their shoulders in celebration, and carried him through the uproarious crowd.[16]

Muldoon quit the police force in 1881 and began touring the country as the champion of his beloved Greco-Roman wrestling. He ran a professional operation, sending advance men into the towns on his schedule to wrestle locals and generate excitement ahead of his arrival. He also took to matching himself against wrestlers from Europe and Asia. As the American, Muldoon always came out on top. Wrestling was serious business to him, and he presented it as such. During a particularly slow-moving match in San Francisco, when a fan yelled out for Muldoon to break his opponent's back, Muldoon stopped the match and declared to the crowd that not only would he not be breaking anyone's back but that if such talk continued, the show would be stopped and everyone could go home.[17] Somber and seemingly humorless, as his popularity grew, he began lecturing audiences on sobriety, hygiene, and fitness. He came to be known as both "The Iron Duke" and "The Solid Man of Sport"—nods to his incessant endorsements of healthy living and probity, though Muldoon himself both drank and smoked.

He enjoyed the neat coincidence of coming along just as many newspapers were beginning to devote more space to sports. Though sports were handled cautiously by more serious publications, by the end of the 1800s, Joseph Pulitzer's *World*, William Randolph Hearst's *Journal*, and James Gordon Bennett's *Herald* all included dedicated sports sections staffed with writers whose jobs were as much about crafting narratives and cultivating personalities as they were about reporting results. Wrestling, and to a greater degree boxing, received a significant boost when an Irish immigrant named Richard Kyle Fox decided to dedicate space in his weekly *Police Gazette* to sports.[18]

The *Police Gazette* had been in existence since 1846, but under Fox's leadership, it was transformed into something the likes of which people had never seen before. Bitter and deeply bigoted ("'good taste' can be applied to him with as much reason as 'nice fellow' to Genghis Khan," wrote author Gene Smith), Fox filled the *Gazette*'s pink-hued pages with sports news, theatre gossip, and reports of murder, suicide, and disorder of all kinds. His headlines ranged from amusing to vilely provocative and blatantly racist and nativist. He specialized in debauchery, accompanying the paper's lurid prose with richly detailed woodcut illustrations that froze the chaos and suffering in time. By the early 1880s, Fox was selling 150,000 copies of the *Gazette* per week, his subscriber base focused on barbershops, taverns, and working men's clubs and halls, where the paper was passed eagerly between male patrons.[19]

Fox also used the *Gazette* to sponsor boxing and wrestling matches, offering championship belts and guaranteeing outrageous purses. His work exploited the tension and dislocation many American men felt as the new century loomed, with many suddenly packed into cities and working in offices and factories instead of on open farmland. Aspiring athletes used the *Gazette* to issue challenges to one other—or sometimes just to anyone looking to put up money for a fight. Fox also published a set of rules that were used in matches around the country. Rules, and the specifics of which holds were allowed and which weren't, were important if betting was going to take place. Even if the crowd knew that it was always possible for a match to be rigged, in order for them to lay money on it, they needed to at least understand the contest's terms.

The coverage afforded to Muldoon and his contemporaries in the *Police Gazette* and other outlets helped the popularity of wrestling increase across the United States. When Muldoon retired in 1894, he was one of the most famous athletes in the country and was still the undefeated Greco-Roman champion. There was change coming, though, and Muldoon must have sensed that he had no choice but to get out of its way.

William Brady was already a successful theatre and boxing promoter by the time he tried his hand at professional wrestling. He'd produced several Broadway plays, including the one that would eventually secure his fortune: *Way Down East*. He'd led boxer James Corbett to the heavyweight championship in 1892, as well, transforming him along the way into "Gentleman Jim" in a ploy to attract a more respectable group of spectators to his fights. In 1898, in something of a radical career move, Brady took over the career of a wrestler named Yusuf İsmail. In the months they worked together, they remade wrestling into a spectacle that William Muldoon would have barely recognized.

İsmail was born in 1857 in the village of Cherna, in what is now the northeast corner of Bulgaria. A successful wrestler in his homeland before moving to Paris in his late thirties, he was six feet tall and paunchy, with lumps of muscles as big as baseballs that he could make bounce and wiggle. In Paris, he found employment as a dock worker while wrestling in the evenings for an enterprising businessman named Jean Doublier.[20] Doublier featured İsmail as part of a group of Turkish wrestlers in shows held at the city's Folies Bergère theatre. French writers soon dubbed İsmail "The Terrible Turk," a racist handle that dated back to the Turkish conquest of Constantinople in the fifteenth century. İsmail drew crowds throughout 1895, his most notorious match ending with him so infuriating the audience with his refusal to release an opponent from a hold, that police were forced to enter the theatre to keep fans from climbing into the ring to attack him.[21]

In 1898, İsmail relocated to New York with the French promoter Antonio Pierri. Pierri struggled to get attention for him from the city's wrestling fans and soon, desperate for money, sold İsmail's contract to William Brady. "[Pierri had] filled the poor devil full of how much money he had to back him with and how important his connections were," Brady wrote. "When he got to New York, however, he found the

Frenchmen didn't have a cent." Under Brady's direction, İsmail paraded down Broadway dressed in a red turban, baggy green pants, and a gold-laced jacket. ("He looked like the *pièce de rèsistance* of a Shriner's parade," Brady joked.) Brady reserved him a table in a restaurant where he could be clearly seen from the street and set him to work eating multiple steaks and desserts. Brady made sure to have newspaper writers tagging along every step of the way, convinced he could create a local media sensation. He told reporters that İsmail was a soldier in the Turkish army, that he was the personal assistant of Sultan Abdul Hamid, that he slept twelve hours a day, and that he never bathed for fear it would sap his enormous strength. "As I look back on him now, I find it hard to believe he was real," Brady later wrote. "I've never seen his equal as a publicity gag."[22]

The papers most prone to sensationalism printed it all. They listed İsmail as being as tall as 6'6" and placed his weight anywhere between 250 and 350 pounds. "No one who saw the Turk could forget him, or, apparently, describe him accurately, for all accounts of his dimensions vary," wrote the *New Yorker*'s A. J. Liebling. "He must have stupefied the beholder, like an avalanche or a waterspout. People who saw him were too frightened to take notes."[23]

With Brady as his manager, İsmail performed to a standing-room-only crowd in Madison Square Garden on March 26, 1898, paired against a thirty-six-year-old German-born wrestler named Ernest Roeber. Roeber was 5'8", with blond hair, clear blue eyes, and a thick chest. He met İsmail on top of a sixteen-foot-high elevated wooden platform with a large mat laid out for padding, its sides kept open without posts or ropes to give fans a better view of the action. At the start of the match, İsmail pursued Roeber around the platform. After just a minute of circling, Roeber lost his footing and fell backward, landing hard against the Garden's tanbark floor. Several people in the crowd thought he had been killed and began to push their way forward. The Garden filled with shouts of "Kill the Turk!" With the threat of a riot brewing, a cordon of policemen formed around İsmail and marched him through the crowd and back to the dressing room while physicians tended to Roeber.[24]

Roeber survived, of course, and Brady made plans to match the wrestlers against each other again, this time at the prestigious Manhattan Metropolitan Opera House. On April 30, 1898, the crowd that turned out for the rematch filled the Opera House from the gallery to the stalls. Additional seats were positioned on the stage, and those too were filled.[25] The scene turned rowdy early. When the wrestlers went down to the mat, the fans in the orchestra section lost sight of them and were forced to stand up to see. Fans seated in the boxes behind them, in turn, shouted out for them to sit down. They threw rolled newspapers, climbed over each other's backs, ripped their seats apart, and littered the aisles with cigar butts; women swung their umbrellas, and one man even swung his cane at the spectators blocking his view. "From the quarters which the George Goulds, and the Seward Webbs, and the W. C. Whitneys call their own quiet little boxes, came roars to 'Smash him!'," wrote the reporter covering the match for the *New York Herald*. "The city has never before witnessed so disgraceful a spectacle."[26]

The match descended into an almost comical scene as İsmail and Roeber traded pokes and jabs. Brady leapt into the ring shouting "Foul!" and was met by Roeber's cornerman, boxer Bob Fitzsimmons, who shoved him backwards. "I went away from there hastily, with Fitz coming after me, that hairy freckled right hand of his cocked and ready," Brady wrote.[27] Fights broke out in the audience as spectators in the box seats began to throw their chairs, while those jammed into the orchestra pit climbed onto the stage and into the ring. To restore order, the police took over the ring and brought the fracas to an ignoble halt. It didn't look much like wrestling, but it made money. Roeber would later remark that the $800 Brady paid him for the match was the most he ever made in a single night.[28]

Brady booked İsmail for appearances in Ohio and Missouri before taking him to Chicago for a match against a wrestler from Ridgeway, Wisconsin, named Evan Lewis. Lewis was part of a group of wrestlers popularizing a fresh style of wrestling called catch-as-catch-can. His matches were decidedly more violent than those of his Greco-Roman contemporaries. One sportswriter declared that they were nothing more than "unmitigated brutality."[29] Lewis adopted the nickname "Strangler," a nod to his famous stranglehold, in which he wrapped his burly arms around an opponent's neck and forced them into unconsciousness. In one match, he was said to have locked an opponent in a stranglehold for so long that their face turned black.[30] The handle was given to Lewis by Parson Davies, a Chicago-based sports promoter, high-stakes gambler, and operator of one of Chicago's largest betting houses.[31] Davies understood, perhaps as early as anyone, the potential for well-organized, well-promoted wrestling matches to draw large audiences. Evan Lewis was his star: rough, unapologetic, and awe inspiring.

"Catch" wrestling, as catch-as-catch-can came to be known, had arrived in America via Lancashire, England, and Lewis had learned the style directly from his English contemporaries. Catch was freer and faster than any other style of wrestling. Holds could be applied anywhere on the body, and punishing one's opponent into submission became as acceptable as pinning their shoulders down.[32] This new style leveled the field between wrestlers, too, diminishing the primacy of brute force and placing a value on speed, flexibility, and a capacity to endure pain. "As a physical exercise, there is no sport which calls for so much strength, endurance, and agility, combined with cool judgment," is how catch wrestling was described in the *Spalding Library*'s 1912 guide to the sport. "With men who love to oppose their strength to that of others, no sport is so popular."[33]

American audiences, drawn by the quick, violent action and loose rules of engagement, took to catch immediately and claimed it as their own. It made Greco-Roman wrestling seem even more ponderous and antiquated than it already was. For some, catch harkened back to an older, even more brutal type of no-holds-barred competition called "rough-and-tumble" fighting. Rough-and-tumble was most popular in the southern United States during the eighteenth century. Fighters bit, scratched, gouged, butted, and throttled their opponents. One witness to a 1774 bout remarked that "every diabolical stratagem for mastery is allowed and practiced."[34] The only rule governing the battles was that they ended as soon as one man said that he'd had enough. That, and a fighter shouldn't gouge out the eye of an already one-eyed opponent.[35]

İsmail and Lewis's match on June 20, 1898, brought out 10,000 people to Tattersall's, Chicago's immense glass-ceilinged auditorium on Dearborn Street. To ensure that order was maintained, the match's referee entered the ring with a pair of pistol handles poking out from each of his coat's flask pockets. Any signs of irregularity, he said, would be severely punished.[36] Lewis and İsmail wrestled fast and physically, with İsmail winning only after using Lewis's famous stranglehold against him. "I was licked," Lewis said after the match. "The Turk is a better man."[37]

İsmail returned to New York, and with his contract with Brady expiring, set sail for home on the French liner *La Bourgogne*. In dense fog southeast of Halifax, on July 4, 1898, the ship crashed into a British vessel and began sinking quickly. In fewer than thirty minutes, *La Bourgogne* was lost, along with 549 of its passengers. Reports soon made it back to New York that, in the panic, some crew members had stampeded passengers trying to make their way into lifeboats. Some were even said to have stabbed and beaten people trying to pull themselves into rafts. İsmail was one of the most famous people on board the ship, and his name was prominently mentioned in the early accounts of the sinking.

Never one to let an opportunity for publicity pass, one of Brady's associates fabricated a story that İsmail had been among the crew members fighting past the women and children in the rush off the ship. Once in the water, their story went, İsmail was too greedy to let go of the forty-pound money belt that contained the payout from his American tour—thousands of dollars in gold coins that he was said to have demanded in lieu of paper money. The weight of the belt, they told reporters, pulled him down to his death. The story was pure bunk but has continued to be repeated more than 120 years after İsmail's death.[38] It also obscured a darker truth about the exploitative nature of Brady and İsmail's relationship; "I doubt that his managers ever let him have enough money to affect his buoyancy," Jack Curley would later remark.[39]

Brady left professional wrestling after İsmail's death and never tried to repeat his success. İsmail's legacy is visible in the nonstop parade of broadly drawn foreign terrors who would stalk wrestling rings for years to come. More than 100 years after his untimely death, a statue and museum were built in his honor in his home village of Cherna.

"From its earliest days as a mass entertainment, beginning after the Civil War, pro wrestling was the exclusive domain of showmen and con artists, people who were more interested in dollars than true sport," wrote Lou Thesz, a professional wrestler who began wrestling full-time in the early 1930s while still a teenager.[40]

Many turn-of-the-century wrestlers worked and trained as part of traveling carnivals and athletic festivals, where they would undoubtedly have had plenty of opportunity to rub shoulders with the sharpers, magicians, sleight-of-hand artists, and pickpockets who rarely lingered far behind. P. T. Barnum incorporated wrestling into his traveling circus in the late 1880s, and other businessmen would soon follow suit. On an elevated platform called a bally in front of the tent housing the ring, sideshow talkers worked the crowd with their distinctive patter. The term "ballyhoo" comes from their exaggerated claims and too-good-to-be-true appeals. It was thought to have originated at the same 1893 Chicago World's Fair that Jack Curley had worked as a teenager. The goal of all this was to "turn the tip," to convince as many members of the assembled crowd to buy a ticket for the show as they could. Inside the athletic show tent, spectators squeezed together in front of the ring, their perspiration and cigar and cigarette smoke swirling together to make the humid air feel about twenty degrees hotter than the air outside.[41]

The highlight of the show was when the carnival's star wrestler searched the crowd for a local hoping to take a chance in the ring. Audience members wagered on whether the volunteer could last for the agreed-upon amount of time; if the local survived, they took home the whole pot. If they lost, the money went to the carnival. In a ploy to help loosen up betting, the audience members who took up the challenge were sometimes secretly carnival employees themselves. Called "sticks," their job was to make the match look as convincing as possible, lulling would-be town toughs into thinking that they, too, might stand a chance. As with other rigged games, like the ring toss or rope ladder, the rubes had to be made to believe the game could be beat, even when it was cooked from the inside out.

Matches could be, and often were, painful affairs. Grain tarps were sometimes laid over wood floors to serve as makeshift rings, and rolling on the rough surfaces could cause painful boils and carbuncles to form on a wrestler's skin or tear the flesh off their knees and feet.[42] Ears that were lumpy and deformed from the clotted blood collected in them due to repeated blows, known as cauliflower ears, became the trademark of the truly competitive wrestler.[43] To make sure they came out on the winning end of any wager, carnival wrestlers had to be strong enough to overpower opponents and dangerous enough to get themselves out of tough spots when needed. When taking on all-comers, all it took for a wrestler to be put out of a job was for a particularly skilled local or a single plucky farmer willing to bite or throw elbows to catch them unaware.

To protect themselves, the best wrestlers learned to locate and exploit the pressure points of their opponents' bodies, digging into them with their fingers and fists. If that wasn't enough to discourage an eager opponent, they employed painful, sometimes crippling maneuvers called "hooks." A skilled hooker, as the most elite professional wrestlers came to be known, only needed to grab hold of an opponent's ankle, wrist, or head to inflict unbearable punishment on them. It was about manipulating bones and tendons into positions in which they were not meant to be placed. And while the holds didn't always look like much to the audience, they could result in torn ligaments, separated shoulders, broken bones, or worse. One hooker named Charles Olsen, who toured successfully in the early 1900s, was involved in two matches in which his opponents suffered fatal injuries.[44]

Hookers measured each other based on power, quickness, a knowledge of holds and corresponding escapes, and simple guts and grit.[45] "If you're a hooker, you can wrestle with anyone," Dick Cardinal, a wrestler who began performing at carnivals in the 1950s, told an interviewer. "You can wrestle with the very best wrestlers and have a chance to beat them. Once a guy's hooked, he's hooked. It doesn't make any difference who he is."[46]

Men were not alone in dominating the stage. Female wrestlers, such as Grace Hemindinger, Alice Williams, and Marie Ford, worked the same circuit of carnivals, backrooms, and theatre stages as their male counterparts, wrestling both against other women as well as in mixed-sex matches.[47] In 1891, a tough, powerful, 5'8" strongwoman known as Minerva became the first recognized women's wrestling champion. Though little reliable documentation is available on her early years, it is likely that Minerva was born Josephine Schaeur in 1865, in Hamburg, Germany, as she told an interviewer, though some research has her being born in New York. She married an American strongman named Charles Blatt sometime in the late 1880s, and the couple traveled across the Americas and Europe performing in strength shows. Some stories have her being able to lift a baby elephant, others a horse. Minerva was placed in the *Guinness Book of World Records* for a hip and harness lift of close to 3,000 pounds that she performed in 1895 in Hoboken, New Jersey. "Her strength was just natural," Blatt said of his wife.[48]

Generally mild-mannered, she refused to suffer fools. Relating the story of a heckler to an interviewer in 1892, she said, "I warned him to keep quiet, and finally [he] dared me down off the stage. I jumped over the railing in front of the stage and went for him. Grabbing him by the throat, I threw him across the tent against a pole. I was so angry."[49]

Somewhere in all the swindling and violence, staged and otherwise, wrestlers got even better at putting on a show. Freed from having to contend with the same jumble of state and local laws that governed boxing, wrestling matches could be held with little concern for police action. In the early years of the twentieth century, businessmen, such as Baltimore's Gus Schoenlein, set up shop as promoters and staged wrestling shows in their hometowns on a fixed schedule. They brought in traveling professionals to perform, as needed, and turned local talent (and often themselves) into stars. The demands of running wrestling as serial entertainment, however, called for athletes versed in an entirely new set of skills.[50]

Successful wrestlers developed methods to engage audiences and keep matches looking competitive right up until the very end. "Conducted honestly, wrestling is the dullest of sports to watch," wrote the *New Yorker*'s A.J. Liebling, "but wrestlers with an honest background can lend a fake verisimilitude to their work that non-wrestlers find it hard to duplicate."[51] They learned that a match that lacked action, ended too decisively, or came to a close before spectators had gotten their money's worth tended to discourage repeat customers. They learned to "work," as they called it, carrying lesser talents through matches that looked, to the untrained eye, like an honest competition. "If an acknowledged superior athlete and showman wanted to make a gross inferior look good in the eyes of the hometown folks, it was done with artistry," wrote wrestler Ed Lewis, who began his career in the early 1900s and would go on to achieve outsized fame. "To the audience, the loser went down in fighting glory."[52]

To build interest in rematches, they kept endings inconclusive and learned to feign injuries. "If a local boy would lose by an injury, he would be taken to the local hospital with a concussion, a wrenched back or limb, or internal strain," Lewis wrote. "Press bulletins would be issued daily by the leading doctors, who were sometimes fans but not averse to the ethical advertising they were getting. Hastily, it must be added that they were absolutely sincere in their diagnoses. There is hardly an old-time wrestler alive today who will be not be able to regale on how he took in these practitioners."[53]

Some came to understand that audiences responded passionately when a wrestler defined by their inclination to break rules or inflict unnecessary punishment on an opponent wrestled against another who invoked sympathy. One wrestler in particular, Leo Pardello, was known for his rowdy, violent matches meant to provoke and revolt attendees. Convinced that a ticket buyer who hoped to see him lose was as good as one who hoped to see him win, Pardello was pure menace in the ring.[54] He was burly and tough, with thin hair and a pair of prominent cauliflower ears.[55] His avowed purpose, remembered one wrestler, was to make people hate him. He glowered at the audience and beat his opponents into seeming unconsciousness. Some of Pardello's opponents would bite down into bladders of red ink hidden in their mouths to simulate blood, leaving horrified audiences stunned. After a show on Coney Island, Pardello and his opponent had to return to the ring and reassure the crowd that the match had been an act to keep them from calling the police.[56]

As wrestling became more established, questions of its honesty became harder to shake off. If a carnival wrestler were called a fake by an overconfident audience member, locking them into a front face lock or a double wrist lock would be sufficient to remove any questions or doubts. This wasn't an option when the question came from a reporter, a legislator, or a fan you hoped to turn into a regular ticket buyer. "The wrestling public wanted to eat its cake and have it too," wrote sportswriter Grantland Rice. "It wanted all the excitement and action of a faked match, carefully rehearsed, but it also wanted all this action to be on the level."[57] An air of secrecy developed around the wrestling business, an unwritten code intended to keep a sense of legitimacy around how the business and matches operated.[58] When confronted by doubters, wrestlers would defend their own integrity and that of their profession in any way they could. "We protected it because we believed it would collapse if we ever so much as implied publicly that it was something other than what it appeared to be," wrote Lou Thesz. "Protecting the business in the face of criticism and skepticism was the first and most important rule a pro wrestler learned."[59]

FIGURE 4. Frank Gotch, Farmer Burns, and Ole Marsh pose together in Humboldt, Iowa, 1901. Courtesy of Mark Hewitt, Susan Grant, and Michael Murphy.

CHAPTER 3

Americans Believe Him Next to Invincible

MODERN PROFESSIONAL WRESTLING may have been born in carnivals and saloons, but it came of age on the farms and in the downtown theatres of Iowa. Its first major stars and some of its most controversial figures were all born in the state and learned the trade there. Some found national fame; others found infamy and prison. How closely they all worked together and the full degree of their interconnectedness can't be known, but they would orbit each other and frequently cross paths for the better part of the early 1900s.

During those years, no wrestler was more famous than Frank Gotch. His hometown of Humboldt now has a street, a day, and a 67-acre park named in his honor. "The story of American wrestling in the first stages of its glory is the story of the career of Frank Gotch," wrote *Ring* magazine's Nat Fleischer.[1] Gotch is remembered today as a quick, intelligent, and tenacious competitor. He tore through the professional ranks and came to embody the sport in a manner comparable to Babe Ruth in baseball, Jack Dempsey in boxing, and Bobby Jones in golf, all of whom he preceded by more than a decade. "With the development of Gotch as a champion," Jack Curley would later write, "wrestling was moved out of a setting of circus and mire to a place of comparative public confidence."[2] His matches were front-page affairs—not just in Iowa and the Midwest but everywhere he appeared. Just how many of them were straight-faced contests and how many were stage-managed put-ons is completely open to speculation.

Frank Alvin Gotch was born on April 27, 1877, the ninth and last child of German immigrants.[3] Gotch showed an interest in wrestling early and built his reputation by taking on other local grapplers anytime and anywhere a contest could be had. "When men had time from the hard work of the outdoors and assembled together, their fun generally consisted of physical games of strategy," wrote George Bicknell, a Humboldt resident who saw many of Gotch's early matches. "Each man would place his arm around the waist of the other, clasp the other hands together, and go at it. It was the roughest type of exercise."[4] For his first professional match, Gotch dressed in overalls that he'd cut off at the knees and wrestled against a local chicken rancher.[5]

Gotch's life changed in 1899 when he came under the tutelage of Martin Burns, an eccentric, illiterate, nationally known wrestler nicknamed "Farmer." Gotch came to Burns's attention after wrestling one of Burns's associates, a wrestler named Dan McLeod, in a cinder-littered field near the Humboldt railyard during a country fair. "I was picking cinders out of my anatomy for a month after that match," Gotch later wrote.[6] In Jack Curley's recounting of the day, McLeod and Gotch wrestled for four hours for wagers of almost $10,000, but based on other accounts of the match, it's likely that the contest lasted closer to an hour.[7] Regardless of the exact details, Burns was so taken with the way Gotch handled himself against the veteran McLeod that he began training him.

Born in Cedar County, Iowa, in 1861, Farmer Burns was lean, somber, and near-biblical in his habits. He claimed to eschew alcohol, caffeine, tobacco, and swearing.[8] He preached a gospel of relentless self-discipline and self-improvement. Surprisingly prescient as a businessman, he envisioned an America filled with gyms and health food stores and a population obsessed with physical fitness. "My hope," he wrote, "is that I may live to see the day when every large city will have organized athletic clubs for businessmen with facilities on hand for the building up of every man's physical constitution."[9]

He was also a ceaseless self-promoter. Burns told reporters that he slept with a canvas bag of lead shot draped across his throat to strengthen the muscles in his neck, and he developed a reputation for being able to survive a twelve-inch drop from the gallows while in a hangman's noose. One of his favorite gimmicks was to stand with his head and neck flat against a wall and challenge people to squeeze his neck to try to cut off his steady stream of patter.[10]

Burns was nearing thirty with a wife and children when he finally began earning enough to quit his job as a laborer and turn to wrestling full time. He took to traveling the country, performing with carnivals and vaudeville troupes, but much of his income came from running elaborate betting schemes. Arriving in a town under an assumed name, he would take work as a dishwasher or farmhand, gradually letting it be known to the locals that he liked to wrestle on the side for money. He hardly looked the part of an athlete. Recounting one of Burns's more successful hustles in *Harper's Weekly*, author Henry Smith Williams described him as "lean [and] cadaverous looking," with a face so drawn and pinched that he appeared to be suffering from consumption.[11] But even his deceptive appearance was part of his bigger plan. Once he'd secured a match and betting odds were set, the combination of his sickly countenance and brash behavior made locals all the more eager to lay stakes against him.

To drive up betting even more, Burns would let it be known that he'd attracted substantial amounts of financial backing from out-of-state businessmen. They would cover all bets, he assured the townspeople, so they should wager as much as they liked. Sensing a chance at some easy money, many were often more than happy to do so. Once Burns's financial backers arrived in town to cover whatever bets the townspeople had been convinced to make, the match would be held anywhere a crowd could gather and money could be safely gambled. Burns invariably made short work of his opponent; by all accounts, he was a uniquely skilled and lethal wrestler. If all went well, he would gather his winnings and slip out of town quietly before anyone could piece together that they'd been had by a pro.

Burns was one of a group of wrestlers who came to be known as barnstormers. These free-wheeling, itinerant wrestlers traveled the country taking down the best local athletes an area had to offer. They relied on assumed names and disguises to avoid detection and on their considerable skills to avoid defeat. There is no evidence that they considered their lives dishonest. Burns himself valued honesty above all else. "If a man is honest with himself and his fellows everywhere, and upon every occasion," he would later write, "he is the proud possessor of a good feeling that enables him to perform great tasks, and at the same time to keep on a continual search for better things."[12] Barnstormers lived by the well-worn and widely accepted maxim among gamblers and con artists that you can't cheat an honest person and a dishonest one has it coming.[13]

On April 20, 1895, Burns won a version of America's wrestling championship from Evan Lewis in a messy match in Chicago that drew accusations of being rigged before it even took place. As Burns's fame grew, it became more difficult for him to slide into towns as an unknown. He set himself up as a businessman, running gymnasiums, selling mail-order courses on wrestling and self-defense, and managing wrestlers. When he met Frank Gotch in 1899, he sensed that he'd stumbled onto something special.

In May 1901, Gotch traveled to Dawson City, Alaska, with a hard-shelled wrestler and burgeoning businessman called Ole Marsh. Born in 1869 in Decorah, Iowa, Marsh was a talented athlete who was as skilled at mixing it up with locals as he was at convincing sportswriters to cover his matches. In publicity photos, he appears open-faced and almost jocular, a marked difference from his contemporaries, who frequently posed grimacing and stone-faced.[14]

Marsh and Gotch's trip to Dawson was intended as a kind of proving ground for Gotch, as well as a chance to pick clean whatever remaining Alaska Gold Rush money they could from miners looking to gamble it away. Playwright and screenwriter Wilson Mizner traveled to Dawson in 1897 and found it, as his biographer wrote, "overrun with crooks, conmen, fugitives from justice, card sharps, adventuresses, and sporting ladies."[15] Marsh had already been to Dawson and knew what to expect, and though the area had calmed down some by the time he returned with Frank Gotch, it wasn't by all that much.

Gotch traveled under the name Frank Kennedy, posing as a veteran of the Spanish–American War looking to work the mines and wrestle on the side. After establishing his local bona fides by winning wager after wager against local opponents, he wrestled against Marsh in a series of increasingly dramatic matches in the theatres of Dawson. They traded victories, making sure that the ending of each match was inconclusive enough to keep people coming back for more. In one, Gotch took a breathtaking fall from the ring into an orchestra pit. Terrified that they'd witnessed the wrestler's death, the crowd fell into silence, only to break into yelling and cheering as Gotch climbed out of the pit and back into the ring. The gamblers who wound up losing big on these matches suspected that they'd been taken but couldn't pin down exactly how or when the wrestlers had pulled off the con. Dusting out of town with

Marsh before the end of spring, Gotch was said to have cleared as much as $40,000 in just a few months.[16]

Working under the management of Ole Marsh and Farmer Burns, Gotch wrestled across the United States and into Canada in the early 1900s. Tough and exacting, sportswriters transformed him into an athletic sensation. "As cold art, it was impossible for wrestling to go beyond Gotch," the *Saturday Evening Post*'s Milton MacKaye would later write.[17] Still in his late twenties, Gotch was boyishly handsome, with dark brown hair, long muscular arms, and a broad back and chest. He had learned his trade from the best in the wrestling business, but the success that soon came his way must have caught even him by surprise.

Gotch's reputation was made over a thrilling series of matches against a hard-bitten, one-eyed former mill worker from Bedford, Ohio, named ·Tom Jenkins. Born in 1872, Jenkins had worked yanking heated iron bars out of a furnace and shaping them with rollers in an Ohio factory before establishing himself as a top wrestler. "That job," he later said, "taught me to be quick." Beginning in 1903, Gotch and Jenkins drew thousands of spectators in Buffalo, Kansas City, and Bellingham, for matches that were riveting, blood-soaked, affairs.[18] At one, Gotch used his fingers to scrape and dig at Jenkins's only good eye. Officials at another likened it to a cockfight. At each appearance, the steady flow of cash being bet on both men made claims of match-throwing inevitable, but as Gotch's reputation grew, those cries grew fainter. A strange kind of doublethink set in; professional wrestling may not have always been for real, but Frank Gotch undoubtedly was. "Suppose I did lay down that first fall," Gotch circuitously explained to reporters after an action-packed match against Jenkins in Cleveland. "I won the match, didn't I? And that was what I was there for. . . . There was never a prize fight or a wrestling match pulled off that someone did not yell fake."[19]

When the pair met in New York on March 15, 1905, Madison Square Garden was full to the upper gallery with spectators. By then, Gotch's reputation had grown to such a degree that, after the match was over, a sportswriter at the *New York Telegraph* declared it, "strictly on the level, free from any suspicion of an inside understanding. . . . That match did more for the good of wrestling than anything that ever happened before."[20]

Watching all of this from a measured distance was Jack Curley. Given the right kind of promotion, he must have thought that Gotch could attract even larger crowds. Curley worked with Gotch on matches in 1907 and 1909, and he kept in close contact with the young star. Soon, their names would be tied to one of the most debated matches of the twentieth century.

Far removed from the violent world of American wrestling was Russian George Hackenschmidt. Born in 1878 in Dorpat, Estonia, he began his career as a professional strongman. "So far as I can remember," he later wrote, "I was, from my earliest years, devoted to all bodily exercises."[21] Intelligent and temperamental, he possessed an impossibly well-developed physique that was known for driving crowds into hysterics. His muscles, one reporter marveled, "might have served for a horse."[22] A physical wonder, he liked to display his agility to onlookers by jumping over chairs or in and out of barrels.

Trained in the circuses of Moscow, Hackenschmidt was an astute performer. In 1902, he relocated to England in the hope of advancing his professional prospects. After struggling initially, he began working with manager Charles Cochran, a theatrical promoter whose professional roots were in vaudeville and who would later become a close associate of playwright Noel Coward. Cochran encouraged Hackenschmidt to embrace showmanship in his matches and convinced him of the primacy of entertaining a crowd. "It was obvious that the music hall public did not want straight wrestling," Cochran later wrote. "They wanted a show, and a show they were given."[23]

Hackenschmidt began drawing packed houses across the country, including at the Alhambra, London's most prestigious music hall. His name sang out from newspaper headlines, show posters, and billboards. "London became wrestling mad," Cochran later wrote. "The boys in the street were always trying conclusions on the pavement. Supper parties often culminated in 'holds' being discussed and demonstrated."[24]

On Hackenschmidt's first tour of America in 1905, he defeated Frank Gotch's rival, Tom Jenkins, to become recognized as wrestling's world heavyweight champion. When Hackenschmidt returned three years later, he was famous enough to meet privately with President Theodore Roosevelt. "If I were not President of the United States," Roosevelt told him, "I would like to be George Hackenschmidt."[25]

Frank Gotch and George Hackenschmidt, the two most famous wrestlers in the Western world, met each other for the first time in a wrestling ring on the evening of April 3, 1908, at Chicago's Dexter Park Pavilion. Although there had been marquee matches in America before it, America's hero versus the world champion was something else. It was front-page news around the world, a contest between flag-bearing, near-mythical heroes. "The Stars and Stripes must rise or fall with Frank Gotch," exclaimed one sportswriter in the *Washington Post* during the lead-up to the match.[26]

Still, the match was a risky proposition for everyone involved. Its promoter, a Wisconsin-based businessman named William Wittig, had outbid several other promoters, including Jack Curley, for the rights to handle the event. Wittig guaranteed each man $10,000—an exorbitant amount of money at the time for participants in a wrestling match. And besides earning the right to call themselves the world champion, the winner stood, as well, to gain lucrative opportunities to tour the United States, England, and elsewhere. Underscoring the hoped-for interest in the match, Wittig poured even more of his money into cameras to film the match for distribution to theatres and enough lighting to turn the Chicago night as bright as day.[27]

Hackenschmidt was understood to be the clear favorite. He was physically stronger than Gotch and more experienced. He was known and respected in multiple countries. He'd publicly predicted that he'd beat Gotch in two straight falls and that he'd only need fifteen minutes to do so. Wittig was hoping for a barnburner, but even with the blustery talk, and with somewhere between 6,000 and 8,000 people in attendance, the match turned out to be a monotonous grind. The first ninety minutes were filled with nothing more than pulling and tugging as Gotch and Hackenschmidt struggled with each other for position. Gotch drew hisses and cries of "Cut it out!" from fans seated ringside for repeatedly driving his thumb and fingernails into Hackenschmidt's eyes and cheeks. Taunting Hackenschmidt, Gotch told him, "Over here in America we wrestle on the level."[28] Hackenschmidt, in turn, rammed his head into Gotch's mouth, drawing blood. There were occasional flurries of action, but by midnight, with the match still just in the first of three planned falls, Hackenschmidt began petitioning the referee to declare a draw. Just after 12:30 a.m., bleeding from his forehead and a cut on his left forearm and concerned about sustaining a permanent injury after having been thrown down hard to the mat, Hackenschmidt tried again to persuade the referee to end the bout. Again unsuccessful, he turned to Gotch and said, "I'll give you the match."[29]

"The end came so unexpectedly that the crowd of 8,000 which witnessed the contest could scarcely comprehend what had happened," wrote the reporter on hand from the *New York Times*.[30] Spectators surged into the ring, followed by police, who pushed many right back through the ropes. Gotch was draped in the American flag that had been decorating his corner and carried out of the ring by enthusiastic fans. Back in his own dressing room, Hackenschmidt sat dejected, the left side of his head severely swollen and his eyelids scraped and cut.[31] When Wittig begged him to explain why he'd surrendered the entire match instead of just a single fall, Hackenschmidt just shook his head and refused to respond.[32]

Several days after the match, Hackenschmidt began complaining that Gotch had fought dirty. He'd covered his body in oil prior to the match, Hackenschmidt claimed, making it impossible to get a hold of him, and doused his hair in chemicals that had dripped into Hackenschmidt's eyes whenever the two men locked up. He'd been distracted, as well, Hackenschmidt said, by concerns that had he defeated Gotch, the jingoistic crowd in Dexter Park would have mobbed him. His claims gained little serious traction but did draw an agitated response from Gotch. "Hackenschmidt never was a better man than I am," he told reporters. "I can beat him any time and am willing to go right out now and wrestle him again."[33] The match had been a dud, but Gotch's win had brought the world heavyweight wrestling championship to America all the same, and his country loved him for it. He was the rugged Iowa farm boy blessed with strength and ingenuity who'd taken on the world and won. "Americans," wrote a reporter from the *New York Times*, "believe him next to invincible."[34]

By the end of 1909, Gotch's matches were drawing thousands of people into theatres and halls around the country. Crowds so large to see a single star were unheard of in professional wrestling. A cartoon printed in the *Chicago Tribune* depicted a smiling Gotch vanquishing his opponent and then cuddling up to a bagful of money. The caption read, "Another Winning Hold."[35] Though the sport still had its doubters, Frank Gotch was above reproach.

At just thirty-three years old and only a decade into his career, he'd grown rich enough to consider retiring from the ring to spend more time on the vast stretches of Iowa farmland he'd purchased. He'd traveled the world but was making plans to settle down in exactly the same place from which he'd started. He'd gone from risking his life hustling miners in the goldfields of Alaska to fame and athletic glory. The age of the barnstormer creeping into a town with disguises and aliases and leaving in a hurry with a pile of money was reaching its end. Improbably, a professional wrestler had become the most celebrated athlete in America.

FIGURE 5. Dr. Ben Roller wrestles an unknown opponent at the Alaska-Yukon-Pacific Exposition in Seattle, 1909. Photograph by Frank H. Nowell. Courtesy of Special Collections, the University of Washington Libraries, AYP616.

CHAPTER 4

I Never Miked an Honest Man

JACK CURLEY RARELY had to seek out opportunity. As often as not, if he waited and watched long enough, it always seemed like opportunity sought him out instead. In April 1909, a friend recommended him to John Cort, a Washington-based theatre magnate, who was looking for a promoter to coordinate the boxing and wrestling shows to be featured at Seattle's upcoming world's fair, the Alaska-Yukon-Pacific Exposition. For his effort, Cort offered him $2,000 per month and a cut of the gate receipts. "That looked mighty sweet to me," Curley wrote.[1]

Curley operated out of Cort's Arena, a 5,000-seat venue located at the head of the fair's exhibit-lined midway. Attendees to his boxing and wrestling shows were immersed in a dreamlike atmosphere as they passed by replicas of Klondike dance halls, a recreation of the naval battle between the *Monitor* and *Merrimac*, and Prince Albert the Educated Horse, who bowed and knelt before spectators. Outside of the arena, a thirty-foot-tall statue of former boxing champion John L. Sullivan greeted attendees, his bare fists cocked and ready for silent battle. Inside, Sullivan himself was appearing daily at the fair in public sparring matches.

He lent a much-needed air of credibility to Curley's shows. The reputation of professional wrestling in Seattle at the time was even more problematic than in most cities. To try to build interest in his matches, Curley hired Dr. Benjamin Roller, a Seattle-based athlete who was already a well-known figure around the Pacific Northwest, as his star attraction. Born just three days earlier than Curley, on July 1, 1876, in Newman, Illinois, Roller had been an accomplished multi-sport standout and practicing surgeon in Philadelphia, where he'd experimented with early treatments for tuberculosis and new methods for administering anesthesia. Traumatized by the death of one of his young patients, he moved to Seattle in 1904 to take a position with the University of Washington.[2] Handsome and refined at just over six feet tall and an evenly distributed 200 pounds, he had begun wrestling professionally in 1906 at the encouragement of Frank Gotch's associate, Ole Marsh, initially as a way to pay off accumulated debt from a real estate deal but also, he said, because he saw in the sport a way to achieve physical perfection. Marsh built Roller's reputation around Washington by matching him against some of the best-known and most feared wrestlers in the country, including Farmer Burns, Fred Beell, and Jack Carkeek.[3] Roller, a wrestling neophyte, was victorious against them all.

Roller's success in 1907 and 1908 was a salve to the damage that had been caused by Ole Marsh's rumored ties to rigged boxing and wrestling matches that had been run out of a boathouse on the banks of Seattle's Lake Washington during the early months of 1906. The boathouse was set behind a dense growth of trees and brush. Planks laid over swampy muck marked the trail to reach it. Gamblers had been lured there by a network of sharps and steerers—well-dressed, educated, slick-talking men operating around the city who were responsible for hooking deep-pocketed prospects with the promise of inside information on the outcomes of bouts.

Inside, the boathouse was outfitted with a makeshift ring instead of living quarters. Its oblong windows were covered over with paper to discourage onlookers, and canvas was stretched tightly from the ceiling joists to prevent athletes from crashing into walls. Matches often took place in near silence for fear of attracting unwanted attention, and spectators were encouraged to lay outrageous bets on what they'd been led to believe were sure things. The matches never played out as planned, though, and more than one bettor was sent home penniless. The con was executed so smoothly that only two victims ever made complaints to city officials about having been swindled.[4]

The operation ran for eight months, bringing in more than $150,000 before the police were tipped off to its existence in August 1906. Ole Marsh, along with two well-known wrestlers, Jack Carkeek and Dan McLeod, were implicated in the scheme but never charged with crimes. Seattle's chief of police, Charles Wappenstein, bedeviled by a lack of evidence and witnesses on which to build a case, responded by vowing to carefully watch any attempts to stage professional wrestling going forward. "There will be no fake wrestling matches as long as I am chief of police," he promised in October 1906. "I shall investigate every match that's made, and if I find that they are not to be conducted honestly, the participants will be arrested and the bout called off."[5]

Despite the charged environment, Marsh and Roller worked together to some success before eventually splitting over a financial disagreement sometime in late 1908. Roller's decision to begin working with Jack Curley in 1909 at the Alaska-Yukon-Pacific exhibition enraged Marsh. He visited Curley at his office, telling him that wrestling was dead in Seattle, and he would be ill-advised to try to revive it.[6] When Curley pressed on undeterred, Marsh confronted him again, banging his fists on Curley's desk and promising him a fight. "[The situation] almost seems unreal," Curley would later write, "for so swiftly did the dramatic sequences follow each other that a skeptic reading the chronicle of them may deem them to be the creation of a romancer."[7]

It was professional wrestling's first skirmish over geography. It would be far from its last. While it can be read either as a genuine dispute between two ambitious businessmen or as an elaborate ploy to attract customers gone wrong, the complete story is impossible to know. The truth is likely (but by no means assuredly) closer to the former. Marsh, according to most accounts, was serious in his desire to sabotage Curley's move into Seattle. Curley, too, would contend that he had received death threats in response to his public criticisms of Marsh.[8]

For much of 1909, Curley monopolized the wrestling scene in Seattle. Curley and Marsh exploited their connections with area reporters to fill Seattle newspapers with broadsides and threats directed against each other. Marsh derided Curley's matches as fakes. Curley called Marsh a scam artist. After weeks of back and forth, the two agreed to settle things with a match between Jack Curley's Ben Roller and Ole Marsh's new wrestler, Bert Warner. Advertised as the "Wrestling Match of the Year" and bolstered by the steady stream of press coverage Curley and Marsh had generated, they booked it for September 24, 1909, during the closing weeks of the Alaska-Yukon-Pacific Exposition.[9]

The night was a fiasco. Surviving accounts describe the crowd's reaction as varying from enthralled to bewildered.[10] It likely went something like this: Three thousand people inside Cort's Arena were buzzing to the point of frenzy. Curley and Marsh stalked agitatedly around ringside. As soon as the match began, in a dramatic and wholly unexpected move, Bert Warner fell to the mat. A man rose from his ringside seat and began reading from a letter Warner had written. In it, Warner accused Curley of insisting that he hand over $1,000 as a guarantee he would lose the match to Roller within an hour. "In order to protect my money, I am going to lose the first fall as soon as I possibly can, and the second just as quickly," the man read on behalf of Warner. "I then want you to insist that the referee be changed, and I want to wrestle Roller on the square, and give the people a run for their money."[11]

With the crowd shouting "Fake!" and confusion setting in, a spectator grabbed a chair and tried to attack Curley before being hustled out by police. Curley began banging on the ring, calling for silence and threatening to shut the arena down. "This 'faint' of [Warner]'s is a palpable fake designed to ruin the match, discredit me, and swindle you," Curley shouted. "We shall see this thing to a finish."[12]

After a long break, Warner and Roller finally agreed to wrestle. The much-hyped match turned out to be a bore. After an hour of mostly defensive maneuvering, a frustrated Roller scooped Warner off the mat and slammed him down, separating his shoulder. The crowd left the arena "intensely disgusted," as one attendee remarked, and unimpressed with the rowdy sideshow that the evening had become.[13]

If wrestling wasn't quite dead in Seattle when Jack Curley had arrived there, it would be by the time he left. He and Marsh continued their back and forth in the local papers for two more weeks. Through the *Seattle Star*, Marsh spread a story that Curley had made arrangements with Frank Gotch to lose his world championship to Ben Roller. Roller retaliated by publishing a letter in the *Seattle Times* accusing the *Star*'s business manager of an attempt to extort Curley. That move got Roller arrested on a libel charge.[14]

The morning of Roller's court hearing on the libel charges, Curley sat edgily picking over a late breakfast. "Roller was in real danger of going to prison," Curley wrote, "for the offense with which he was charged was punishable by two years at hard labor." When he heard a newsboy shouting in the street, he stepped out, bought a paper, and read the news that both Ole Marsh and Bert Warner had been arrested on mail fraud charges. "I cannot tell you what I did or said at the moment," Curley later wrote. "I suppose I was incoherent in speech, outlandish in action. It had worked out exactly as though it had all been a carefully planned melodrama."[15]

Marsh and Warner's arrests were front-page news in Seattle. Claiming they had left town on a hunting trip, the pair had been tracked by police into central Washington, apprehended, and turned over to federal officers as part of a nationwide crackdown on what came to be known as the Mabray Gang. Marsh took the arrest with an air of calm, even stopping to buy several newspapers on his way to the county jail. Handing one to Warner, he coolly remarked, "We'll read these going over in the car."[16]

The Mabray Gang was a loose knit ring of athletes, gamblers, and hustlers swirling around John C. Mabray, an amiable, dough-faced former horse trader from Omaha. Mabray operated predominantly out of Council Bluffs, Iowa, considered one of the country's earliest "right" towns—areas where swindlers could work with limited competition and where support from police and politicians could be secured at a reasonable price.[17] From Council Bluffs, he coordinated a nationwide network of crooked athletes, make-believe millionaires, and as many as 200 steerers.

Mabray and his associates communicated using letters filled with a complicated vocabulary of code and shorthand. They spoke in the language of commerce: buildings from which they worked their cons were "stores," prospective victims were "properties," and areas of operation were "mines."[18] Members were assigned numbers: Ole Marsh was "22"; Bert Warner was "48"; wrestler Jack Carkeek (later arrested in San Francisco in 1910 for helping to run a wire-tapping swindle in the city) was "60."[19] Government officials had begun tracking the group only after one of their letters was mistakenly delivered to the wrong customer who, concerned by the cryptic content, had turned it over to postal authorities.

The broad plan outlined in the letters was always the same. Once a target—referred to as a "mike"—was identified, steerers were deployed to engage them with a story about a group of millionaires headed to town on business and eager to gamble. The millionaires were said to routinely travel with an athlete—a wrestler, a jockey, a boxer, or a foot racer—whom they matched against local competition in high-stakes athletic contests. What the millionaires didn't know, the mike was told, was that their business secretary had become disgruntled after years of arranging matches and not once being cut in on the winnings.

This secretary had found their own athlete, the story continued, who they were certain was a lock to win. The plan was for the secretary to discreetly arrange for the millionaires' athlete to be matched against their own. They would then lay their own bet and clear a fortune. The problem, which is where the mike came in, was that the secretary would raise suspicion by placing the bet himself. All that was needed to bring the plan off was for the mike to handle posting the bet in place of the secretary.

If the mike agreed, it was promised that they wouldn't have to risk a cent of their own money or pay a dollar for their own travel. The fleecing of the ungrateful millionaires was pitched as something of a vacation. The money was meaningless to them, the mike was assured, and they wouldn't miss it at all. In fact, the heartless millionaires had it coming. "It isn't a question of how much money they will lose but how much we think best to let them lose," Bert Warner wrote in a letter to one prospective mike. "They are all very wealthy and $10,000 is no more to one of them than $10 is to you or I."[20] The way the steerer sold it, being the linchpin in the secretary's convoluted revenge scheme was hardly even dishonest.

The only requirement—added only as an afterthought—was that the mike had to produce enough of their own cash to convince the millionaires that they were dealing with a man of means. At no point did anyone suggest that any of that money would be used for actual gambling. This process of hooking a mike could play out over weeks or months, sometimes taking as long as two years. Once hooked, they were like lambs jumping for the knife.

The final act of the con played out with military-like precision. When a mike arrived in the designated town (the plan always involved the mike leaving their hometown), they were introduced to Mabray and his fictional millionaires. Together, they drank, socialized, and talked sports. The atmosphere created by Mabray and other confidence men of his era was alluring yet, once inside, opaque. "To expect a mark to enter into a con game, take the bait, and then, by sheer reason, analyze the situation and see it as a swindle is simply asking too much," wrote David

Maurer in his authoritative history of American confidence games, *The Big Con*. "The mark is thrown into an unreal world which very closely resembles real life; like the spectator regarding the life groups in a museum of natural history, he cannot tell where the real scene merges into the background."[21] Caught up in the heat of wagering and the illusion of mingling with a monied crowd while secretly planning to take them for every dollar they could, the mike proved reliably willing to wager their personal cash alongside the secretary's, even though there was no requirement for them to do so.

During the actual athletic event they were betting on, disaster reliably struck. As if on cue, the secretary's "can't lose" athlete would collapse to the ground, bleeding from the mouth. For boxers and wrestlers, it was a hard shot to the stomach that would bring them down. If it was a horse race, the jockey would tumble from the saddle as they neared the finish line. The gore was produced by the athlete biting down onto a blood-soaked sponge or bladder they'd secretly stuffed into their mouth before the contest. A member of the Mabray Gang, posing as a doctor, would examine them and proclaim them dead.

Uneager to be arrested as accomplices to murder, the spectators quickly became restless. Betting on an illegal sporting event was one thing, but being involved in one that ended with a fatality was something else. It was agreed that all bets would be called off, but that instead of waiting around to divide up the stakes money and return it back to its original owners, each man's original wager would be returned once the secretary, who invariably ended up holding the entirety of the cash, made it back safely to their hometown. Mabray's men then hopped into waiting cars and beat the retreat as quickly as they could, leaving the mike on their own to find a way home.

So convincing was the scam that, in some instances, mikes sent extra money to help cover the medical care or funeral expenses for the athletes. It was often only after weeks had passed and the promised stakes money was never returned that the mike came to understand they'd been had. When the realization sank in, most were too humiliated or afraid to file a complaint with the authorities. Mabray's operation was said to have taken in a total of more than $5 million. One victim later testified to being devastated by their financial losses. Another, a Virginia-based lumber merchant who had been convinced to travel 3,000 miles to Los Angeles to bet on a rigged horse race, said, "It was a tragic thing for me, and once it looked like I might have to walk back to Virginia."[22]

Ole Marsh, Jack Carkeek, and Bert Warner had run a version of the scam out of their houseboat in Seattle in 1906, and after three years, their past involvement with Mabray came back to sink them. Mabray was arrested in 1908, but it would take more than a year for federal marshals to round up the other people identified in his papers. Before Jack Curley's controversial matches at the Alaska-Yukon-Pacific Exhibition, Marsh and Warner would have known there was a risk of their being arrested, but they were hoping that the convoluted system of codes used in Mabray's letters would make obtaining evidence of their involvement impossible. Of the ninety of Mabray's associates ultimately arrested, fourteen, including Mabray, Marsh, and Warner, were sentenced to terms at the federal prison at Leavenworth.

After his verdict was announced, Mabray shook hands with the jurors on his way out of the courtroom. He steadfastly believed his victims shared in the guilt, if for no other reason than their intent. "As soon as a man begins trying to do other people, he is bound to be done," he said. "There have been mikes since the world was born, and there will be plenty of mikes in the end. . . . Americans in business and baseball make all they can out of the rules. That was our game too, but the court says it went too far." Desperately cynical, he told reporters from his cell, "I never miked an honest man."[23]

The revelations concerning the Mabray Gang, and in particular the involvement of multiple well-known wrestlers in the scheme, did nothing to help bolster the public's faith in the honesty of professional wrestling. Despite their close working relationship with Marsh, Frank Gotch and Farmer Burns were never implicated in Mabray's schemes. Following Ole Marsh's arrest, Gotch did all he could to distance himself from his former manager and trainer. "I was six years with Gotch," Marsh later wrote. "Took him from a nobody and made him into a world's champion, then he turned traitor."[24]

Marsh made little attempt to contest the charges. Furious at Mabray for keeping the records that would implicate him, he recounted the revenge that he and Mabray's other former associates had exacted on him to a US Marshal. "Mabray was a big, fat man," the Marshal remembered being told. "Well, they have put him to work in the brickyard. And he has to catch brick[s], which are thrown to him by another convict. Now, the other convict, the man who pitches the brick to him, is one of his former gang members. They are working some sort of system by which they get a fresh man to throw to Mabray about every hour, and while the thrower is fresh and strong, Mabray has to stand it all day by himself. If he fails to catch them as fast as they come, he gets hit by a handful of brick. And you bet they come fast enough."[25]

When the Alaska-Yukon-Pacific Exhibition finally closed in October 1909, Jack Curley and Ben Roller boarded a train to Chicago. Curley's Seattle shows had been a success, but the constant controversy proved exhausting and unappealing to the area's serious sports fans. By the time Curley left, the business of professional wrestling was nearing death there and in other cities as well. If Jack Curley had hopes—never mind a plan—for reviving it, he wasn't letting on.

FIGURE 6. Stanislaus Zbyszko, Chicago, 1909. Image ID: SDN-008153, Chicago Daily News Collection, Chicago History Museum.

CHAPTER 5

When a Mayor Leaves Office
He's an Ex-Mayor, Isn't He?

THE COLOR LINE in professional boxing had been drawn by one-time heavyweight champion John L. Sullivan. Sullivan ruled the sport during his championship reign from 1882 through 1892, but all the while had refused to defend his title against Black fighters. He had framed it as a matter of racial pride, but the policy served him just fine, too, as a way of ducking the worthy challengers, such as Peter Jackson, who also happened to be Black. Subsequent champions followed his lead, and the color line held until 1908. By then, boxing's heavyweight championship had passed to Tommy Burns. Though open to taking on all fighters, it took months for Burns to agree to a bout with a hard-punching thirty-year-old Black boxer from Galveston, Texas, named Jack Johnson. Johnson had to chase Burns all the way to Bushcutter's Bay in Australia, where on December 26, 1908, he trounced him in fourteen rounds to become boxing's first Black world heavyweight champion.

Jack Curley was already well-acquainted with Johnson's power as a fighter by then, and following Johnson's championship win, their relationship would only continue to grow more intertwined and complicated. Curley had first seen Johnson fight in March 1899, in Springfield, Illinois, as part of what was known as a battle royal. Battle royals were cruel and intentionally humiliating events where any number of Black boxers were outfitted with boxing gloves, then blindfolded, and sent into a ring to blindly punch until only one was left standing. Johnson had won that evening, knocking out four other fighters. His pay, he would later say, was "about 30 sandwiches and a dozen beers."[1]

Curley and Johnson formally met on May 5, 1899, at the Howard Theater in Chicago. That evening, Johnson took a dive that was so obvious—resting an elbow on the mat and propping his head in his hand while the referee comically slow counted to ten—that it elicited laughter from the crowd.[2] When the fight's promoter refused to pay Johnson his share of the purse, Curley scraped together three dollars and gave it to the desperate fighter so he could buy himself dinner. "Had anybody told me that this hungry Negro would be heavyweight champion of the world," Curley later wrote, "I would have laughed in his face."[3]

Johnson's championship win over the Canadian Burns had come only eight months after Frank Gotch's widely praised win over Russia's George Hackenschmidt for wrestling's heavyweight championship, but it was met with none of the same nationalistic ardor. In fact, Burns's blood had barely dried on the Bushcutter's Bay ring canvas before sportswriters began sounding cries for a White man—any White man—to step up and defeat Johnson. Writer Jack London was so unhappy with Johnson's victory that he implored one-time boxing heavyweight champion Jim Jeffries to "emerge from his alfalfa farm and remove that smile from Johnson's face. Jeff, it's up to you."[4]

Jim Jeffries was a rough-hewn former boilermaker from Ohio. He had retired as heavyweight champion in 1905, vacating his title in the process. During his reign, he, too, had refused to defend his title against Black fighters, promising that he'd go back to swinging a sledgehammer for twelve hours a day before doing so. When Jack Johnson became heavyweight champion in 1908, the myth of Jim Jeffries, undefeated and resting at home, took on an almost mythological shape to crazed fans who couldn't stand to see a Black fighter claiming boxing's highest prize. Their hue and cry became so loud that Jeffries finally decided to return to the ring. "I was through with the fighting game until Johnson butted into first place," Jeffries told reporters. "But so long as I have never been defeated, I think it no more than right that I should step into the ring again and demonstrate that a White man is king of them all."[5]

"It amuses me to hear this talk of Jeffries claiming the championship," Johnson shot back. "Why, when a mayor leaves office, he's an ex-mayor, isn't he? When a champion leaves the ring, he's an ex-champion. Well, that isn't Jeffries."[6]

The Johnson–Jeffries fight promised to be a blockbuster, and the right to promote it had been won by a brash forty-year-old whose birth name was George but who was best known as "Tex." Tex Rickard was born on a farm outside of Kansas City, Missouri, in 1870. At twenty-five, he endured the death of his wife and only child within the span of just two months. Following the loss, he moved to Alaska, where he made and lost a fortune running saloons in Dawson and Nome. After Alaska, he would relocate again, this time to Goldfield, Nevada, where he turned his attention to sports. In time, he would take the violent, clandestine world of boxing and turn it into a national obsession.[7]

Tex Rickard's gift for promotion and flair for staging sporting events dwarfed his competition, including Jack Curley, whose shows soon came to feel ramshackle in comparison. As a promoter, Rickard was everything Curley was not: arrogant, willing to bet big, and unwilling to lose. And unlike Curley, Rickard had no interest in professional wrestling. Maybe its reputation was too suspect. Maybe the potential for gates was just too small. Whatever it was or wasn't, when it came to boxing alone, he was willing to gamble fast and loose.

Rickard dubbed the Johnson–Jeffries bout "The Fight of the Century." He scheduled it for July 4, 1910, in Reno, Nevada, and pitched it to reporters as a battle for racial superiority. News of the fight filled newspapers for weeks on end. "It seems that every day more printed matter bearing on the Johnson–Jeffries prize fight is written, printed, distributed, and read than most booklovers have in their entire libraries," mused novelist Rex Beach.[8] When the fighters gathered to sign contracts, the room, Jeffries remembered, "was jammed with newspapermen, sporting men, photographers—you'd have thought we were picking the next President of the United States."[9]

Curley had put in a bid to stage the fight, but he never really had much hope of outbidding the determined Rickard. He was, however, part of the group of businessmen who signed Jeffries to appear as part of a boxing and wrestling variety show that also featured both Frank Gotch and Dr. Ben Roller. The show toured the country for twelve weeks leading up to the fight. Curley picked up on Rickard's promotional cues, promoting each tour stop with calls for spectators to come out and "Judge for yourself!" as to whether Jeffries would be able to shake off his retirement and defeat the younger, faster Johnson.[10] The tour finished as a financial success for everyone, with Curley paying Jeffries more than $100,000. With the wrestling business still in the doldrums, Curley made immediate plans to take Jeffries out after the Johnson fight on an even more ambitious nine-month tour, should he win in Nevada.[11]

On a boiling hot Fourth of July in 1910, more than 15,000 fans converged on Reno to watch Johnson and Jeffries finally come to blows. Once the bout was underway, anyone hopeful that Jeffries would function as some kind of White savior was quickly disappointed. Johnson beat Jeffries bloody before finally knocking him out in the fifteenth round. As he returned to his corner, Johnson told his trainers, "I could have fought for two hours longer." Fearing violence if Johnson should win, Jeffries, among others, including one-time Greco-Roman wrestling champion William Muldoon, had implored fans prior to the fight to stay peaceful. Johnson was able to exit the ring safely, but horrific violence was committed in several major American cities, with at least 11 and as many as 26 people killed and hundreds more injured. Musician Louis Armstrong, at the time a ten-year-old paperboy living in New Orleans, remembered being told to run for his life after news of Johnson's victory made it to the city. "Jack Johnson has knocked out Jim Jeffries," a friend told him. "The White boys are sore about it, and they're going to take it out on us."[12]

Immediately following the fight, Jeffries made no attempt to take credit away from Johnson's victory. "I could never have whipped Jack Johnson at my best," he said. "I couldn't have reached him in a thousand years."[13] Less than a year after his resounding defeat, however, he changed his story. In newspaper reports and later in the 1929 book *Two Fisted Jeff*, he claimed to have been poisoned before the fight. The drug, Jeffries said, had rendered him listless and incoherent, and left him incapable of mounting any kind of challenge. It was discovered only after the fight, during a doctor's visit, and had lingered in his system for years. "Since then," he wrote, "there has never been the slightest doubt in my mind that I was 'slipped something'; thus far, however, we never have been able to get legal proof or to learn when and how the drug was given to me."[14] Jeffries's claims were considered preposterous by all but a few fans still unable to accept that their hero had been squarely outmanned.

Jack Curley hadn't even bothered to travel to Reno to attend the fight in person. Instead, he followed the results from New York, later opining that nerves and the pressures of fighting for the hopes of an entire race had undone Jeffries long before he'd entered the ring. As a result of Jeffries's loss, Curley's plans to spend most of the coming months on the road showcasing him were scuttled. Instead, accompanied by Ben

Roller, Curley boarded the *RMS Carmania* on July 8, 1910, and set sail for London.[15]

Curley hadn't seen Europe since he was a child. He would later feign that the trip was meant as a five-month vacation, but by 1910, his life had become a busman's holiday. Any time spent not actively promoting events was spent scouting opportunities for new work. This trip, in particular, was to involve evaluating wrestlers he could import to America, and Curley set to work as soon as he and Roller deboarded in London.[16] He threw dinner parties for sportswriters and feted their children with gifts. He wrote the publicity for his matches himself and had it printed in newspapers word for word. "It was the first introduction of our American methods in London," he later remarked. "[It] was viewed as almost scandalous."[17]

While in London, Curley matched Roller against an Indian wrestler named The Great Gama. Born Ghulam Muhammad, Gama had arrived in the city from India earlier that year and had struggled to find opponents. Curley and Roller had only agreed to the match after a convincing sales pitch from Gama's manager. "We were cold to the proposition at first, but when he convinced us that there were many wealthy Indians of the highest caste in London who would pay well to see such a match, we warmed up to it," Curley later wrote.[18] His advance press for the match, angling it as a competition between the East and the West, caused such a stir in the city that Curley was summoned to the Foreign Office, where he was dressed down by a British official. "The danger that the Indian might triumph was inimical to the security of Great Britain's hold on the subject races," he remembered being told. "It would not do to get it into the heads of these races that one of their numbers could humble a White man at anything. Did I understand? I did."[19]

The match filled the city's Alhambra Theatre, with an overflow crowd left to mill outside in Leicester Square waiting for the result. Despite official warnings, Gama won the match handily, with Roller claiming an injury to his ribs after being tossed around the ring for ten minutes.[20]

In Vienna, Curley paired Roller against an inelegant but oddly charismatic wrestler named Stanislaus Zbyszko. Born Stanislaw Cyganiewicz in 1879 or 1881, in what is now southeastern Poland, Zbyszko stood a modest 5'8", with heavy muscles, cropped hair, and a thick, dark mustache. A one-time circus strongman, he embellished his history more than most, taking an already rich personal background and exaggerating it by claiming at different times to speak eleven languages, to be a highly skilled chess player, to have graduated from Vienna University, to have been a lieutenant in the Austrian army, to be a close associate of European royalty, and to be a lawyer. Zbyszko had become popular in England following George Hackenschmidt's departure for America, not because British fans adored him as they had Hackenschmidt but because they found him crude and his ring style ponderous and hoped to see him lose.[21]

Zbyszko first toured America in 1909. He helped establish the style that foreign wrestlers would follow for decades to come, holding onto his consonant-rich last name instead of flattening it for American audiences. And instead of downplaying his heritage, he reveled in it, touring in areas of the country with large Polish populations and referring to himself as "The Mighty Son of Poland."[22]

As with Ben Roller's match in London against the Great Gama, his match with Zbyszko in Vienna also attracted attention from government officials, this time after Austria's Archduke Franz Ferdinand announced that he would attend. The story Curley would later tell is that he met the Archduke while jogging on the grounds of what turned out to be his private estate and talked him into going. The match was a sellout well in advance, but the night almost ended before it could begin. The evening prior, Zbyszko, claiming an injury to his knee, had telegrammed Curley with news that he would be unable to appear. Convinced he could persuade Zbyszko to change his mind, Curley caught a packed overnight train to Krakow. Arriving in the city at 6 a.m., he rushed in a cab to Zbyszko's house. Suspicious that Zbyszko would try to ignore any knocks at the door, Curley threw a rock through one of the upstairs windows. "Get into your clothes!" he yelled when Zbyszko appeared. "Come with me." He packed Zbyszko into the waiting car and onto the 7 a.m. train back to Vienna, reaching the arena just hours before the match was set to begin.[23] Zbyszko won the match, gamey knee and all.

Despite his occasional setbacks, the trip was far from a failure for Curley. He soaked up the manner in which professional wrestling was presented in major European cities, where grand international tournaments were held in elegantly appointed theatres. He succeeded, too, in reacquainting himself with a wrestler he hoped American fans would be eager to see again. George Hackenschmidt had mostly stayed quiet after his loss to Frank Gotch in 1908, but after a chance meeting on the streets of London, Curley convinced him to return to the United States for a rematch. Professional wrestling might have been close to death, but Curley hoped that, with the right match, he could shock it back to life.

FIGURE 7. Frank Gotch wrestles George Hackenschmidt in Comiskey Park, September 4, 1911. Courtesy of the Chicago Daily News collection, Chicago History Museum, SDN-057297.

CHAPTER 6

The Sodden Earth Never Closed Over a Deader One in the World

BY 1911, FRANK Gotch had become a wealthy man. In addition to vast landholdings in Iowa, he now owned property in Washington, the Dakotas, and Canada. He'd been wrestling's world champion for three years and had soundly dispatched all of his challengers. Along the way, he'd made more money and gathered more fame as a professional wrestler than anyone would have imagined possible. Now thirty-four, he'd flirted not only with retirement but with switching sports so he could challenge Jack Johnson for the boxing heavyweight championship. Given Gotch's unimpressive showings in his younger days against boxers much less experienced than Johnson, it was a move decided wisely against.

It would take a guarantee of $20,000, deposited directly into his Humboldt bank account by Jack Curley, to lure Gotch back into a wrestling ring for a match of real consequence.[1] Perhaps inspired by Tex Rickard's gaudy promotion of the Johnson–Jeffries fight, Curley had set to work building interest in a rematch between Gotch and George Hackenschmidt even before he had firm agreements from the two principles. Once the contracts were signed, he scheduled the bout for Labor Day of 1911 at Chicago's Comiskey Park. Curley hoped for a landmark event, the first wrestling match to gross $100,000 in gate receipts. But what it would prove to be, more than anything else, was scandalous. When it was over, Chicago Mayor Carter Harrison would publicly refer to it as the "Labor Day Swindle at White Sox Park." Newspapers would deem it a flop, with one calling it "probably the most daring and astounding attempt at pillaging the public by means of a fake athletic event in recent years."[2]

George Hackenschmidt arrived in America at the beginning of August and installed himself at a camp just outside Chicago, to begin his training in earnest. "I have waited two years for this chance, and everything depends on it," he told reporters. "I have all the money in the world I shall ever need. I am not in this for money. I want to whip Gotch, want to wrestle the mantle of the champion from him. I shall be the most disappointed man alive if I fail."[3]

Curley pulled out every promotional stop he could. Newspapers covered the lead-up to the match with surprising interest and hyperbole. One compared it to the mythical battle between Ajax and Ulysses in Homer's *Iliad*.[4] Another promised it would "be for blood."[5] All the attention became a liability when, during a training match against Ben Roller, Hackenschmidt became tangled in a hold, fell to the mat, and wrenched his left knee.[6] "I heard three distinct little pops like small corks being drawn, and I dropped to the floor and lay there like a log," Hackenschmidt remembered.

"What's wrong with Hack?" Curley asked Roller later that day.

"Nothing," said Roller, "but the big hound thinks there is."

"Oh, Jack, I'm finished!" Hackenschmidt cried from the next room. "Roller has ruined me. We will have to call off the match!"[7]

Curley calmed Hackenschmidt and, loath to change his plans, gambled that the excitement of the day would convince him to go forward. "My experience with fighters had taught me that few of them, including the greatest, are free of worries about their condition when they enter the ring," Curley later wrote, "but as soon as the bell sounds, they forget their troubles and concentrate their thoughts on beating down their opponents."[8] Curley began limiting Hackenschmidt's press appearances, fueling speculation that something was wrong. Curley later claimed that his goal was to keep knowledge of the injury a secret from Gotch. Reporters would claim that the real goal was to keep it a secret from them.

Less than 24 hours before he was due at Comiskey Park, Hackenschmidt tried to wrestle with a training partner for the first time since his accident. "The moment I put the slightest strain on the knee, whether standing or kneeling position, the pain was so great that I dared not move," he remembered. "The least effort in either attack or defense made it feel as though the leg were about to break. I got up from the mat and went back to my quarters realizing beyond all shadow of doubt that my wrestling days were over."[9]

Uncertain as to the condition of one of his two stars, Curley took Hackenschmidt on a drive later that afternoon. The pair rode in silence, only beginning to speak after they were seated at a table inside a German beer garden. "George, do as you like," Curley told him. "Whatever you decide, my opinion of you will always be just the same."

Hackenschmidt had been weighing whether to call the match off, looking for ways to raise enough capital to repay Curley the considerable amounts of money he knew stood to be lost. "I knew the trouble he would be in if I said I would rather abandon it," Hackenschmidt would later write. "All these things, with recollections of the man's unfailing kindness to me, his unhesitating belief in me as a wrestler, passed through my mind before I answered." Knowing it would mean the end of his athletic career, Hackenschmidt stood up and said, "Jack, I am going through with it."[10]

The *Chicago Tribune* declared September 4, 1911, "A Day to Rest and Wrestle." The newspaper's front page featured a shirtless, heavily muscled, cigar-chomping Uncle Sam seated ringside at Comiskey Park. Clouds and evening rain were forecast, but the afternoon broke clear, the temperature settling in the low 70s. Diehard fans had crowded in front of the stadium the evening prior, determined to secure prime seats, and as the turnstiles started clicking the next day, some 20,000 to 30,000 fans began filing in.[11] Those who couldn't get tickets gathered in front of the *Tribune*'s branch offices around the city, blocking traffic as they waited for bulletins to be phoned in.

Determined to avoid unneeded controversy, Curley selected Ed Smith, sports editor for the *Chicago American* and a respected boxing and wrestling referee, to officiate the match. Looking to further bolster public confidence that the competition would be square, the payoffs for each wrestler were publicized well in advance. It was hoped that both men having been well-paid would send a clear signal that neither would have motivation to take a dive.

With the ring positioned halfway between home plate and the pitcher's box, a handful of press sat circled around it on the infield with fans seated throughout the grandstand and bleachers. One film crew was set up on the pitcher's mound and another in right field to capture the match for planned distribution to theatres. "I pride myself that I know how to dress up a show," Curley later wrote, "and I dressed this one up to the best of my ability."[12]

Backstage, as the day's preliminary matches got underway, Hackenschmidt called for Curley. Before he would go out, he told him, he wanted his payout for the match delivered in cash. Curley set off with a basket, running from gate to gate, raiding the box tills for ones and fives. He rolled the $11,000 in cash together inside a newspaper and handed the two-foot-high bundle to Hackenschmidt, who counted it slowly.[13] "Alright," he said. "Keep it for me until tonight." Hackenschmidt handed the money back, turned away, and walked to the window, Curley remembered, "as though he had forgotten my existence." Hackenschmidt looked out at the overflowing stands full of people. His nerves were on edge. He hadn't slept, and it was going to be a long day. Waiting for the signal to walk to the ring, he felt like a man waiting to be hung.[14]

While the band played the "Star Spangled Banner" and the movie cameras began to grind, Frank Gotch walked across the field, smiling and waving to his wife and mother at ringside. Hackenschmidt appeared next, the crowd yelling hot and loud. Dressed in a pair of long green tights meant to hide the bandages that covered his left leg from hip to ankle, he was said to be pale by the time he entered the ring. Curley would later declare that he'd gone ahead with the match "as a personal favor to me to save the show."[15]

Rumors had already circulated through the crowd about Hackenschmidt's injured knee and lack of training. Still, when referee Ed Smith announced just prior to the start of the match that by order of the Chicago Police Department all bets should be called off and any money wagered on the bout returned, the crowd responded with an angry roar.[16] Jack Curley would later claim that he'd requested the announcement to be made because he detested betting at his shows. George Hackenschmidt took credit as well, later saying that it was he who had demanded that betting be stopped. "You either call off all bets," he claimed to have told referee Smith, "or I walk out right now."[17] Regardless of its impetus, the effect of the announcement was to convince attendees that they were getting ready to watch a fake.[18]

The match began just after 3 p.m. Gotch had promised to wrestle all night, if necessary, but he needn't have bothered. Just eight minutes in, he got his first successful hold on Hackenschmidt's injured left knee, pinning him six minutes later to win the first fall. "I saw needless absolute acts of cruelty on [Gotch's] part that I did not like," remembered Smith. Only five minutes into the second fall, Gotch got another hold on Hackenschmidt's left ankle. He lifted it up off the mat and rammed his knee into Hackenschmidt's right leg, sending him to the mat in a heap. He then positioned his leg between Hackenschmidt's calf and thigh and, using it as a fulcrum, twisted Hackenschmidt's left ankle as he bent his knee. Smith claimed that Hackenschmidt, trapped on the mat, called out, "Don't break my leg!"[19] With no hope of escaping the hold, Hackenschmidt looked at Smith and asked him to declare the match over. "Smith hesitated," Curley later wrote. "There was barely anyone who heard the request. The infield was barren. The spectators were confined to the grandstand. If Smith had given the fall to Gotch with Hackenschmidt's shoulders so far off the mat, he realized he would have been subject to harsh criticism. Leaning over, he urged Hackenschmidt, 'Make it a real fall.' No time then to argue, Hackenschmidt flopped his shoulders back to the mat."[20] The great rematch, three years in the making, was all over in less than twenty minutes. Hackenschmidt never even mustered all that much of a fight. "The sodden earth never closed over a deader one in the world than the hour of 4 o'clock yesterday afternoon closed over George Hackenschmidt," wrote Lloyd Kenyon Jones, reporting from ringside for the *Chicago Inter Ocean*.[21]

In Humboldt, people shouted and danced in the streets when "Gotch Wins" flashed over the wire. Fans gathered outside of the *Tribune* branch offices threw their hats in the air.[22] Hackenschmidt picked himself up off of the mat and returned to his dressing room. Brokenhearted and in tears, he sat talking to reporters. "It was the cheapest world's championship ever won," he told them.[23] As he dressed, his friends stood speechless. "Everything seemed so empty, so drab and colorless," he remembered. "There was nothing for anyone to talk about. It was all so different from the many hundreds of other matches that I had wrestled in my life. . . . Yet, I had no regrets for what I had done."[24] The crowd, wrote the *Chicago Tribune*, filed out feeling "victimized . . . as if something had been done to them, they knew not exactly what, but something."[25]

The match took in almost $96,000 at the gate—short of what Jack Curley had hoped but far more money than any wrestling match before it had earned.[26] He'd shown that the public would turn out for wrestling in large numbers, but after the backlash and disappointment in the match itself, just how soon they would come back for more was an open question. "The sporting public shelled out its coin in large gobs," declared the *Tacoma Times* the next day. "It is highly improbable that it will do so again."[27]

The film of the fight was touted as a twenty-five-minute theatrical event, but it was met with a muted reception by audiences, and advertisements for it disappeared quickly.[28] Everyone, it seemed, except for the match's participants, felt that something about the match wasn't right. Emphatic in his defense of the honesty of the match was Chicago's assistant chief of police, Herman Schuettler, who'd given the order to call off betting. The match had to have been on the level, he argued. If it had been a fake, he said, it would have been more exciting.[29]

If the rematch of Frank Gotch and George Hackenschmidt had failed as entertainment, it had succeeded as a business venture. Jack Curley had managed to pull off a wrestling match on a scale others thought impossible, and he'd cleaned up as a result. According to his own estimate, he walked away from the match with $15,000.[30] Less than a week later, though, his fortunes would change drastically.

Curley had quietly married Mildred Schul sometime in the previous decade. He would later claim that it was a common-law marriage and that no ceremony had been performed. When she filed for divorce mere days after the Comiskey Park debacle, she cited extreme and repeated cruelty during the marriage, including Curley attacking her in a hotel room, grabbing her by the throat, and dragging her around the room. She also claimed that Curley had been married once before and had deserted that wife as well. The resulting settlement effectively wiped out Curley's earnings from his Labor Day success.[31]

The disappointing end to the Gotch–Hackenschmidt rematch had done nothing to help sell wrestling to new fans. Coupled with Frank

Gotch's return to semi-retirement in 1912, as well as with the lack of any star contenders to promote, its popularity sank. It would take more than two decades for another match to top the attendance numbers posted on September 4, 1911. Perhaps most damaging to wrestling, though, was the creation of a firmer legal basis for boxing.

FIGURE 8. The final moments of Jack Johnson versus Jess Willard, Havana, Cuba, April 5, 1915. Courtesy of The Library of Congress.

CHAPTER 7

The Greatest Promotional Odyssey of Modern Times

PROFESSIONAL BOXING GAINED legal status in New York under 1911's Frawley Law, which allowed for fights of up to ten rounds in clubs that posted $10,000 bonds with the state to guarantee honest fights. The law, and the increased volume of bouts that accompanied it, helped to kick off the search for what some called the "White Hope"—the White fighter who would finally prove capable of defeating heavyweight champion Jack Johnson. The originator of the phrase White Hope is thought to be either author Jack London or the improbably named Otto Floto, a sportswriter with the *Denver Post* and a close friend of Jack Curley's. Floto had first applied it to Jim Jeffries, who came to be called the "White Man's Hope" in press coverage of his 1910 bout with Johnson in Reno.[1]

After Johnson's trouncing of Jeffries in that fight, arenas and halls across the United States had filled with White fighters looking to pick up the mantle. Many were altogether new to boxing, and many, Curley later joked, while "undoubtedly White, certainly were not 'hopes.'"[2] Writer John Lardner mockingly defined a White Hope as "a White heavyweight who had not recently been knocked out by another White heavyweight." "In the heat of the search," Lardner wrote, "well-muscled White boys more than six feet two inches tall were not safe out of their mothers' sight."[3] A White Championship was even invented, and a tournament of White Hopes was held in New York on May 26, 1911, to fill it. Jack Johnson watched the eleven hapless fighters who'd bothered to show up punch it out from a special ringside box. It was obvious to everyone in attendance that none seemed likely to present him with any real challenge. "Learning anything, Jack?" a reporter asked Johnson. "I'm learning plenty," he replied, with an enormous laugh.[4]

Privately, though, Johnson was suffering. Police were harassing him, and on at least one occasion, he had been assaulted on the street. Jack Curley knew this as well as anyone. Still, while Curley did not invent the White Hope nonsense, he was not above cashing in on it. He'd seen the crowds that greeted Jim Jeffries on the 1910 tour he'd managed and understood just how much money stood to be made from matching Johnson against a White fighter whom the public could believe had a reasonable chance of beating him. Curley, wrote Alva Johnston in the *New Yorker,* "insisted that White supremacy should rest . . . on fair play in a roped arena, with ringside seats selling for twenty-five dollars apiece."[5]

His first attempt came via a fighter named "Fireman" Jim Flynn, a tough and mean thirty-two-year-old boxer from Hoboken, New Jersey, whose contract Curley had been lucky enough to be holding when, on September 15, 1911, Flynn upset Carl Morris, the most heavily promoted of the new crop of White Hopes, in a fight so violent that its referee had to change his blood-soaked shirt midway through it.[6] The win made Flynn the most logical challenger, and Johnson agreed to fight him while standing with Curley in the parlor of Johnson's Chicago home during a New Year's Eve party. Curley scheduled it for July 4, 1912, his thirty-sixth birthday, and booked Las Vegas, New Mexico, a small town 120 miles outside of Albuquerque, as the site to host it.[7]

Las Vegas businessmen and government officials welcomed the event and the tourism they hoped would accompany it. The Santa Fe Railroad, with a stop in Las Vegas on its Chicago to Los Angeles line, promised Curley that they would run special trains to carry fans to the town as well as pay for a stadium. Town representatives pledged $100,000 to make sure the fight happened and put Curley and Flynn up in the city's finest hotels. They were less welcoming to Johnson, who was forced to hire an armed guard and carry a revolver tucked into his pants after receiving a death threat from the Ku Klux Klan.[8]

On May 22, 1912, with the fight a little over a month away, Curley married Marie Drescher, the eighteen-year-old daughter of a wealthy Denver couple, in a whirlwind Wednesday morning ceremony at the town's Castaneda Hotel.[9] They had known each other for less than a month. "Experience had taught me that no big fight is put on without difficulties," Curley remembered. "And with everything running so smoothly at Las Vegas, I began to wonder when the break would eventually come."[10] Come, it would.

Days after his wedding, Curley was publicly named in a divorce case playing out in a Chicago courtroom. Ellsworth B. Overshiner, a Chicago businessman, had discovered a cache of letters his wife had exchanged with Curley, some dated just days before Curley's marriage to Marie. In one, Curley mooned, "Yours till the cows come home." It was humiliating for Curley and undoubtedly upsetting for his new, young wife.[11]

Next, the Santa Fe Railroad conceded to pressure from heiress Helen Gould and the Christian Endeavor Society and reneged on its promise to run dedicated cars. Worse, they withdrew their agreement to build an arena. Curley instead used the money put up by town boosters to start construction. On the day of the fight, carpenters were still nailing down the ring floor as groups of spectators made their way to the venue.[12]

Nothing about the event turned out to be easy. Curley even struggled to find a film company that would work with him. The day of the contest, the San Francisco firm he had finally managed to hire had so little film available that Curley had to stand at ringside and signal to them by waving his hat when to turn the cameras on and off to make sure they conserved what film they did have on hand for the fight's high spots.

In the ring, Johnson made short work of Flynn, frustrating him with taunts that he followed up with shots to the head. Bleeding heavily and disregarding warnings from the referee, Flynn resorted to trying to strike Johnson's chin with the top of his head. By the ninth round, Flynn was clearly a beaten man. Sensing that the referee was uncomfortable awarding the victory to Johnson on a disqualification, New Mexico police entered the ring and stopped the fight.[13]

The arena had been built to hold more than 17,000 people, but only between 3,000 and 5,000 had attended. Despite the anemic turnout, Curley would later claim the fight was successful enough to avoid becoming the financial disaster many had predicted.[14] However, given that Johnson was paid his standard guarantee of $30,000, it's unlikely that Curley turned a profit. His experience in Las Vegas should have scared him off from promoting such prominent and risky events, but three years later, he would try again, staging one that was even bigger.

Following the Flynn fight, Johnson opened his three-story Cafe de Champion on West Thirty-first Street in Chicago.[15] It featured solid silver spittoons, electric fans, white-gloved waiters, and a two-story-tall electric sign that read "Jack Johnson" with proud defiance. Business thrived, but Johnson struggled with incessant harassment from local officials. Hounded by depression and frustrated with Johnson's pursuit of other women, his wife Etta committed suicide in the cafe's third-floor bedroom only three months after the opening. Jack Curley stepped in to make the funeral arrangements, and when Johnson's sister fainted during the service, Curley carried her outside.[16]

In June 1913, Johnson was convicted of violating what was known as the Mann Act, a three-year-old federal law formally called the White-Slave Traffic Act, which outlawed the transportation of women between states "for the purpose of prostitution or debauchery, or for any other immoral purpose." The law purported to target human trafficking, but its poorly defined use of the phrase "immoral purpose" made it a handy tool to punish a variety of presumed offenses. The Justice Department had hoped to use the Mann Act to prosecute Johnson since its passage. Their opportunity to arrest and pursue charges against him came after the mother of Johnson's new fiancée, a White woman named Lucille Cameron, created a media firestorm after learning that her daughter was engaged to Johnson.

During the resulting investigation, an anonymous letter received by the Bureau of Investigations office in Chicago led agents to a woman named Belle Schreiber, who offered evidence that Johnson had paid for her railroad fare to Chicago in late 1910 and had helped her get started in business as a madam. "Oh well," Johnson said after an all-white jury found him guilty after less than two hours of deliberation, "they crucified Christ, why not me?" Johnson was sentenced to one year in federal prison. While free pending his appeal, Johnson fled the United States, sneaking onto a train to Canada. From there, he caught a boat to Paris.[17]

By Fall 1914, the times, as Jack Curley later put it, were slack. He and Marie had relocated to an apartment on Riverside Drive in New York. Their son, Jack Jr., was born on March 9, 1913. Their daughter, Jean, was born one year later on March 12, 1914. Curley adored the children and pampered the family with gifts and expensive clothes. "We had a chef, a French maid, a car—and chauffeur—and I didn't have a dime," Curley later said.[18]

With professional wrestling in the doldrums and Jack Johnson unable to fight in the United States, Curley had no realistic options for staging a money-making event. He could barely afford the lunch he had scheduled at the Hotel Astor with his friend and sometimes business partner Harry Frazee, at which he'd hoped to hit Frazee up for a $2,500 loan to cover his debts. Frazee, Curley learned, was struggling as well, but he connected Curley with L. Lawrence Weber, a theatrical entrepreneur interested in staging a fight for boxing's heavyweight championship. Weber told Curley that if he could find a White fighter with a real chance of beating Jack Johnson, he would pay to stage the match.[19]

Suddenly back in the game, Curley turned his attention to finding a suitable challenger. He landed on Jess Willard, a six-foot-six boxer from Saint Clere, Kansas, known for his unnaturally long reach and for throwing hard uppercuts, one of which had unintentionally killed a fighter named Bull Young in 1913. Willard was acquitted of murder at the trial that followed, but the incident ruined fighting for him. "I never liked [boxing]," he would later confess to a friend. "In fact, I hated it as I never hated a thing previously, but there was money in it. I needed the money and decided to go after it."[20]

Looking to pit a reluctant fighter against another living in exile, Curley set out to make his match. Writing in the *New Yorker*, Alva Johnston would later call Curley's resulting efforts "the greatest promotional Odyssey of modern times."[21] It took him six months of unceasing work, during which he traveled more than 15,000 miles. "I had many difficult decisions to make, some of them on the spur of the moment," Curley would write of the time. "Here and there I made mistakes, of course, but on the whole, I figured, or guessed, correctly."[22]

The first hurdle was signing up Willard. Curley hammered out the basic details of an agreement with him while sitting on a baggage truck on the arrival platform of a train station in Kansas City. Willard agreed to fight Johnson for almost no pay, knowing that significant money stood to be made from personal appearances across the country should he win.

With Willard signed on, Curley turned next to pinning down a commitment from Jack Johnson. But just finding Johnson in the chaos of warring Europe was daunting. He'd moved to St. Petersburg in July 1914 to try to escape creditors but was forced to move to London after Germany declared war on Russia just a few weeks later.[23] Deep in debt, Johnson, boxing's reigning heavyweight champion, was reduced to working music halls around England with an act where he played the bass fiddle, sparred, and mugged for the crowd. He was a man without a country and quickly running out of options.

After finally tracking Johnson down to a flat in St. Mary's Mansions in Westminster, Curley made plans to meet him there in November 1914. Talking through the details of the fight over a meal of chicken and biscuits that Johnson himself had prepared, Johnson demanded his standard rate of $30,000 plus training expenses. Curley obliged, and the contract for Johnson to defend his championship against Willard was drawn up and signed the next day.[24]

Now that the fight had been agreed to by both contestants, Curley's next issue was where to hold it. Considered a fugitive because of his conviction under the Mann Act, Johnson was not legally allowed to enter the United States. Curley's idea was to hold the fight in Mexico so American fans could easily attend. He landed on Juarez, just across the border but inaccessible to US law enforcement, as the ideal location. Curley met with the then governor of Chihuahua, the revolutionary Mexican General Francisco "Pancho" Villa, in March to make arrangements. Villa was supportive of Curley's plans, as the fight would lend his regime credibility and the anticipated proceeds would go a long way in supporting his war against General Venustiano Carranza, then in control of the southern portion of Mexico. He guaranteed Curley peace in Juarez along with the use of his troops to secure the venue chosen for the event—the city's race track.[25]

With the location settled, the promotion could begin in earnest. It fell to Curley to sell Willard, who sportswriter Grantland Rice had described as carrying "as much magnetism as a carload of sawdust," to an eager public as the last best hope for beating Johnson.[26] In January, the pair filmed *The Heart Punch*, a slapdash melodrama shot in a single day that centered on Willard as a cash-strapped boxer with a sick baby and a wife who wants him to hang up his gloves. On the other side, a promoter played by Curley offers him big money for a fight. Willard takes the money, wins the fight, and hurries home to his family with the medication needed to save his child.[27]

The next problem was smuggling Johnson, one of the most famous figures in the world, into a small town just across the Rio Grande without attracting the attention of American authorities. Johnson planned to depart from Havana, Cuba. Suggestions to route him through New Orleans were instantly discarded as too risky. Instead, a landing at the Mexican port city of Tampico was agreed to, with Johnson to make the 1,000-mile trip to Juarez by land. The idea seemed airtight, but after General Carranza made it clear that he would happily turn Johnson over to the US government should his forces apprehend him, Johnson reconsidered fighting in Mexico altogether.

With just two weeks to go and his grand promotion hanging in a perilous state, Curley was up late one evening wandering the streets around his hotel. It was an old routine that he followed whenever he was deep into pulling an event together—stay up late, keep alert, watch for something to happen. "You always see something interesting," he said of his habit, "if it is only a dog running up and down the street."[28] That evening, he walked into a Western Union office just as a cable arrived announcing that all scheduled passenger boats out of Havana would be canceled. With unrest in the country, and concern over the prospect of German U-boats prowling the Gulf of Mexico, Cuba had forbidden ships from sailing to several ports. The fight, Curley now knew, would need to come to Johnson. Curley caught the first train from El Paso into New Orleans and from there boarded a ship to Havana. Arriving "seasick, dilapidated, and worn," he found Havana in the height of the horse-racing season and packed with tourists.[29] He met with Cuban president General Mario Garcia Menocal, and after arranging a three-week delay in the date, rescheduled the Johnson–Willard heavyweight championship bout for Easter Monday, April 5, 1915, at the Oriental Park Racetrack, ten miles outside of Havana.

The day of the fight started overcast, with a cool breeze blowing in off the sea. As thousands of spectators started on their way to the venue early, with some making the ten-mile trip from Havana on foot rather than waiting for a space on the packed trolley cars, Curley tended to a chaotic scene at the racetrack. Two hours before the fight was to start, as low tumbling clouds threatened rain and workmen wrapped the heavy ring ropes in black tire tape and laid blankets for padding below the ring floor, messengers had to be dispatched back to Havana to find a bell, the purchase of which had been overlooked, so the timekeeper would have something to ring between rounds. Noticing the lush hills that circled the racetrack, Curley dispatched guards to each one to prevent bootleggers with telescopic lenses from shooting film of the fight. He was also due at Johnson's camp to pay the $29,000 balance of Johnson's guarantee in cash. By 12:40 p.m., the sun finally broke through and shone brightly down on the racetrack. On the back stretch, jockeys exercised their horses in preparation for the races that would follow the bout.

With the temperature inside the ring topping one hundred degrees and close to 20,000 spectators in the stands, time was finally called at 1:53 p.m. Johnson and Willard punched it out for twenty-four rounds.

Willard was outfought in most, and in rounds thirteen and fourteen, referee Jack Welch thought for sure that Johnson would knock him out.[30] Willard stayed on his feet, though, and by round twenty, the pace of the fight slowed visibly as Johnson began to wear down in the intense heat.

Prior to the start of round twenty-five, the fading champion asked Curley to have his wife, Lucille, escorted away from her seat, telling him, "I don't want her to see me knocked out."[31] As the round started, Willard landed three hard punches to Johnson's face and body. A fourth landed on Johnson's jaw and sent him falling first into Willard and then down to the mat. Johnson landed on his back with his knees bent and his right hand over his face, as if trying to keep the sun out of his eyes. As the referee counted him out, Johnson's bent legs slid down, leaving him flat on his back in the sweltering heat. Jess Willard was declared boxing's new heavyweight champion.

As thousands of fans chanted, "*Viva El Bianco!*" those closest to the ring crowded in to congratulate Willard. The Cuban cavalry soon followed, sabers drawn, to protect the boxers. Curley went to Johnson's corner to cut off his gloves.

"Let me keep these," Johnson told him.

"How do you feel?" Curley asked.

"All right," said Johnson. "Everything is all right—the best man won."[32]

Johnson turned to survey the crowd. "Now all my trouble will be over," he told his trainer. "Maybe they'll let me alone."[33]

Curley had managed to bring the spectacle off, but getting out of Havana would prove to be another challenge. Immediately after the fight, he announced gate receipts of $110,000, with some newspapers placing the take as high as $160,000.[34] At midnight, police arrived at the stadium and arrested both Curley and Harry Frazee after a carpenter and chauffeur they'd employed expressed concern to Cuban officials that members of the fight's management team were planning to leave the country without paying their bills. Hauled into a Havana courtroom, Curley significantly revised his estimates on the gate receipts, claiming that they amounted to only $56,000. He told the court that the fight hadn't even pulled in enough to cover expenses.[35]

The next day, for unclear reasons, Curley and Frazee were released from police custody. They hurried to the dock to meet the ship that would take them back to the United States. Once onboard, Curley was locked inside one of the ship's state rooms with just $350 left to call his own.[36] Outside, a throng of angry creditors descended the gangplank and tried to raid the boat. "Havana was getting its last crack at fight promoters and was making the most of it," wrote a reporter from the *Los Angeles Herald*.[37] The group sailed out of Havana with a pile of bills in their wake. An embarrassed Johnson covered some of them with his cut of the purse, but many went unpaid. Curley would later contend that he had settled all of his bills before leaving Havana, "contrary to stories circulated at the time by persons who did not precisely wish us well."[38] The preponderance of stories to the contrary suggests otherwise.

In Key West, Florida, a horde of people pushed and jostled their way to the wharf to greet Curley and Willard as they disembarked the *Governor Cobb*, the crowd knocking over the wooden barricades and rope barriers in their way.[39] Curley, Willard, and their entourage boarded a train headed north to New York, and at each stop, crowds clamored to congratulate Willard. "I have made many journeys with celebrities I have managed or with whom I have had some other official connection, but never in my experience has there been anything like this," Curley wrote of the trip. "Every depot at which we stopped was an island set in a sea of humanity. Men, women, and children besieged the train, clamored for a sight of Willard, roared with praises, swept police lines aside in an almost hysterical effort to get close to him."[40]

Arriving in Pennsylvania, Curley stopped to speak with a reporter from the *Washington Post* to give a statement on Johnson, the man he'd known and worked with for more than fifteen years. "I found Johnson a man before, during, and after the fight," he said. "It doesn't make any difference what he's done outside the ring, he was a brave, game, generous warrior inside of it. He is the first man since John L. Sullivan who has been man enough to acknowledge defeat without a hue and cry of being tricked and doped out of his title."[41]

It would be a rocky summer. Curley knew that his most significant payday would come from exhibiting the film of the Havana fight to boxing fans who had been waiting seven years to watch Johnson lose. Fight films were a significant source of income for everyone with a stake in them, which, in the case of the Havana films, included Curley, Johnson, Willard, and several others. Some estimates put the film's value in the United States alone at as much as $100,000.[42]

Since 1912, federal law had prohibited the importation and transportation of boxing films. That the passage of the law, called the Sims Act, coincided with Johnson's reign as boxing's heavyweight champion was hardly a coincidence. Passed just seventeen days after Johnson's July 4, 1912, fight with Jim Flynn (which Curley had also promoted), the explicit purpose of the Sims Act, as declared by House Democrat and bill cosponsor Thetus W. Sims, had been to prevent "moving-picture films of prize fights, especially the one between a Negro and a White man, to be held in New Mexico on the 4th of July."[43] It is impossible to imagine that Curley and his associates were unaware of the Sims Act. What is likelier is that they were gambling that government officials, overjoyed by Willard's victory, would happily relax their restrictions. They figured wrong.

Unable to procure the chemicals needed to develop the film of the fight while in Cuba, Curley hadn't even had the chance to view the reels before they were impounded by customs officials in Florida. As a co-owner of the film rights, L. Lawrence Weber challenged the legality of the Sims Act up to the Supreme Court, finally losing in a unanimous decision in December of 1915. "[We] had some mighty fine legal advice, and they couldn't see how to get it done," Weber said. "We brought quite a bit of influence to bear, with no result. We didn't even get a favorable nibble."[44]

Jack Johnson had planned to personally exhibit the film to audiences throughout Europe, but access to a copy quickly became a sticking point between him and Curley. Curley would later claim that just moments before the Havana fight was to begin, a lawyer representing Johnson had demanded a higher ownership percentage in the film rights for his client. "Oh hell," said Harry Frazee as he held the contract against Curley's back and signed it. As revenge, Frazee duped Johnson into leaving Cuba with canisters of stock footage unrelated to the fight.[45] In Johnson's account of the story, likely closer to the truth, he left Havana empty-handed other than with a promise from Curley to have the films sent to him in London as soon as they were ready. When no film arrived, Johnson began monitoring the London American Express office for any trace of a delivery. When an associate of Curley's arrived at the office to receive a package of film canisters, Johnson stepped in and muscled the film away from him. He edited out the footage of Willard's knockout punch and began exhibiting the film.[46]

The incident fractured the relationship between Johnson and Curley. Johnson would later claim that Curley had agreed to pay him $50,000 and arrange his safe return to the United States in return for his losing to Willard. "When I found that they had not kept their word in paving the way for me to return home, I became not only cognizant of the fact that I had been flimflammed but that I was up against a pretty raw deal," Johnson later wrote.[47]

Curley dismissed Johnson's accusations as pure fantasy. Evidence does exist that Curley arranged a meeting with federal officials in Chicago about allowing Johnson to return to home.[48] Curley also had a connection to William Jennings Bryan, Woodrow Wilson's secretary of state, whom he'd managed on a speaking tour when Bryan was campaigning for the Democratic nomination for president in 1899.[49] The two had stayed friends; Bryan was impressed with Curley's disdain for alcohol, and it's conceivable that Curley made some overtures to him on behalf of Johnson. Either way, Curley was unsuccessful in whatever attempts he made to help Johnson. Whether these efforts were undertaken out of loyalty or some kind of obligation can't be known for sure. Still, as Johnson's biographer Geoffrey Ward would write, it seems unlikely Curley would have ever offered something so far-fetched as a guaranteed return to the United States, and equally unlikely that Johnson would have believed him even if he had.[50]

Though Curley didn't know it at the time, it was the Johnson–Willard fight for which he would always be best remembered. It captured the most headlines and was unmatched in its sheer audacity and the improbability of success. While he would continue to keep something of a hand in boxing for the next two decades, the Johnson–Willard fight would be the last major bout over which Jack Curley would command as much control. His future would be in professional wrestling, whether he wanted it to be or not.

FIGURE 9. The Masked Marvel, New York, ca. 1915–1916. Courtesy of Steve Yohe.

CHAPTER 8

Call Me Desdichado

IN THE SUMMER of 1915, Manhattan was bursting with more professional wrestling than it had ever seen before. A score of top-flight foreign wrestlers who had fled to America during the early days of World
War I were suddenly in New York and available to work for cheap.
That November, a former actor and theatre promoter named Samuel
Rachmann announced an event that would feature the best of them, a
wrestling tournament that would be grander and more ambitious than
any previously attempted in the city. Rachmann's background is mysterious. He is known to have been born in the late 1870s in Galacia, a
small territory of Austria straddling the modern-day borders of Poland
and Ukraine, and to have worked in Berlin before arriving in New York
as part of a historic wave of immigration. Between 1900 and 1914, more
than thirteen million people arrived in the United States, transforming
the country—New York City, in particular.[1]

With his international wrestling tournament, Rachmann was imag-
ining something akin to the events he'd helped to stage in Europe. He
planned to saturate Manhattan with twelve consecutive weeks of nightly
wrestling shows at the Manhattan Opera House, a 3,000-seat theatre
near the corner of Thirty-fourth Street and Eighth Avenue. "Swedes,
Finns, Turks, Greeks, Poles, Huns, Italians, Spaniards, Portuguese,
French, Germans, Swiss, Danes, English, and Americans will compete,"
teased the *New York Times* in early November.[2] It would be remarkably
expensive, but Rachmann was taking a calculated risk. He promised his
performers a weekly salary, some as little as $100, while the better-known
attractions were promised a percentage of the higher-earning gates.[3]

Rachmann's tournament aimed squarely for Manhattan's theatre-
going crowd. In his ads, he promised to deliver, "The classic sports of

High Olympus viewed from the comforts of an opera chair." "It seemed to be a show conducted by an artist, with artists, for artists," remembered "Strangler" Ed Lewis, who performed at the tournament.[4] Rachmann appreciated the close connection between wrestling and theatre, and he orchestrated each evening to be filled as much with entertainment as with sport. As a lead-in to the matches, he presented slapstick acts along with acrobats and musical performances. On the tournament's opening night, amid a sea of international flags, thirty-three wrestlers representing more than a dozen countries paraded around the stage while a medley of national anthems played.

Rachmann judged performers based on their ability to excite the audience.[5] Each evening's card was organized with a sense of burlesque, mixing matches that were designed primarily for comedy with others that featured more serious athletics. Wrestlers chased each other around the ring and fought into the wings of the opera house. Some stamped their feet in outrage and frustration when they lost a match. A Finnish wrestler named Sulo Hevonpaa would drape his robe over the chairs at ringside, only to have other wrestlers come out and wipe their feet on it. Le Colosse, a French wrestler weighing close to 400 pounds, made broad pleas to tournament officials in his native language, while the audience laughed at his inability to communicate. "Farmer" George Bailey claimed he could hypnotize opponents and began his matches by attempting to do just that, convincing one to run wildly around the stage. A Greek wrestler named Dimitrios Tofalos, a former Olympic weightlifter, came to the ring dressed in a tuxedo and would sing opera before changing into his wrestling gear.

One evening ended with the curtain falling on two wrestlers who refused to break their holds on each other. As the theatre staff extinguished the lights and the audience filed out, the sound of the two wrestlers groaning in the dark could still be heard from the stage. "It would be impossible to describe exactly what occurs every night," wrote the *Brooklyn Times Union*'s John Fleeson, "still I can say, without fear of contradiction, that there is more genuine comedy and laughter in this tournament than in many a play now running."[6]

It was a large house to fill night after night, though, and seeing the same wrestlers on the same stage in the same kinds of matches began to wear on audiences. Attendance began lagging as the tournament dragged into its second month and reports appeared that Rachmann was facing several thousand dollars in losses.[7] Ever the showman, Rachmann opted to gamble on an even more elaborate tactic to save his production. On a Friday evening in early December, a man in a hood with holes cut into it for his eyes, mouth, and prominent nose climbed in front of the opera house lights to issue a challenge to every wrestler in the tournament.[8] Dubbed the Masked Marvel by reporters, he became an immediate sensation. In each of his tournament matches, he appeared unbeatable. He heaved the massive Le Colosse about the ring like he weighed nothing. When one opponent tried to escape from the ring by running into the wings of the theatre, the Marvel chased him down, dragged him back onto the mat, pinned him, and then scooped him up into his arms and carried him away.

"Bravissimo!" cried the audience, though the Marvel never stayed long enough to soak in the applause. After each match was through, he raced back to the dressing room, put on his coat and hat, and hurried out into the Manhattan night, sometimes hopping into a waiting taxi or onto a motorcycle and riding away. When he did mix with the public, the Marvel was a publicity man's dream. Asked by fans to reveal his identity, he grandly responded, "Call me Desdichado," referencing the legend of Ivanhoe. "I assure you he has a very good reason for wearing the mask," teased his manager, Ed Pollard. "No, I cannot tell you just what that reason is—but it will come out in time."[9]

The Marvel proved to be the attraction the tournament needed. Spectators in formal wear soon filled the floor and opera boxes on evenings he appeared. On some evenings, females accounted for up to half of attendees. Noting the unexpected number of women in attendance, Rachmann adopted a new slogan for the tournament: "Don't cheat your wife, bring her along!"[10] "Every third person in the audience was a woman," wrote Zoe Beckley, who covered the tournament for the *Washington Post*. "I went to stay five minutes and remained there three hours and a quarter, being then pried, reluctant, from my seat. Don't ask me what it was all about. The funny part is that you don't have to understand it to enjoy it."[11]

It is not clear just who came up with the idea for the Masked Marvel. A masked wrestler had appeared in Paris in the fall of 1867 and thrilled audiences by handily defeating the city's most popular competitors. It's likely that Rachmann was at least aware of this, and it is possible that he was resurrecting the idea in America. It is notable that the Marvel's contract to appear in the tournament gave credit solely to Rachmann for the idea of a "Mysterious Masked Wrestler."[12] Newspapers claimed the idea came from the tournament's press agent, Ben Atwood. The idea had been given to him, Atwood said, by Mark Leuscher, a theatre producer who had had a hit with a masked dancer in the Ziegfield Follies whom he called, "La Domino Rouge." Credit for choosing the wrestler who played the Marvel was given by some to Jack Curley, whose relationship with Rachmann was vague at best but who was thought to have provided some of the funding to stage the tournament.[13]

The secret of who exactly the man in the mask was didn't last long. Reporters took to following the Marvel home after matches. Confronting one who had trailed his car out to the Bronx, the Marvel, still wearing his hood, growled, "You keep following me and I'll wring your neck. Do you get that?"[14] By the end of December, not even a month after he'd emerged from the Opera House audience, writers at the *Brooklyn Daily Eagle* were publicly naming Mort Henderson, a wrestler from Altoona, Pennsylvania, as the Marvel.[15] The reports, though, did nothing to dim his appeal. To tournament crowds, the Marvel remained a favorite, and he refused any calls to unmask.

The mystery man was indeed Mort Henderson, and despite his growing popularity, he was still being paid just $100 per week for his work. In January, he quit the tournament, telling Rachmann that Jack Curley had offered him more than ten times his weekly salary to wrestle a single match as part of a show Curley was planning to hold at Madison Square Garden later that month. Henderson stopped showing up for his tournament matches, prompting Rachmann to slap him with an injunction on January 25, 1916, just two days before Curley's event was to take place. The suit, which was widely reported on in the city's papers, named Henderson as the Marvel and revealed that his contract with Rachmann called for him to win and lose his matches as directed.[16] With Rachmann's injunction blocking Henderson from working as the Masked Marvel for a rival promoter, Curley faced the prospect of an opponent-less main event for his Garden debut. He scrambled to find a replacement, but after a spirited conference with Rachmann, his lawyers, and other advisers, Curley successfully negotiated to have the injunction dropped.[17]

On January 27, 1916, Curley's Madison Square Garden show took place as planned. Thousands attended, with the box seats around ringside filled by couples in evening dress, their diamonds and furs mingling uneasily with the heavy clouds of cigar smoke. "Folks who live on Fifth Avenue and the Upper West Side were there, foreign-looking people from the artist colony in Washington Square, and all the familiar faces you see along Broadway," reported the *New York Times* the next day.[18] For the main event, Curley matched Henderson against a rising young star from Nebraska named Joe Stecher. Stecher dominated the match, winning over the crowd by pinning Henderson twice in less than fifteen minutes. With his foothold in Manhattan now established, Curley would turn to making the city his new base of operations, pulling the center of the wrestling world along with him.

Rachmann finished out his tournament as planned, but with his star attraction gone, attendance sank. He quit wrestling almost immediately, turning next to movies and live theatre. He was one of the most imaginative and far-seeing businessmen to be attracted to professional wrestling yet. Though he was only briefly involved with it, his influence can't be overstated. With his eye for dramatic detail and the gleefulness with which he pushed against the accepted boundaries of what a wrestling match should be, Rachmann had anticipated the shape wrestling would come to take by better than a decade.

FIGURE 10. Promotional poster for Joe Stecher. Reproduced from the original held by the Department of Special Collection of the Hesburgh Libraries of the University of Notre Dame.

CHAPTER 9

The People Booed;
They Thought Frank Was Faking

BY THE BEGINNING of 1916, anyone keeping tabs on professional wrestling knew that real money stood to be made by whoever could bring off a match between Frank Gotch and Joe Stecher. When Gotch formally retired in April 1913 as the undefeated heavyweight champion, it was Stecher, a bashful twenty-two-year-old athlete from Dodge, Nebraska, with a boyish face and a big smile who succeeded him as the title holder.[1] But even though Gotch hadn't appeared in a wrestling ring for almost three years, he still embodied the sport like no one else. He'd defeated all of his challengers, including his most famous, George Hackenschmidt, who he beat in two straight matches that, while unseemly, had settled the question all the same as to who the better wrestler was. He'd gone almost seven years without losing a match. He'd conquered America and Europe and gotten rich in the process.

The right offer, it was thought, would coax him back for one last show. A Chicago promoter had offered him $25,000, but Gotch countered with a demand for $35,000. Jack Curley had attempted to bring Stecher and Gotch into Manhattan, but Gotch refused, arguing that the match would draw much better in the Midwest. The winning bid came from Gene Melady, a prominent promoter in Nebraska who, working in tandem with Curley, made an offer to hold the match in Omaha. Melady had been a former amateur boxer and college football standout as part of Notre Dame's first football squad, after which he'd made a fortune dealing livestock. To entice Stecher and Gotch, he proposed building a stadium to host the match in time for Labor Day 1916. The $150,000 gate he was hoping to rake in would be the biggest professional wrestling had ever seen.

Joe Stecher had begun wrestling professionally when he was nineteen. With his moony eyes, large hands, slim waist, wide hips, and long arms and legs, he was an unusual sight in his wrestling trunks. He fit neatly, if not exactly, into the Gotch mold—a simple Midwesterner with a no-nonsense approach and a body said to have been made strong by hard work. He appeared, remarked the sports editor at the *Evansville Press* when he met Stecher for the first time in 1915, "to be a big farm boy just come to town to look for work in one of the local factories."[2] Stecher even liked to tell reporters that he'd promised his mother that he would never participate in anything crooked.[3]

Stecher won his matches quickly and consistently, and fans who had staked their money on him returned home with big winnings. He was dubbed "The Scissors King" in homage to his most popular hold, in which Stecher would trap an opponent's chest between his legs and squeeze them into defeat. Stories about him described how he'd developed the unusual power in his legs by crushing sacks of grain between his thighs. Jack Curley was so excited about Stecher that, given the chance to talk him up to sportswriter Damon Runyon, he took hold of *New York Evening Journal* sports editor Wilton Farnsworth and demonstrated Stecher's signature move on him. "Don't make any mistake on this fellow," Curley told Runyon. "I've been in the wrestling game many a year, and he's the greatest I ever saw—bar none."[4]

Stecher had won Frank Gotch's vacant world heavyweight championship on July 5, 1915, defeating a wrestler named Charlie Cutler in front of a sold-out crowd on an idyllic Nebraska night at Rourke Park in downtown Omaha. Fans had traveled from across the Midwest for the big match and Stecher did not disappoint them.[5] The ring was pitched under a dozen blazing white arc lights. When Stecher came into view, the crowd broke into a roar, cheering and chanting his name.[6] A local Reverend was so overcome by the crowd's reaction that he recounted it in a sermon: "Such cheering I never heard. It made the flesh creep and the blood tingle."[7] Stecher defeated Cutler in straight falls, a cordon of police rushing into the crowd as soon as the match ended to cut a path for him to return to the dressing room. "When he gets a body scissors on an opponent—good night—it's like a gigantic boa constrictor," Cutler remarked. "Frank Gotch cannot now, nor never could throw him."[8]

As Gene Melady began preparing in earnest for the Labor Day Gotch–Stecher match, questions about Gotch's health and enthusiasm lingered around the planning. Would he still be able to put on a convincing show? Would he consent to losing to the upstart Stecher, and if not, could Stecher beat him in a straight match? What would it mean for Stecher's promising career, should he lose? In April 1916, Gotch set off from Denver with the Sells–Floto Circus for a national tour scheduled to run through November. It was the perfect way for him to simultaneously get back into ring shape and build interest in his comeback. His guarantee for the seven months of work with the circus was more than $30,000. "Well," Gotch excitedly told reporters, "I'm back in the harness."[9]

It was obvious from the very first dates, though, that Gotch was a changed man. Less than a month in, his weight plunged dramatically. "There is something radically wrong with me," he said.[10] In something of a panic, he left the tour to recover. Just a month later, convinced that his health had returned, he resumed his schedule of appearances. He declared that he would go forward with the Stecher match as planned. Frank Gotch was back and ready to wrestle.

Whatever the sport, determining the champion was a complicated affair. Having a single recognized champion with a clearly maintained list of credible challengers was taking on increased importance as professional sports became better organized. With championships came contenders, and with contenders came rivalries and drama. This made sports more fun for fans to follow and gave them an air of legitimacy. It provided people with something to argue about and with something to believe in. A structure for awarding championships gave shape and meaning to something that might otherwise look aimless and blurry.

Still, this level of organization in professional sports was novel. Boxing's first recognized heavyweight champion of the modern era was John L. Sullivan in the 1880s. Every title holder since had been able to draw a straight line from their claim back to his; so and so defeated so and so, who had defeated so and so, and so on. Major League Baseball's first World Series was played in 1903 and was born out of a period of ruthless competition between club owners. Professional football was still in the early stages of organizing itself into leagues comprised of a steady roster of teams, and the first Super Bowl, as we know it today, wouldn't be played until 1967.

But when it came to professional wrestling in 1916, things were particularly convoluted. The sport lacked even the most rudimentary governing body and was populated with athletes and businessmen steeped in the fine art of putting one over on audiences and, when necessary, on each other. Joe Stecher's championship claim was already tenuous at best—a matter only made more complicated by Frank Gotch's steady stream of reminders to sportswriters that Stecher had never actually defeated him in the ring. Worse, there was no way to prevent a rival wrestler or promoter from creating and advancing their own championship claim should they choose to do so.

Since becoming champion the previous July, Stecher had worked at a breakneck pace. His matches had taken him across the country, from Kentucky to California, up to Minnesota and Illinois, and down through Texas. He'd developed, as well, an intense professional rivalry with another young wrestler appearing around the Midwest named "Strangler" Ed Lewis. Strangler Lewis was born Robert Friedrich in Sheboygan Falls, Wisconsin, on June 30, 1890. In top condition, he stood 5'10" and weighed 230 pounds. Sway-backed and bulky, he had gigantic wrists and forearms, a 54-inch chest, and a neck like a telephone pole. A charismatic master of self-invention, he boasted of being an athletic instructor at the University of Kentucky despite not having any known affiliation with the school. He claimed, too, to have adopted his ring name not as a nod to his famous predecessor, "Strangler" Evan Lewis, but simply because he liked the sound of it.[11]

In 1909, Lewis traded his twelve-hour-a-day job in a Rhinelander, Wisconsin, paper mill stacking 100-pound bundles of paper for 20¢ an hour to try and build a career in wrestling.[12] He was just another struggling local grappler when, in 1914, he came to the attention of Billy Sandow, an ambitious young manager with extensive connections in the wrestling business and a flair for publicity.[13] Sandow was born Wilhelm Baumann in Rochester, New York, in 1884. As a twelve-year-old, he met the promoter William Brady and was so taken with Brady's flashy presence that he turned his attention to performing and managing athletes.[14]

Sandow would come to see wrestling in the same terms that Brady had first imagined it in 1898 when he was shepherding Yusuf İsmail around New York. Sandow came to understand that more than boxing and more than theatre, professional wrestling held the potential to be uniquely rowdy, immersive, and unhinged from the limits of reality. At the age of eighteen, Sandow moved to Chicago, where he began performing in vaudeville as a strongman and wrestler. He cut an impressive figure, with a manicured physique and a head full of dark curly hair. As a businessman, he was a fierce negotiator and became known for driving impossibly hard bargains. "He never admitted he was wrong," Lewis later wrote of Sandow, "and would destroy anyone in his way."[15]

Nimble with language and always happy to talk with any journalist who would listen, Sandow engineered a reputation for Lewis as a human ripsaw who left a body count of broken wrestlers in his wake. Like Joe Stecher with his body scissors, Sandow had Lewis adopt an identifiable hold to claim as his own. For his signature headlock, Lewis would trap his opponent's head in his bulky arms and squeeze before flopping him to the mat. Sandow even patented a headlock machine built by his brother Alexander from a wooden dummy head split down the middle, with railroad springs connecting the two halves, which Lewis would take into the ring with him to demonstrate his strength.

When Lewis and Stecher wrestled for the first time in October 1915, in Evansville, Indiana, their careers were on almost equal ground. Stecher was the sport's recognized champion, but Lewis's career had taken on a momentum all its own. Cautious and well trained in defensive wrestling, he wasn't about to hand Stecher an easy victory. As the match began, the pair shuffled around the ring and avoided mixing it up. The slow pace of the match drove the fans mad, and they took to yelling at the pair to engage. After two hours, a frustrated Stecher began rushing at Lewis, who tumbled over the ring ropes and landed on a chair. A ringside examination declared him fit to continue, but Lewis quit the match anyway. After checking himself into the hospital, he issued a statement claiming that he had suffered a groin injury. The Evansville mayor, Benjamin Bosse, declared the match a fake and seized the gate receipts. "How, don't ask," Lewis later wrote. "Mayor Bossie [sic] is supposed to have turned the money over to some charity, but where the money went no one seems to know to this day."[16]

The fans hated the match, yet they stayed to watch it all the same. Plans for a rematch were drawn up immediately.

Stecher and Lewis wrestled again on July 4, 1916, in Omaha. With Gene Melady in charge of promotion and the much-anticipated Gotch–Stecher Labor Day match just two months away, Stecher needed a good showing. Lewis had frustrated him once, and Stecher knew that if he allowed that to happen again, he risked squelching much of the enthusiasm building around him.

The day started with a drizzle, and by the match's 4 p.m. start, the weather had turned muggy and damp, with a bright sun beating down. The ring had been constructed under a large canvas cover to keep the sun off the wrestlers, but the 18,000 spectators in attendance sat exposed in the baking-hot Nebraska air.[17] The match would prove to be as miserable as the weather. Each time Stecher made a move to engage, Lewis backed away or oozed out of his grip. Significant amounts had been wagered by Stecher's fans on him beating Lewis in under an hour. "Those Nebraska chaps, loaded with Eastern money they had won previously on Stecher against some of the best in the country, had bet wildly," remembered the match's referee, Ed Smith.[18] "Some of those farmers even bet their farms that the champion would win two falls within an hour," remembered Billy Sandow.[19] When that first hour passed, and those bets had turned into losses, many in the crowd took to heckling and jeering the slow-moving wrestlers.

In the ring, what little discernable action there was consisted of Stecher and Lewis pressing their foreheads together and pulling and jerking on each other as they looked for an advantage. As the match dragged into its third hour, a group of children set off fireworks in the middle of the grandstand, causing a mild panic. As darkness set in and parts of the crowd began leaving for home, Melady, who'd neglected to have a lighting setup installed, took to the ring and moved for the match to be called off and resumed in the morning. His suggestion was met with such intense disapproval from the audience that he sent his staff to round up lanterns. Cars were driven over from the infield parking lot to ringside and their headlights directed toward the ring as well.

Close to 9 p.m., after yet another hour of disappointing wrestling conducted in near darkness, referee Ed Smith finally shut down the match. "In the name of humanity," he said, defending his decision, "the match was over."[20] Some spectators estimated afterwards that there had been as little as thirty seconds of actual wrestling during the entire five hours Lewis and Stecher had been in the ring. Tired and frustrated, the crowd responded by throwing rocks, bottles, half-eaten food, and seat cushions at the wrestlers.[21]

Promoter Gene Melady had built his reputation on his promises only to stage honest competitions. Following this Fourth of July fiasco, he raced to save face and salvage hope for bringing off Stecher's match with Frank Gotch in September. If this was what honest professional wrestling looked like, it was unlikely that people would keep paying to watch it.

Two weeks later, on July 18, 1916, Frank Gotch arrived in Kenosha, Wisconsin. He was scheduled for a light public training session against a wrestler named Bob Managoff. During the match, Gotch twisted and reached for Managoff, a motion he'd made in other matches an incalculable number of times. This time, though, as he turned, his foot became entangled between two ring mats. The speed of Gotch's movement snapped his left fibula. He fell to the mat in shock and had to be carried out of the ring to a waiting car.[22] "The people booed," Managoff later recounted. "They thought Frank was faking."[23]

"This is the first accident I ever had on a wrestling mat in the seventeen years I have been in the game," Gotch said from the hospital. "It happened so quickly that I had no chance to see what was happening."[24] After being sent home to recover, Gotch's condition only seemed to worsen. As his weight continued to fall, any hope of his returning to the ring by Labor Day was abandoned. Though he didn't know it yet, Frank Gotch's wrestling career was over.

By the end of 1916, his blockbuster match against Gotch a now-distant memory, Joe Stecher needed a rest. Now twenty-three years old, he'd kept up a heavy schedule of matches and training since becoming champion and was bringing in $1,000 or more for each of his appearances. "When one of my wrestling matches is over, I want to know when the first train leaves for Dodge," he told reporters. "I would advise all boys born and reared on farms to remain there."[25] On December 6, 1916, he married his eighteen-year-old girlfriend, Frances Ehlers, a dark-haired bank president's daughter from Scribner, Nebraska, in a private ceremony in a suite on the ninth floor of Omaha's Hotel Fontanelle. After the wedding, the famous couple walked unnoticed out of the hotel's side door and boarded an eastbound train to begin a working honeymoon.[26]

The first match on Stecher's itinerary was on December 11, 1916, in Springfield, Massachusetts, against a former Olympic silver medal-winning amateur wrestler from Finland named John Olin. Olin knew he couldn't match Stecher's ring skills but had hoped the pair could put on an entertaining show for Olin's hometown fans. That message never made it to Stecher, who had by then earned a reputation for being uncooperative with opponents. The match was messy, with Olin refusing to give up easily and blocking all of Stecher's attempts at offense. It ended close to 1 a.m., with Olin and Stecher outside the ring, trading punches in the first row of seats. A frustrated Stecher turned and walked back to the dressing room, losing the match on a disqualification.[27]

Four months later, on April 9, 1917, Stecher was back in Omaha for a match with a twenty-nine-year-old rising star named Earl Caddock. The match's opening two falls lasted almost three hours. Stecher returned to his dressing room to rest before the start of the final fall, just before 2 a.m. When the announcement was sent that it was time for the match to resume, his manager, Joe Hetmanek, sent back word to the referee that Stecher had been hurt and was forfeiting the match.[28] When the referee declared Caddock the winner and new heavyweight champion, the crowd broke into hysterics.

Stecher was said to be sitting slumped in a chair in his dressing room, looking dazed and with tears running down his face. "I won't go back and you can't make me go back and nobody can make me go back," he told his brother Tony. "Joe Stecher was not himself," Hetmanek told reporters the next day. Stecher would later claim that he could have continued the match and had only failed to return because he hadn't been informed that the match was resuming.[29] Still, worn down by two years of relentless travel and suddenly free of his championship, Stecher took the loss as a chance to disappear altogether from wrestling for the next five months.

Any quixotic hopes of keeping some kind of straight line of claims to wrestling's heavyweight championship were irrevocably dashed when John Olin, fresh off of his disqualification win over Stecher in Springfield, took to calling himself champion. In December 1917, Jack Curley declared still another wrestler—a tall, muscular, smooth-faced Polish athlete named Wladek Zbyszko—to be his heavyweight champion. Zbyszko had been brought to America in 1913 by his older brother Stanislaus, and Curley had plans to make him into a star.

Along with Earl Caddock, this made for a total of three grapplers simultaneously laying claim to some version of wrestling's heavyweight title. The situation underlined the lack of cohesion in the sport, and although it served to further tarnish wrestling's already flea-bitten reputation among sportswriters, it did not seem to alienate fans. Attendance at matches grew at a steady pace. It was clear that interest was building, but how long it would last and what, if anything, could be done to keep it going was anyone's guess.

At noon on December 16, 1917, Frank Gotch died at his home in Humboldt at the age of forty, with his wife and four-year-old son at his side. The mystery illness that had been plaguing him since his aborted comeback attempt was finally diagnosed as uremia, a poisoning of the blood caused by untreated kidney failure.[30] By the time of his death, his best days of running wild with Gold Rush gamblers in Dawson, of performing in front of thousands, and of being a sports hero to the hundreds of thousands more who followed his career through countless news articles, were already well behind him. He'd transformed himself into a successful businessman and philanthropist, started a family, and settled into an abundantly comfortable middle age. He'd taken to politics, as well, having considered a run for governor of Iowa and later campaigning for William L. Harding when he ran for the office in 1916.[31] Gotch's health, though, had been steadily declining. He'd been in and out of hospitals with different illnesses and injuries. His clothes, typically tailored and elegant, had been hanging loosely on his deteriorating frame for months. His drawn appearance at his final public engagement that May had shocked fans who remembered him as the husky world beater of just six years prior.[32]

Life paused in Humboldt, Iowa, on December 19th to allow Gotch's funeral procession to move uninterrupted to the tiny snow-covered cemetery on the edge of town. Flags were lowered to half-mast, and schools and businesses closed in his honor. Special trains carried mourners from Fort Dodge and Des Moines, and hundreds of people gathered outside of the town's stone-walled Congregational Church to pay their respects.[33]

Gotch had been responsible for making pro wrestling a nationally recognized sport. He'd carried it off the farms and out of the tiny theatres of Midwestern towns and into stadiums and arenas. He was as famous for his athleticism as his contemporaries in boxing and baseball and was said to have amassed a fortune valued at upwards of $750,000 dollars.[34] His death stunned fans and threw the business of professional wrestling suddenly, unexpectedly, wide open.

PART II

In This Way,
The Hippodrome May
Be Continued Indefinitely

1918–1941

FIGURE 11. Jack Curley (*third on the left*) presents the New York Heavyweight Championship to Wladek Zbyszko (*center*), 1917. Courtesy of the Milo Steinborn Collection, the H. J. Lutcher Stark Center for Physical Culture and Sports, the University of Texas at Austin.

CHAPTER 10

The Knockers and Scandalmongers Will Be Chased to the Woods

ON JULY 4, 1918, Jack Curley celebrated his forty-second birthday staring down a diminishing set of options. He had moved his family from Riverside Drive and was renting a large eight-room home in Kensington, a community with just a few dozen homes spread across 155 acres on the Great Neck peninsula of Long Island. Great Neck, a one-time fishing village, was emerging as a community of successful artists, writers, and performers with a vast concentration of glamour and wealth. His business prospects had dimmed, but money poured out of the Curley house as quickly as it came in. "We spent on the basis of $20,000 a year," Curley's wife Marie later said. "Well, he spent most of what he made."[1] Curley had a "fondness for going on shopping sprees and spending money on absolute un-necessities," remembered a friend. "He let the dough run through his fingers like water."[2]

Boxing, in a limited capacity, had been more or less tolerated in New York City since the passage of the Frawley Law in 1911. That changed in 1917 when improper payments to government officials from boxing promoters, including at least one made by Curley, were uncovered.[3] This came on top of the death of a boxer named Stephen McDonald, who was killed in Albany during his first professional fight after taking a hard punch to the chest—all while his father watched the bout from ringside. Instead of calling the evening off, the promoters, with the blessing of the state official in attendance, carried on through four more bouts. "The tragedy did not seem to affect the large crowd that witnessed the fight at all," reported the *New York Times*. "At first, it was thought to be an ordinary knockout. The killing of McDonald—when it became known in the audience that he had died—seemed merely to whet the appetite of the spectators."⁴ The next day, New York governor Charles Whitman began calling for an immediate end to all fights. In May, the state legislature passed the Slater Bill, outlawing boxing in the state.⁵

"The fatality in the ring at Albany must be deplored," wrote Curley in a newspaper editorial intended to stave off legislation. "We are sorry. But it is no more than happens in football, racing, and other sports, as well as in any circus many times during the year. As for graft, if there is graft existing and proved—because personally I know of none—there has also been graft in many departments or public administration. The remedy has always been to cleanse the department and discontinue it. Bank cashiers have been known to steal the bank's funds, but the remedy has never been to do away with all the banks." His logic failed to persuade lawmakers.⁶

Curley still had a hand in managing Jess Willard, boxing's reigning heavyweight champion. But since defeating Jack Johnson, Willard had fought only once. His absence was so conspicuous that sportswriters took to derisively calling him "the pacifist heavyweight champion."⁷ Blame for the dearth of title defenses fell alternatingly on Willard and Curley, who were accused of everything from greed to fear and laziness. In July 1917, looking to minimize any further drains on his already strained finances, Willard fired Curley as his manager.

On July 27, 1918, Curley staged what was to be his last significant boxing event, a bout between Fred Fulton and an exciting twenty-three-year-old fighter named Jack Dempsey. The fight, which was staged in Harrison, New Jersey, was a logistical and financial disaster.⁸ Fewer than 13,000 people came, leaving Harrison Park, the 25,000-seat ballpark chosen to host the fight, less than half full. At 7 p.m., just before the main event was to start, as a cool early evening breeze fanned the audience, attendees sitting in the outfield bleachers rushed forward and claimed seats closer to the ring. Even more people dropped into the stadium from over its exterior walls and took seats without paying. Curley fought his way into the ring, where he threatened to shut the evening down early. "You tell those people to get back in their seats or I'll call the show off," he told the ring announcer. "I'm not going to lose $15,000 this way." The announcement was met with jeers. Fearing a full-on riot should he make good on his threat, Curley let the fight go forward, though he almost needn't have bothered. Dempsey knocked Fulton out cold with a right to the jaw in the first round after just twenty-three seconds. Fulton would later call the fight a frame-up, claiming he'd been led to believe Dempsey would go easy on him for eight rounds with the hope of building interest in a return fight between the two.[9]

Dempsey's win over Fulton helped him land a championship fight against Jess Willard. On July 4, 1919, in a fight promoted by Tex Rickard in Toledo, Ohio, Dempsey annihilated Willard in just three rounds to become boxing's new heavyweight champion. The beating Willard took was so severe that rumors, certainly false, circulated following the match that Dempsey had either doctored the tape used to wrap his hands with a hardening agent or hidden a foreign object under his gloves.[10]

With promoting regular fights in New York no longer an option, his relationship with Jess Willard severed, and Tex Rickard taking on an ever more prominent role in boxing, Curley found himself struggling to find his place in the sport in which he'd spent his life working. "The problem with [Jack Curley] as a boxing promoter was that he was several years ahead of his time," wrote Damon Runyon. "He was putting on matches at a loss, when a few years later, corresponding matches would have been tremendous winners."[11] "Boxing always was a hoodoo for Curley," wrote sportswriter Ed Smith. "When it came to staging boxing shows—well, Jack just wasn't there, that's all."[12]

Jack Curley had expressed his love of professional wrestling to reporters easily and often, but he had never had to rely on it as his primary source of income. As his opportunities for staying active in sports promotion ran ever thinner, it looked increasingly likely that he would have no other choice. Despite graduating into larger halls and even into arenas in some cities, professional wrestling remained no better organized than it had been when William Muldoon had been appearing in the back room of Harry Hill's forty years earlier. And though there had been flashes of popularity, the sport's reputation had also improved little over that time.

To make pro wrestling operate on the level he imagined it could, Curley knew things would have to change.

In early 1918, he worked to get agreements from a group of his fellow promoters and managers to share talent and cooperate in the staging of wrestling matches. The business of professional wrestling at that time was, as Strangler Lewis later wrote, one of "pseudo-magnates and competitors for a czar's position, each more or less jealous of each other and eager for power."[13] Curley was the most accomplished and experienced promoter in the group, and while exactly what he said or promised to secure these agreements is unknown, he did walk out of the negotiations wielding far more power than when he went in.

What was publicly reported was that he had argued for matches to be decided by a single fall and for the establishment of time limits. Unlike boxing, wrestling remained free from time constraints. Matches could—and frequently did—unwind at an unbearable pace, with no punctuations to the boredom. If a wrestler chose to stall or play defense for the entire evening, there was little his opponent could do to force him to engage. Curley argued that time limits would solve this problem. Fans wanted action and drama, and for the business to be successful, wrestling matches would need to supply both. "Boxing is outlawed in most of the states, while wrestling is lawful everywhere. With the right sort of rules and regulations, we can put the sport on its feet and keep it there for all time," Curley said. "The sport will take on such a boom that the knockers and scandalmongers will be chased to the woods. . . . The idea that the grappling game died when Gotch passed away is preposterous."[14]

In January 1918, with New York as his base, Curley began staging regular wrestling shows at Madison Square Garden. It soon became evident that the boxing ban New York had enacted the year before had unexpectedly increased demand for wrestling. Folks who might not have been caught dead at a match a few years prior were now not only buying tickets but joining in the hysterics, shouting and yelling and getting themselves all worked up.

Five thousand people were said to have been turned away for a March 1918 match between Wladek Zbyszko and Strangler Lewis. Inside the packed arena, in addition to the prominent spectators at ringside who threw hundred-dollar bills into the ring during the pre-match drive for donations to the Knights of Columbus, hundreds of women, many in evening gowns, dotted the audience. During the match, Lewis and Zbyszko repeatedly brought the crowd to their feet. After Zbyszko head-butted Lewis, sending the dazed Strangler through the ropes and out of the ring, a menacing and rowdy group of audience members surged forward, shouting, "Kill the Pole!" As Zbyszko fled toward the dressing room, frantic audience members threw chairs at him, one striking him in the back of the head. The reporter from the *New York Times* who covered the match called it, "the wildest wrestling bout New York has ever witnessed."[15]

Curley would put on a total of a dozen shows, rotating Lewis, Zbyszko, Joe Stecher, and Earl Caddock in and out of each evening's main event and selling out the arena seven times before his final show in March of 1920.[16] He would certainly have booked more matches during that period had not Lewis, Caddock, and Stecher all been pulled into military service at different points during World War I.

The quartet matched up with each other in varying combinations over and over in matches held across the country as well—Lewis and Zbyszko in Savannah and Louisville; Stecher and Lewis in Chicago and Omaha; and Caddock and Zbyszko in Des Moines. The matches routinely ended in dramatic, uncertain, and sometimes infuriating fashions; again and again, they ran out of time, a vague injury would stop a match cold, or a pinfall would occur under suspect circumstances. In one match, a wrestler was pinned after pausing to tie his shoe, in another after trying to break up an argument at ringside.[17] In tandem with the matches, Curley (representing Zbyszko), Billy Sandow (representing Lewis), Gene Melady (representing Caddock), and Tony Stecher (representing his brother Joe) tirelessly batted very public challenges and accusations among themselves. No sooner would one man's wrestler get a win over another's than stories would appear decrying the match as illegitimate or a referee's decision as unfair or incorrect. At the same time, the promoters made constant appeals to reassure fans that the matches were on the level. Billy Sandow liberally threatened litigation against any hints that Strangler Lewis's matches were faked, while Curley made embarrassingly earnest pleas for the public's trust.[18]

Keeping fans off balance was essential, and the effect was a seemingly transparent, though impossible to penetrate, swirling fantasy world. Sandow, in particular, worked with near delight at planting red herrings with writers.[19] The most skilled and eager fabulist of the bunch, he extended the quasi-fiction enacted by the wrestlers in the ring into the sports pages. He plainly understood that pro wrestling's best chance for survival in a shifting sports landscape was as a circus-like spectacle that mixed athletics with a meta-type of surrealism.

The changes made for big box office pulls. In New York, the apex of Curley's run came on January 30, 1920, when he pitted Joe Stecher against Earl Caddock in a contest for what was being called the unified heavyweight championship. Besides clearing up the convoluted wrestling championship picture, the match would prove, Curley hoped, that "there is genuine and countrywide interest in wrestling."[20] On the night of the match, Madison Square Garden was filled to the doors, with as many as 10,000 attendees paying as much as $22 for a ticket while thousands of others outside were turned away at the gate. Seven cameras whirred at ringside while four giant lamps poured hot white light down from the rafters. A procession of uniformed US Navy and Army personnel escorted Stecher and Caddock as they walked to the ring. The pair wrestled a clean match devoid of any histrionics or rough tactics. After two hours, Caddock tied Stecher up in a half-nelson, snaking his arm under Stecher's armpit and around the back of his neck. Stecher drew a long breath, lifted Caddock up onto his shoulders, and hurled him to the mat, where he wrapped his legs around Caddock's waist, trapping him in the famous leg scissors. Stecher grabbed hold of Caddock's wrists, forced them down, and pinned him to become the new heavyweight champion.[21]

The evening was said to have cleared anywhere from $50,000 to $80,000 in ticket sales, and even more stood to be made from screenings of the match film. It was significant money for professional wrestling, but just how much of it stayed with Curley is unclear. Stecher and Caddock were said to have been paid $20,000 each for their work, and the advertising and incidental costs for the evening had been substantial.[22] Still, the overflow crowd and positive press coverage helped to firmly establish Jack Curley as the wrestling czar of Manhattan. It wouldn't be an easy ride.

FIGURE 12. William Muldoon (*second on the left*) meets with the New York State Athletic Commission. Courtesy of Steve Yohe.

CHAPTER 11

Much That Is Undesirable and Unfair
Has Crept into the Sport

THE STECHER–CADDOCK MATCH had been one of Jack Curley's most successful promotions yet, but chaos lay close behind. Curley's marriage had been unhappy for years, and in March, his wife Marie sued him for divorce after he was caught in a Houston hotel room with an unnamed woman. The divorce was finalized in June. Just six months later, on December 12, 1920, Curley married his third wife, Bessie Grubfeld, in Connecticut.[1]

As threats to professional wrestling went, legal, well-organized boxing was perhaps second only to government oversight. In the spring of 1920, Curley found himself contending with both. That May, the New York legislature passed the Walker Bill, which would soon become the model for boxing legislation throughout the United States. The new regulation allowed for bouts of up to 15 rounds, required decisions by referees and judges, and mandated the licensing of boxers, managers, trainers, physicians, and promoters. The Walker Bill was followed by the Simpson Bill, which created the New York State Athletic Commission. In addition to oversight of boxing, the three-member commission was also tasked with ensuring "sportsmanlike and scientific wrestling contests."[2] It was a monumental task, but one of the men chosen to help guide the new body had an extensive understanding of exactly how professional wrestling worked.

William Muldoon, the former Greco-Roman champion, was appointed to the New York State Athletic Commission that June. Upon taking office, he set to running things with an iron fist. Under his leadership, sour-faced regulations were issued for wrestling matches intended to make them, in the commission's words, "honest and fair." The new rules created a laundry list of offenses that would no longer be tolerated, including gouging, scratching, and displays of bad temper, as well as head holds, toe holds, and scissor holds meant "especially for the purpose of punishing an opponent."[3] "Much that is undesirable and unfair has crept into the sport," Muldoon's commission declared, "so it is the intention of the new commission to clean house, so to speak."[4]

With boxing now on firm legal ground, Tex Rickard saw an opportunity to gamble even bigger on it. On July 2, 1921, he staged his chanciest promotion yet: the heavyweight championship fight between Jack Dempsey and the French boxer Georges Carpentier in Jersey City, New Jersey. "The chance [Rickard] took was tremendous," Curley later wrote. "The enterprise [was] the most daring I have ever seen brought to a successful conclusion."[5] The bout drew more than 80,000 spectators and was boxing's first million-dollar gate. Dempsey knocked Carpentier out with a right hook in the fourth round of the violent and mostly one-sided affair to retain his championship. "I thought he would kill me," a shaken Carpentier told Curley that evening as the two drove together back to Long Island. "I mean that."[6]

Rickard also partnered with circus magnate John Ringling to take out a ten-year lease on Madison Square Garden. "The man who controlled the largest arena in the East would control the promotion of every great sporting spectacle to come," he said.[7] Running regular shows at the Garden brought with it intimidating fixed costs that Curley had deemed too steep to try taking on himself. To meet them, Rickard drew up plans to keep the Garden busy year-round. While boxing would be his main focus, his plans soon expanded to include arranging his own wrestling shows. Sportswriters portrayed Rickard's move as an encroachment into Curley's domain and a direct shot across the bow in a war between New York's two best-known sports promoters.[8]

The news of Tex Rickard's sudden interest in professional wrestling set off alarm bells across the business. Rickard scheduled his first wrestling show for November 14, 1921. It was to be the first night of matches held under the official oversight of William Muldoon's New York State Athletic Commission, with athletes licensed by the state competing under state-approved rules. In the main event was a ferocious up-and-coming wrestler from Ravenna, Nebraska, named John Pesek.

Pesek was an enormously gifted athlete with an almost impenetrable Czech accent and the unusual talent of being able to walk on his hands.[9] Pesek maintained a close working relationship with Billy Sandow and Strangler Lewis and had wrestled against Lewis several times. He was known in the wrestling business as a "policeman," a skilled and aggressive wrestler who was used by promoters to measure the true ability of other wrestlers. "Savage guy. Cruel when he had to be," was how a contemporary of Pesek's remembered him. "No one could take him. How he learned to wrestle, I don't know. . . . It was instinctive, something he did as naturally and easy as he breathed."[10]

Wrestlers acting as "policemen" were trusted to rough-up uncooperative opponents when needed in order to discredit them as deserving a match with whomever was the current heavyweight champion. While the arrangement all but guaranteed they'd never be champions themselves, it kept them busy working in well-paying matches around the country. "The bigger they were when they tried to get by me, the farther they wanted to get away from the Lewis camp after the match was over," Pesek later said of his role.[11]

For Pesek's opponent, Rickard scheduled a thirty-four-year-old wrestler from former Yugoslavia named Marin Plestina. Weighing well more than 200 pounds, Plestina was a large and experienced competitor. He'd been trained by Farmer Burns and was managed by Ole Marsh, Jack Curley's nemesis from his Seattle days. Marsh had been released from prison after serving just less than a year of the fifteen-month sentence he'd received for his involvement with the Mabray Gang. He'd taken over managing Plestina in 1917, boosting him to reporters and branding him the "Trust Buster." The pair issued challenges to the group Marsh labeled the "Big Four": Joe Stecher, Strangler Lewis, Wladek Zbyszko, and Earl Caddock. "These so-called champions do not dare to meet a real wrestler on the square," Marsh wrote in one of his challenges.[12] It was intentional, he claimed, that matches between prominent wrestlers invariably ended in controversy and that outcomes were kept inconclusive. "Look at the 'trust' matches and it will be seen that someone always gets hurt, or they lose on a foul or 'wrestle' a draw, or they bar a hold, but they never let a match end so that the public may know which man is the best," Marsh told reporters. "In this way, the hippodrome may be continued indefinitely."[13]

Marsh had been talking about the existence of a so-called wrestling trust for years.[14] The trust, he claimed, was a tightly sewn group of managers and promoters, led by Jack Curley, who dictated the outcomes of matches and controlled access to opponents and arenas. Any wrestler who refused to work according to the orders handed down by the group was blacklisted. "All of the big fellows down East are under the thumb of Jack Curley," Marsh said. "Curley can sit in his office and match any of them by simply writing down their names. Moreover, he can tell as soon as they are matched how the match will end. . . . The public are bound to learn in time how they are being buncoed and will demand a square deal."[15]

Dr. Ben Roller, Curley's old friend from Seattle, joined the chorus when he authored an eight-page article in the magazine *Physical Culture*, titled "What's Wrong with Wrestling." In it, Roller outlined in bracing detail the inner contours of the wrestling business, including a claim that one unnamed promoter had boasted to him of paying sportswriters as much as $9,000 for favorable coverage of matches. Roller described how Curley, along with other promoters like Gene Melady and Billy Sandow, worked to arrange matches for their stars, and how the matches were plotted to ensure that a clear winner could not be determined.

Fault for this situation, Roller argued, lay not with the wrestlers themselves but with the public. Stecher, Lewis, and Zbyszko, he wrote, were skilled, honest wrestlers. Stecher, he even claimed, had never knowingly faked a match. It was the tendency of sports fans to lose interest in a competitor once they'd lost a contest, Roller argued, which left wrestlers and their managers with no choice but to avoid decisive defeats anyway they could. Professional wrestling had once been honest, Roller wrote, and it could be made so again. He predicted that if clean, legitimate wrestling were given a fair chance to take hold, a delighted and clear-eyed public would flock to arenas to support it.[16]

Stories that he was functioning as some kind of corrupt kingmaker made Curley furious, though his responses to them were rarely direct. Speaking to reporters, his voice rising in anger, he told them, "I am called the trust. If half the accusations were true, I would indeed be a great man. All other promoters, managers, wrestlers, sportswriters, officials, war departments—all would be my dupes and tools. Isn't it ridiculous?"[17]

If fans were paying attention, few seemed overly put off by the negative press. For some, suggestions of a shadowy cabal hiding in plain sight that had the power to rig an entire sport must have only added to the enjoyment they experienced at matches; they were thrilled when a match electrified them and when one didn't, they were justified in directing shouts of "Fake!" or "Put those crooks out!" towards the ring.[18] And trying to see through and stay ahead of the supposed machinations could become its own kind of sport. "It's not an utter impossibility," speculated a sportswriter with the *Des Moines Register*, "that [Ole Marsh] is part of the trust, and that his man is being deliberately held back in order to inject new life into the game when the four big contenders fail to attract."[19]

Professional wrestling, by chance and by design, had become a conspiracy inside a conspiracy.

On September 23, 1921, two months before Marin Plestina was to wrestle John Pesek in the main event at Madison Square Garden, a letter was written by an agent at the William J. Burns International Detective Agency to Warden W. I. Biddle at the US Federal Penitentiary in Leavenworth, Kansas. It contained a simple request: "Friend Billie:—I am writing you this to ask you for a special favor if you can consistently see your way to grant it. I would like to have you send me a photograph and criminal record of one George A. Marsh, alias Ole Marsh, who was sent to your institution in 1911."[20]

Just who hired a detective agency to investigate Marsh is unknown. It is a fair assumption that any of the managers or promoters Marsh had run afoul of in his crusade against the wrestling trust would have had an interest in obtaining material to discredit him ahead of Plestina's New York debut. Jack Curley was certainly already familiar with Marsh's prison sentence and had spoken openly in the press about his past dealings with him. The New York State Athletic Commission was said to have been investigating Marsh's background as well, prior to issuing him a manager's license.

It took the Penitentiary less than a week to respond.[21] Whoever received the information next made no attempts to keep it to themselves. By October, stories that excavated Marsh's past association with the Mabray Gang began appearing in newspapers. They carefully outlined Marsh's host of past aliases, as well as his time served at Leavenworth. Curley had cards printed that depicted Marsh in prison garb situated among a rogue's gallery and had them sent to reporters.[22] The implication, left unsaid but easily apparent, was that the man purporting to expose the shameful operations that made professional wrestling run had his own rich history of swindles for which to account.

To compound Marsh and Plestina's problems, on the day of Plestina's match with John Pesek, a New York morning paper ran a bulldog edition with claims that one of them had been injured and, as it was too late to call things off, that evening's match would be a fake.[23] Copies were passed among fans milling in front of Madison Square Garden, causing many to think twice about buying a ticket. Inside, Tex Rickard stormed into the press section, found the story's writer, and banned him from the Garden for life.[24] Back in the dressing room, Pesek complained of a broken arm and tried to call off the match, even as fans were beginning to take their seats. Medical staff assigned by the Athletic Commission examined him and declared him fit to compete.[25]

Madison Square Garden was less than a quarter full by the time Pesek and Plestina entered the ring. For Ole Marsh, three years of work spent building Marin Plestina into a headlining attraction appeared ready to disappear in a flash. As the match got underway, Pesek pursued Plestina mercilessly. Over and over, he dug his thumb and fingernails into Plestina's right eye and head-butted him in the face and shoulders. Despite outweighing Pesek by fifty pounds, Plestina seemed bewildered and overwhelmed by the aggressive tactics. He made no attempt to retaliate against Pesek and failed to mount any offense.

As the match wore on, the booing from the crowd grew louder. Some left their ringside seats and tried to climb into the ring. After forty-five minutes of ugly brawling, the referee finally disqualified Pesek for his rough tactics, bringing the disastrous night to a close.[26] "Looks as if someone had put something over on me," Tex Rickard said after the match, gritting his teeth hard on an unlit cigar as he watched the Garden empty of spectators.[27]

Conflicting explanations for Pesek's actions emerged immediately. His manager, Larney Lichtenstein, dropped Pesek's contract and claimed no responsibility.[28] Pesek declared exactly the opposite. "Everything I did in my match with Marin Plestina was ordered by Larney Lichtenstein," he wrote in a telegrammed statement to sportswriters.[29] William Muldoon and his Commission acted immediately, suspending Pesek, Lichtenstein, and Billy Sandow, who was seen instructing Pesek from ringside during the match.[30] Jack Curley, who had no formal connection to the match, was fingered by multiple writers as the person responsible for the fiasco, including an outrageous story from one of his former employees that claimed a paranoid Curley, convinced that his office was under surveillance and determined to undermine Tex Rickard, had met Pesek on a street corner with orders to injure Plestina.[31]

It's likely that the commission would have suspended Curley had they had been able to do so, if for no other reason than the preponderance of suspicion around his involvement.[32] However, because he'd been staging his shows exclusively in the city's smaller regimental armories since losing access to Madison Square Garden, Curley had never been required to secure a promoter's license, leaving the Commission with no authority over him. Professional boxing and wrestling in armories had been allowed with the consent of the State National Guard, and by staging his shows in them, Curley had exploited a loophole in the state's new laws.

That changed once Muldoon's Commission was granted jurisdiction over all wrestling and boxing in the state, regardless of where it was staged. Empowered with even more sweeping authority, one of the commission's first acts was to decide that the number of wrestling clubs already exceeded any possible demand. They concurrently refused to issue a new license to any promoter, leaving Tex Rickard as the sole wrestling promoter in the city.[33] Curley argued his case in front of a packed committee hearing but got nowhere, and Muldoon held firm. With no license to promote in New York, Jack Curley suddenly found himself out of the wrestling business.

The commission, however, wasn't finished with their clampdown. When Strangler Lewis came to New York in late November 1921 to wrestle for Tex Rickard against Stanislaus Zbyszko, Muldoon had him sign an affidavit stating that he would put forth a legitimate effort to win. "Just a word to the so-called wrestling trust," Rickard boomed. "The members of that organization are going to wrestle honestly at Madison Square Garden or they are not going to wrestle anywhere in this state. I shall insist on honest wrestling or none at all."[34] Compared to the disorder of the Pesek-Plestina bout, the evening of Lewis and Zbyszko's match passed without incident. A heavy rain kept the crowd small, and all of the evening's four matches wrapped up in an unusually speedy ninety minutes. In the main event, Zbyszko and Lewis wrestled an exciting but all too brief match that had the crowd shouting and howling their disapproval.[35]

An unbowed Muldoon, unhappy with the evening's turnout and the crowd's unenthusiastic response, groused to reporters. "For the first time in thirty years, New Yorkers saw an honest contest for the heavyweight wrestling championship. Judging by the way it was received . . . I do not think they appreciated [it]."[36]

Despite his struggles with wrestling, Tex Rickard had succeeded in making his first year at Madison Square Garden profitable. Fans streamed to his evenings of boxing in the fall and winter, and for the scorching summer months, he installed a white-tiled indoor swimming pool that he made available to the public, and which he used to stage races and water polo matches.

Rickard had planned to kick off a new series of wrestling matches in 1922, but all that changed after his arrest in January on charges of sexual assault against a fifteen-year-old girl. Without providing details, Rickard's defense team railed against the allegations, calling them a frame-up pulled off by a group they identified only as "Wall Street district blackmailers."[37] They relied on aggressive attacks on the accuser's background, inconsistencies in the prosecution's timeline of events, and a string of high-profile witnesses (including the son of President Theodore Roosevelt) to land a "not guilty" verdict for Rickard that March.[38]

Rickard's interest in professional wrestling all but evaporated following the trial. Madison Square Garden would go dark to matches for the next six years. They would still be staged at smaller venues around the city, but the turnout on some nights was fewer than 100 people—this for a show that would have attracted thousands just a few years prior.[39] It was a hard comedown after the boom years of the late 1910s, but come 1922, pro wrestling in New York couldn't draw flies.

FIGURE 13. A holiday card from Billy Sandow, Toots Mondt, and Strangler Lewis. Reproduced from the original held by the Department of Special Collections of the Hesburgh Libraries of the University of Notre Dame.

CHAPTER 12

The Crowd Seemed Bent on Inflicting Bodily Harm

WRESTLING MIGHT HAVE died in New York City, but there was plenty of money to be made elsewhere. Strangler Lewis had had a brief run as wrestling's heavyweight champion at the end of 1920, beating Joe Stecher in a heartstopper of a match that December in New York, but he lost the title only five months later to Stanislaus Zbyszko. When Lewis got his second chance, he made sure to hold onto it. On March 3, 1922, Lewis regained the heavyweight championship by defeating Zbyszko in Wichita, Kansas. Rumors circulated following the match that Lewis had promised to lose the title back to Zbyszko before the year was out, as would have been expected in previous years. But whether the so-called wrestling trust had ever actually existed, and whether Lewis, Caddock, Stecher, and the Zbyszko brothers had ever knowingly circulated the championship among themselves, the days of Lewis and Billy Sandow cooperating with the group were over. In possession of the heavyweight championship, and with Jack Curley's influence significantly diminished for the time being, Lewis and Sandow seized on the opportunity to exercise an outsized influence over professional wrestling.[1]

Strangler Lewis became the face of professional wrestling during the Golden Age of Sports. Billy Sandow crafted for him the image of a jigging, jet-setting, bone-crushing sensation. The pair courted sportswriters and associated with some of the decade's most celebrated athletes, boasting that Lewis outearned them all. Instead of contending with New York's hostile press and the overbearing New York State Athletic Commission, Sandow concentrated on building a string of partnerships with promoters in cities in the Midwest and on the West Coast, where Lewis drew well. They traveled relentlessly, sometimes by train and later in a private Laird Swallow biplane. Between March 1922 and January 1925, Lewis defended his championship more than 120 times in nineteen states, as well as in parts of Canada, France, England, Belgium, and Italy.[2] In his autobiography, which Lewis began with an unknown ghostwriter but never finished, he mapped the rapidly changing wrestling world of the mid-1920s:

> At the time, there were probably about 25 heavyweights who were worthwhile opponents who could put up any kind of a contest against the champion, but there were, of course, lesser lights with transitory ambitions, whose orbit was their own city, county, or state and whose local fame was their chief stock in trade. As wrestlers they might be heavy, fairly strong, and tough, but that was about all. They did not have 'color.' A larger city would be 'localized' by one of the 25, who might discern that the sport was popular and had a drawing potential. He would come into town to wrestle the local boy or two, and be able to beat them. Others of the 25 would be brought in and invariably lose to him, thus building him up thru the months or years. He, in turn would take a journey from his hometown and accommodate them and increase their local prestige. . . . When a local situation was judged ripe, that is, their hero had no more Bulgarian lions, Estonian werewolves, Belgian tigers, or Russian bears to conquer, when there were no more champions of Texas, New York, the Pacific Coast, and elsewhere to come to taste bitterly the mastery of their peerless one, it was logical that he should hurl defiance at the champion of the world. . . . The enthusiasm of what sometimes amounted to a year's build-up was sure to be a sell-out at the largest local arena. The champion came, he saw, he conquered, but more often than not, not too decisively. The issue was not always resolved cleanly. The champion would lose a fall, someone would be injured. The referee would show marked favoritism, or bad judgement and was sometimes run out of town. . . . After a return engagement or two, it would be time for another turn to be taken by a newcomer, and the show would go on. Human memory is short and the routine so simple that it was always new.[3]

Sandow and Lewis relied on tenuous cooperation among a network of wrestlers and a string of young, ambitious promoters to build interest in and maintain the veneer of believability around Lewis's matches. Working together, and just as often in competition with each other, these promoters would come to dominate the business of wrestling over the next decade. In Missouri, a businessman named Tom Packs turned St. Louis into one of the best stops on Lewis's circuit of towns.[4] In Philadelphia, Sandow and Lewis worked with a one-time violinist for the Chicago Opera Company named Ray Fabiani. Their connection in Boston was a gregarious former wrestler named Paul Bowser. Bowser had learned to wrestle while working as a circus performer, and his wife, Cora Livingston, was the most successful female wrestler of the 1920s.[5] Bowser loved harness racing, and he loved betting—and not always in that order. His influence over professional wrestling would only grow in the coming years, and by the end of the 1930s, he would be arguably the most powerful promoter in wrestling.

In California, they worked with a former wrestler and strongman from Austria named Lou Daro, who had begun staging wrestling shows in the fall of 1922. He'd first opened shop in Sacramento but moved south after being denied permission to promote shows in the city due to accusations that his matches were faked. With his expensive suits, heavy German accent, and an ever-present carnation in his lapel, Daro couldn't be missed. By October 1924, he'd so solidly established wrestling in Los Angeles that he was able to bring out 10,000 fans to see Lewis wrestle in the city's Washington Ball Park. Just four months later, Daro signed a multi-year contract to hold regular shows at the city's brand new, 10,000-seat Olympic Auditorium. An apocryphal story told in later years about Daro's dedication to his craft recounted him having been asked to speak at the funeral of a friend. When Daro took the podium, he said, "This man was such a good friend of mine that, if he were alive tonight, he would be attending the wrestling match I am promoting, which begins at 8:30"—and then went on to list his headline attractions.[6]

Sandow and Lewis's most important relationship was with a wrestler named Toots Mondt. Born Joseph Mondt in Garden Grove, Iowa, on January 18, 1894, Mondt had a round, friendly face and spoke with a booming voice. As a teenager, Mondt had worked as a clown along with his older brother in local carnivals, but he found himself drawn instead to wrestling. One writer described him as looking "like a mountainous cherub," but in the ring he was a dangerous grappler.[7] At the age of

twenty-seven, he was hired as the wrestling coach at what would become Colorado State University, and after meeting Sandow and Lewis
in late 1922, Mondt began working with the pair as a trainer and fre-
quent opponent for Lewis.[8] Mondt was a rare find: a respected wrestler
who could act in the role of "policeman" but who, like his fellow policeman John Pesek, wasn't above prioritizing entertainment over sport
when needed. "I was like what the mob would call a hitman, though,
of course, I never killed anyone," Mondt later said. "But if a guy got too
big for his tights and too obstreperous for the wrestling organization,
they'd call me."[9]

Mondt also possessed a sharp mind for business. In partnership with
Sandow and Lewis, he became involved in grouping wrestlers together
into package shows and organizing circuits of towns for them to perform in. He had a hand, as well, in plotting storylines for performers
that would keep fans engaged over multiple trips to the matches.[10]
Wrestlers were designated as either "O.K." or "Not O.K." in letters exchanged between Mondt and others, entirely on their willingness to
work according to a script.[11] Some would later claim they were forced
to post large sums of cash or the deeds to their homes as collateral, a
kind of dive taking insurance, against winning a match they'd been
instructed to lose.[12] Mondt could be loyal to people he favored but also
unsparing in his punishment for anyone he felt had crossed him. Shrewd
and unforgiving, he was accused of stealing money out of wrestlers' pay
envelopes, as well as physically assaulting performers who didn't follow
his instructions exactly as he'd laid them out.[13] "He was a born con
artist, corrupt to his soul, always looking for an angle to make a buck,
and pro wrestling was the perfect venue for him," wrote wrestler Lou
Thesz. "The son of a bitch would steal the cream out of your coffee."[14]

For much of the nineteenth century, the dominant genre in theatre, as
far as audiences were concerned, was melodrama. From their very be-
ginnings, often placed in France in the early 1800s, melodramas were
seen as the theatre of the people. The heroes and villains were instantly
identifiable, and productions were engineered for mass entertainment,
showcasing spectacles designed to shock and arouse. They often em-
phasized action, sensationalist and overwrought performances, and a
stark moral polarization between good and bad. They could be crude

and violent, or overstuffed with sentiment and self-righteousness. They could also slyly incorporate political commentary and social critique into their otherwise stock constructions without stiffing the audience on thrills.

By the 1890s, a specific kind of melodrama had risen in prominence. Named for their range of ticket prices, "10–20–30" shows promised attendees "blood and thunder," so named for two of the genre's most common special effects.[15] These shows featured scenes of intense danger and graphic action that relied on ever more complicated staging and stunt work. During a 10–20–30 show, a live fire may have raged or an actual automobile seem to race across the stage. Actors might take leaps from dangerous heights or risk being cut in half by the spinning blade of a real buzz saw.

A 10–20–30 show that couldn't reliably whip an audience into a fierce lather at multiple points during its performance stood little chance of filling the house. Crowds for these productions were frequently rowdy, vocal, and participatory, whooping and hurrahing, or hollering and hissing. Spectators attended 10–20–30 shows hoping to get carried away and lose themselves in the onstage action. Some even found thrills in the possibility that actors could be injured, maimed, or worse, should a showstopping special effect go wrong.

The peak for 10–20–30 melodramas in the United States came around 1907. Competition from the new style of naturalistic drama being popularized by modern playwrights like Henrik Ibsen and Eugene O'Neill, as well as nickelodeons, eroded the hold of melodramas on the theatre-going public.[16] Nickelodeons, which first appeared around 1905, were often little more than storefronts outfitted with makeshift screens and seats, which charged just five cents for admission to a program of short films that ran non-stop. By 1909, moving-picture theatres could be found in all but the smallest of American cities.[17] The films they showed were more intensely realistic than a 10–20–30 show could ever hope to be. The fall of melodramas, and the 10–20–30 show in particular, was quick and complete when, by 1910, almost every theatre in New York previously dedicated to them had been reprogrammed to feature movies. The conventions of the melodrama never actually disappeared, though, but were just absorbed into other kinds of mass entertainment.[18]

There is no single event that marks just when professional wrestling matches of the twentieth century began to incorporate hallmark conventions from the popular form of nineteenth-century theatre, but the process was unmistakably accelerated during the second heavyweight championship run of Strangler Lewis. Lewis and Billy Sandow were both masterful showmen, and consciously cast themselves in the role of the villains. In retrospect, they seem to have even taken delight from infuriating fans. During matches, Lewis's opponents would invariably mount formidable offenses that would bring Lewis close to defeat, but in the end, all fell victim to the Strangler's dreaded headlock and were left seeing stars. As Lewis's second, Sandow invented whole cloth the archetype of the scheming wrestling manager, which would persist for decades to come. He distracted referees and opponents with his antics and infuriated fans by coaching Lewis from ringside during matches.

These changes had been coming in fits and starts for thirty years, and in many ways, professional wrestling and popular theatre had never really been all that far apart. Before relocating to arenas more narrowly intended for sporting events, wrestling matches were often held in burlesque halls and vaudeville theatres.[19] Samuel Rachmann had overtly connected theatre and wrestling with his 1915 Manhattan Opera House tournament. Charles Cochran, the English promoter who guided the early career of George Hackenschmidt, would turn exclusively to theatre in later years, and William Brady, the headline-generating promoter who'd taken Yusuf İsmail, "The Terrible Turk," from living in a New York tenement to being a sell-out attraction in Eastern cities in the late 1890s, became a major producer of 10–20–30 melodramas after leaving wrestling. "It's impossible to draw a hard and fast line between the theater and the arena," he later wrote. "The fundamentals of getting people to pay money to see something happen are the same in any field."[20] By the early 1930s, Jack Curley would even be promising to deliver his audiences "blood and thunder."[21]

Though they couldn't incorporate motor vehicles or spinning saw blades or set the ring on fire (all of that would come in later decades), wrestlers of the 1920s began to deliberately ratchet up their performances by incorporating increasingly dangerous maneuvers. They learned to work crowds, sensing, as Lewis would later write, just how much villainy or valor they could stand.[22] They learned how to pace their performances, how to build tension, and when to orchestrate its release.

They learned to interpret crowd noise to understand what earned an audience's sympathy, cheers, or anger. It was only when crowds became quiet that there was reason to worry. The shrieks and shouts would suddenly become a blanket of silence enveloping the ring. It would last about 15 seconds, during which time a wrestler's thoughts turned immediately to finding a clear path back to the dressing rooms.[23] When the silence broke, the result was often a fury of hurled garbage, shouted death threats, charging spectators, or worse.

As with a great melodrama, a great wrestling match had a way of drawing spectators into a primal kind of morality play—little scenes of right against wrong, justice versus injustice. And more than with any other form of entertainment, professional wrestling fans came to grant themselves license to participate in the show.[24] In Boston in May 1924, police forcibly ejected fans protesting a Lewis victory. That same year, in Chicago, knives and glass were thrown after a Lewis victory. In Philadelphia, Lewis would need a police escort in order to make his way out of the ring.[25]

To some varying degree, audiences knew that the matches they were watching couldn't possibly be on the level, and so perhaps they felt doubly offended when the outcomes didn't go as they'd hoped. Some even took it as a reminder that fair play wasn't always rewarded and that suckers never got an even break, that even in the fantasy world of pro wrestling, life wasn't fair. Throwing trash or food or crumpled-up newspapers, or going as far as to reach out and attack the match's offending wrestler as he ran from the ring, was the one opportunity they got to hit back against a government, an economy, a legal system, a whole way of living that they somehow knew wasn't on the level, and that never seemed to work out in their favor.

"The public wants to see their hero win and their villain lose," Lewis later wrote. "When this is upset, emotional stresses sometimes snap."[26]

Largely shut out of wrestling and rumored to be running out of money, Jack Curley was finding new ways to stay busy. He worked out of sight of the New York State Athletic Commission to supply wrestlers for cards around the city, and he spent five months in Europe scouting athletes in fall 1922.[27] Upon his return, the opportunity fell to him to manage actor Rudolph Valentino's three-month tour of the United States and Canada. Valentino was at the peak of his movie fame but locked out of making new films due to a contract dispute with his studio and sinking into debt. He had signed on as a spokesperson for the Mineralava cosmetics company and agreed to a tour of eighty-eight cities, performing in a show that combined his dancing with a beauty contest. Curley would later say that when he agreed to manage the tour, he had never heard of Valentino: "Someone came up and said, 'There's Valentino,' and I said, 'Who in the hell is Valentino?' because I don't go to the pictures much and when I do it's generally to get a few minutes' nap."[28]

The touring party Curley managed consisted of an eleven-piece band and twenty-odd staff, all traveling in a private railroad car outfitted with Turkish carpets and gilt mirrors. The show blew in and out of towns, traveling overnight between tour stops.[29] Curley gamely courted reporters and helped manage the frenzied crowds that greeted Valentino's arrivals. At the end of each show, he contentedly bundled up the wads of cash collected from the evening's box office before pulling back out of town.[30] During its height, the tour was grossing $100,000 per week. "We swept the country while the ladies almost mobbed him everywhere we went," Curley later said of the tour. "And the biggest expense was the new buttons we had to buy for his suits to replace the ones the fans would pull off for souvenirs."[31]

Curley was said to have been close with Al Smith, who was elected governor of New York in November 1922.[32] Smith's new position gave him significant influence over the State Athletic Commission, though just how much personal involvement he had in its decisions following his election is unknown. In January 1923, Cycle Sporting Corporation, headed by a New York promoter named Matthew Zimmerman, was granted a license to organize wrestling shows at Manhattan's 71st Regiment Armory, the hulking brick-and-stone fortress that dominated Park Avenue along Thirty-third and Thirty-fourth Streets in Manhattan. Zimmerman employed Curley as a promotional agent, but Curley's near-constant presence at the matches suggested that his involvement ran much deeper.[33]

In April, in a move seen as a check on William Muldoon's almost absolute authority, Governor Smith split the commission into separate regulatory and licensing committees, with the licensing committee holding sole power over issuing and revoking all licenses related to boxing and wrestling.[34] Though most were watching to see what changes this new order would bring to boxing, the new committee's most immediate action was to reshuffle control of professional wrestling in the state. In a startling decision issued that December, the committee denied Tex Rickard's permit to promote any further wrestling events. The decision forced him to cancel a series of matches for which he'd already released advertisements. Three weeks later, Jack Curley appeared in front of the Athletic Commission and was fully reinstated as a promoter. He was officially back in the wrestling business.[35]

FIGURE 14. "Big" Wayne Munn. Courtesy of Steve Yohe.

CHAPTER 13

With a Touch of Bronchitis

BY MOST ACCOUNTS, Jack Curley and Billy Sandow were getting along swimmingly. If there were lingering hard feelings between them over Sandow and Strangler Lewis's efforts to monopolize the wrestling business while Curley was hobbled by his tangle with William Muldoon and the New York State Athletic Commission, no one was letting on.

In February 1924, Curley was called in a panic to Room 1410 of Chicago's Hotel Morrison to negotiate a compromise during a heated meeting between Sandow, Lewis, Stanislaus Zbyszko, and Joe and Tony Stecher. When Lewis first won the heavyweight championship from Joe Stecher in 1920, he and Sandow were said to have given the Stecher brothers $25,000 as a promise that Lewis would eventually consent to losing the title back. Since then, the Stechers had lent much of the deposit back to Sandow and Lewis in anticipation of Lewis returning the championship. After growing convinced that Lewis and Sandow would neither agree to another match with Joe nor repay the loans, the Stechers threatened to take their complaints public.[1] Zbyszko, too, had grown more openly frustrated since his loss to Lewis in 1922, and had hinted that he would also be open to selling his story to reporters. Though the details of the agreement that Curley helped the group reach are unknown, his intervention was sufficient to keep everyone in the same tent for the time being.[2] The seams that were keeping the group together were straining, though, and just how much longer the fragile peace would hold was very much in doubt.

By the time Curley reopened business as a licensed wrestling promoter in New York in early 1924, he was using a number of Billy Sandow's stars in his shows. Among them was a curiosity Sandow had been developing for months, a 6'6" ex-college football player named Wayne Munn. Munn was born in Colby, Kansas, on February 19, 1895. After a standout football career at the University of Nebraska, he had tried his hand with middling to no success at selling cars, preaching, and, finally, boxing. The one field he seemed not to have considered, given his complete lack of training for it, was professional wrestling.

To Sandow, Munn's inexperience did not necessarily pose a barrier to entry. Sandow had managed to keep the heavyweight championship on Strangler Lewis for more than two years, but by 1924, gates were down, Lewis was tired, and their associates were unhappy. It was hard for anyone to argue that a change was not in order.[3] Munn, the young, wholesome American-born giant with unimpeachable collegiate athletic credentials, was to be his response. Sandow, Lewis, and Toots Mondt set to training Munn, planning his matches, and hand selecting his opponents. They also set him up with a de facto manager, a longtime promoter out of Kansas City named Gabe Kaufman. They gave Munn the dried-out nickname of "Big" and posed him for publicity photos meant to emphasize his height, with somber-faced men standing beneath his outstretched arms, the tops of their heads nuzzling his armpits. They fed puff pieces to local writers and tried to land stories in any newspaper they could.[4]

In the ring, Munn's matches were kept short, sometimes as brief as just three minutes. By the time he wrestled Toots Mondt in Kansas City on December 11, 1924, he could perform for as long as half an hour.[5] His win over Mondt that evening, a decisive affair in which he dumped Mondt in two straight falls in front of 10,000 people in the biggest city on Sandow's circuit, was a patiently planned bit of stagecraft intended to springboard Munn into a championship match with Strangler Lewis the following month. Mondt was by far the best-known wrestler Munn had faced up to that point, and the conclusive thumping Munn delivered in the match bestowed upon him a whole new kind of shine in the eyes of fans.

On the evening of January 8, 1925, 15,000 people packed into Kansas City's Convention Hall eager to see Munn take on Lewis. Munn was greeted with a hail of applause, a squall of boos and catcalls falling on Lewis and Billy Sandow as they approached the ring. Despite being the crowd's favorite, few in attendance thought Munn stood any real chance of actually winning. It was something of a shock, then, when he made short work of the champion Lewis in the first fall, and again in the second when he lifted the 230-pound Strangler into the air and tossed him over the ring ropes and down to the floor. Billy Sandow leapt into the ring, shouting, "It's a foul, a dirty foul!" and demanding that the referee call the match off. Some in the crowd hissed and hooted at Sandow until they were red in the face. Others tried to force their way past the police and into the ring, where aides were tending to Lewis's limp body. "It was a scene of wildest chaotic confusion," wrote the reporter covering the match for the *Kansas City Times*. "Men and women, who go about the ordinary affairs of life sanely, were standing on chairs and shouting at the champion in the ring."[6]

"You big bum," came one shout aimed at Lewis as he was carried back to the dressing room. "I hope you're hurt!"[7]

It took several men to help a bandaged Lewis return to the ring for the final fall, and once inside it, he never had a chance. After just fifty seconds, Munn lifted him up again, slammed him to the mat, and pinned him. When the referee declared Munn the new heavyweight champion, the crowd cheered and pushed again toward the ring to celebrate.[8] Lewis spent the night at nearby St. Luke's Hospital. Newspaper reports the next night carried word that he could be out of action for as long as a year with a wrenched back and pelvis—if he'd ever be able to return to the ring at all.[9]

Lewis, it turned out, would be back in almost no time. Munn's win should have been considered invalid, Billy Sandow argued upon his return, because Munn should have lost the match for having tossed Lewis out of the ring during the second fall. Munn countered that Lewis had all but tossed himself. "I didn't throw him over," Munn said. "I held him high, and he wriggled out of my clutch."[10] Sandow's eyes turned to planning a rematch—one he hoped would be even larger than Curley's staging of the Gotch–Hackenschmidt match just fourteen years earlier. Sandow picked an open-air arena in Michigan City, Indiana, and set the date for Decoration Day, May 30, 1925.

The scheme had no precedent in professional sports. Sandow had baldly constructed an attraction in a supposed competitive field and manufactured for him a claim to the championship that he wholly expected the public to respect. Just a few years earlier, gamblers had put their thumbs on the scale of the 1919 World Series, bribing members of baseball's Chicago White Sox to perform poorly during games, but even the men behind that plan had hedged their bets up until the very end, harboring serious doubts that the fix would come off.[11] There had been no shortage of scandals, too, in boxing, horseracing, and other sports. But with Wayne Munn, Sandow was orchestrating something altogether new, manufacturing a counterfeit competitor from scratch, and constructing an entire sporting universe to support the myth that they were the genuine article. This was a humbug of a different order. It begged the question of just when an athletic event stops being a sport altogether.

Now that Wayne Munn had been handed Strangler Lewis's championship, the problem became keeping it on him. Even though each of Munn's opponents was hand-selected from the group of wrestlers affiliated with Billy Sandow, their cooperation could never be fully guaranteed. Munn would be vulnerable in any match to which he agreed. To buy time until his rematch with Strangler Lewis, Munn signed a contract to tour vaudeville theatres. The contract was noticeably unusual in that it prohibited him from wrestling onstage or accepting challenges from audience members.[12] To keep fans engaged who were following along only through newspaper stories, Munn and Lewis used the press to knit a complex fiction, trading jabs and threatening each other with lawsuits that never materialized.[13]

For Munn's first title defense, he defeated former champion Stanislaus Zbyszko in straight falls in Kansas City. "I have never wrestled a man so strong, and I don't believe there is a man in the game that can throw him," Zbyszko told reporters after the match, swallowing his gall.[14] Zbyszko had spent most of 1924 on his back, agreeably losing matches he could have otherwise won. Work was steady, but more and more often, he was being picked to be the loser. He wanted to win so badly that sometimes, during a match, if he sensed an opportunity to catch an unsuspecting opponent by surprise and upend the match's planned outcome, his breathing would audibly quicken. He never followed through, though, and the losses piled up.[15]

Zbyszko had been a featured attraction in English music halls in the first decade of the 1900s and was an on-again, off-again star in the United States. His brother, Wladek, had been Jack Curley's favored performer for a number of years, while Stanislaus's career stalled after he was imprisoned in Russia for almost six years as an enemy combatant in the early days of World War I. After his release, he told fantastic tales about his time in captivity, including one about having to wrestle for his life against an Estonian inmate who had accused Zbyszko of being a spy. Zbyszko claimed that in the confusion that followed his victory, he commandeered an automobile and escaped into Poland. In reality, there were no such adventures; his imprisonment had left him penniless and had robbed him of his prime athletic years. In February 1920, Zbyszko had arrived back in the United States nearing the age of forty and out of ring shape.[16]

Still, he managed to reestablish himself in wrestling, even enjoying a brief run as the heavyweight champion in 1921. But by 1925, at 5'8" and well more than 200 pounds, with fleshy arms like a pair of sledgehammers, lumpy cauliflower ears, and a bald head that looked, as one sportswriter noted, like a peeled onion, he was the portrait of the lumbering ogre-like wrestler that was passing out of fashion.[17] When he would screw up his face and try to strike an intimidating pose for photographers, he had a tendency to come off as looking confused. Though in his mid-forties, Zbyszko was pegged by writers as being in his fifties.[18] They took to calling him "Old Man," a nickname that undoubtedly hurt his immense pride.

Zbyszko would occasionally grouse to reporters about his situation, but only occasionally. Since his return to the United States, he'd managed to rebuild some of his wealth, and, along with his brother Wladek, he owned a hotel in Krakow, Poland, and a large plot of land on Saco Bay in Old Orchard Beach, Maine, which the brothers outfitted with a hotel and rental cottages.[19] These ventures were financed, in part, by Zbyszko's wrestling career. If he wanted to continue working, it meant doing whatever Billy Sandow told him to do, no matter how much he disliked it.

All of this maneuvering around Wayne Munn wasn't benefiting Jack Curley, who was eager to feature his own roster of talent and his own heavyweight champion at his shows in New York. Curley had been supportive of Munn initially but had begun making noise about his desire to match him up against Joe Stecher. Stecher could and would have dismantled Munn had the two ever wrestled. It was a match that Curley had to have known Sandow would refuse, and his insistence on stumping for it may have been enough to finally cause a split. In February 1925, newspaper reports appeared claiming that Stecher had confessed to the sports editor of the *Omaha Daily News* that he'd participated in fixed matches. Stecher immediately denied making any such confession, calling the story "a case of malice."[20] "[Stecher] didn't say anything of the kind," Curley boomed, "and he's going to sue for libel if he doesn't get a retraction."[21] Just who was responsible for the story was never stated, but a furious Curley reacted to its publication by all but declaring open warfare on Sandow and Munn. "Munn is not even a good third rater," Curley told reporters. "If he wrestled for any length of time, the crowd would soon see how little he knows about the game and what a champion he really is." Curley, Sandow shot back, was "a discredited promoter."[22]

An even more damaging piece for Munn was printed that February. Billy Sandow's brother, Max Baumann, had inexplicably sat down with a reporter for the *Wichita Eagle* for a wide-ranging conversation during which he claimed that it was a wrestler's ability to draw a crowd that made him a real wrestler, and that it was gate receipts that should determine the champion. "If the matches get out the crowds," said Baumann, "that is all that is necessary." He asserted that if showmen were being elevated over honest competitors, it was wrestling fans, not businessmen, who were to blame. The public didn't care who held the championship or even whether they'd earned the title. If the champion was a great entertainer, he said, then that was enough. The statements were an embarrassment. "Time and again," the reporter concluded, "the writer has been asked why the newspapers do not openly oppose the wrestling trust. If the fans do not care enough about it to protest, if they continue to support the trust wrestlers, if they turn out in thousands for such an event as the Lewis–Munn affair, and go away all enthused, if they demand yards of news on such affairs, then why should the papers kick?"[23]

Wayne Munn was turning into a punchline, and Decoration Day was still three months away.

The gangster Arnold Rothstein, a key figure behind the controversial 1919 World Series between the Chicago White Sox and the Cincinnati Reds, was known to tell associates that anything could be fixed, from a game of checkers to a World War.[24] Jack Curley, for his part, disagreed. In fact, he was of the opinion that no sporting event could be truly fixed.

Even if you thought you had everything in the bag, and that everyone was on the same page with how things were to go, you could never say for sure just what was going to happen once the thing got started. Someone could be outbidding you to sway the contest their way. An athlete, overtaken by a sudden attack of integrity, could change their mind during a match, and instead of taking a dive could decide to go for the win. And you could never account for someone just plain losing their head amid the heat from the fantastic lights and the roar of the crowd. There were just too many interests at play. Nothing could be so tightly sewn up, Curley thought, that a sufficiently motivated party could be kept from upending your plans. The best you could hope to do was to cover as many of the angles as possible, and then pray the dice turned your way.[25]

It took Stanislaus Zbyszko just less than thirteen minutes to prove the point Curley had spent two decades trying to make. Zbyskzo's plan for the evening of April 15, 1925, had been to show up at the Philadelphia Arena, lose to Wayne Munn in the evening's main event, and then return to his room at the Hotel Sylvania without complaint. Just when exactly that plan changed depends on who you believe.

Eight thousand people crowded into the arena that Wednesday evening, expecting to see Munn hurl and humiliate the once-great Zbyszko. "If I can throw Zbyszko within ten seconds, I'll do so," Munn boasted to reporters before the match. "I don't think there is any doubt but that I will still be the world's champion."[26] At nearly twice Munn's age, his bald head barely reaching Munn's shoulders, one might have even been forgiven for thinking that Zbyszko didn't belong in the same ring with the young heavyweight champion. "Philadelphians gathered to the match with the steadfast mien of people attending a wake," wrote the reporter from *Time* sent to cover the evening. "They admired Zbyszko's courage but deplored his bravado."[27]

Once the match got underway, though, the dead air in the arena became charged. Zbyszko repeatedly fended off Munn's advances. Knocking Munn off balance, he circled behind him, wrapped his arms around Munn's waist, heaved him up and off of his feet, and threw the big man down to the canvas. Zbyszko followed him to the mat, where he grabbed hold of his forearm and forced his shoulders down for the pin. In just eight minutes, he had taken the first fall and punctured the myth of "Big" Munn. Suddenly, old and ponderous Stanislaus Zbyszko didn't seem out of place at all.

The crowd began to scream and shout, standing on the arena's wooden chairs to get a better look. Gabe Kaufman collected the dazed Munn, hurrying him out of the ring and back to the dressing room. Suspicious of what could happen to him once he was out of sight of the audience, Zbyszko opted to return to his corner and wait inside the ring for the match to resume. Billy Sandow met him there, and, bending close, whispered into his ear. Some reports claim that Sandow informed Zbyszko that Munn had fainted in the dressing room, and that a substitute wrestler was being sent into the ring to finish the match.[28] Whatever was said, Zbyszko responded by emphatically shaking his head, "No." He had Sandow in a bind and he knew it; Munn had no chance of beating Zbyszko in the second fall, but if he failed to return to the ring, he'd be forfeiting the match and his championship.[29]

Munn and Kaufman did return, resigned to see the match through. The second fall lasted just half as long as the first. Zbyszko again dropped Munn onto the mat, wrapped his arm into a hammerlock, and forced his shoulders down for the pin. After little more than twelve total minutes of wrestling, the match was over. Stanislaus Zbyszko, to everyone's surprise, was wrestling's new heavyweight champion. At ringside, Gabe Kaufman's wife fainted into the lap of Wayne Munn's wife. Photographers and spectators poured into the ring. Zbyszko's second, an aged boxer named Lew Palmer, gathered a team of police to escort Zbyszko from the ring, pack him into a cab, and send him back to his hotel. Stashed away in his room, Zbyszko tried to sleep but wound up slipping out of the hotel at 2 a.m. and walking the city streets until dawn.[30] "I never expected to beat Munn so decisively and quickly, and my victory was as much of a surprise to me as it apparently was to the spectators," he diplomatically told reporters the next day.[31]

The race to make sense of the freshly jumbled wrestling scene immediately commenced. Following the match, word circulated that Munn had been suffering from the effects of a 104-degree temperature. He'd been given two doses of strychnine prior to the match to treat his illness, which made him groggy and blurred his vision, Munn claimed. "I don't want people to think I'm blaming my defeat on being ill, but I was sick when I went into the ring against the advice of physicians and friends and, above all, my wife," he said. "It was suicide."[32] His wife claimed that Munn had been in no condition to enter the ring but had done so only out of an obligation to his fans. "All of us talked to Wayne and begged him to refrain from meeting Zbyszko, but he refused pointblank," she said. "Besides, if he admitted he was ill, they would have called him yellow."[33] The official diagnosis, she said, was acute follicular tonsillitis, with a touch of bronchitis.[34]

Complicating their statements was the fact that the club physician who had examined Munn before the match had not detected a fever.[35] Munn had also visited with the Pennsylvania State Athletic Commission the day of the match but had given no indication of being ill. In fact, one commissioner remembered him as being perfectly jolly.[36] The evening prior, he and Gabe Kaufman had been the special guests of Philadelphia Athletics vice-president John Shibe for the team's season opening win over the Boston Red Sox.[37]

Sandow, too, went to great lengths to explain away Zbyszko's win, still claiming that Strangler Lewis was the legitimate champion.[38] People saw in the outcome what they wanted to see. Some were convinced Zbyszko had pulled off a deliberate double cross, overwhelming a helplessly outmatched imposter and outwitting Sandow and Munn. Others felt the match had been honest, and Zbyszko had simply taken advantage of an ill man. Still others saw a different storyline playing out, an elaborate double bluff intended to throw sand in the eyes of fans who thought they'd sussed out Sandow's plans for Munn and the heavyweight championship.[39]

Jack Curley had traveled down to Philadelphia to watch the Zbyszko–Munn match. He offered little immediate commentary on the outcome other than to gloat. "The wrestling business in the Middle West has been run by the dirtiest gang of crooks that ever lived, and I've been trying to tell the public so for months," he told reporters. "Munn—why the big stiff couldn't throw a fit if he had epilepsy, but he was big and strong and looked the part, so a lot of people thought he was a real champion."[40] Years later, Curley would tell friends that he'd approached Zbyszko in his dressing room before the match and promised him $50,000 if he defeated Munn. It bothered him that Zbyszko had resigned himself to losing to a lesser athlete. "My artistic sense rebelled at the thought of his submitting to anyone as inartistic as Wayne Munn," he said.[41] It's impossible to know what really was behind Zbyszko's decision, but within a week of his win, Curley was making plans for a championship match between him and Joe Stecher. Zbyszko's guarantee for the match was exactly $50,000.[42]

To bring off the Zbyszko–Stecher match, Curley worked with promoter Tom Packs of St. Louis. In a not-at-all subtle rebuke of Billy Sandow, they scheduled it for May 30, putting it in direct competition with Sandow's still-planned match between Strangler Lewis and Wayne Munn on the same day. At St. Louis's University Field, under a scorching hot May sun, Stecher defeated Zbyszko to regain the heavyweight championship in front of 13,500 people. Zbyszko lasted ninety minutes in the oppressive heat. He must have understood that given his age and the unmistakable changes taking place in wrestling, this might be his last chance at starring in a big show. And after it was all over, though reporters would still sometimes refer to him as "Old Man," it must have stung a whole lot less.[43]

Three hundred and fifty miles away in Michigan City, Indiana, Strangler Lewis defeated Wayne Munn, an outcome that was a shock to no one. Lewis used the victory to claim his own version of the heavyweight championship. Sandow had been planning the match for months. It was supposed to have been the largest wrestling spectacle ever staged. In the end, somewhere around 10,000 people turned out to watch. The show was a success, but nothing on the scale for which Sandow had aimed.

The back-to-back losses to Lewis and Zbyszko did everything to deflate the excitement around Wayne Munn. With his reputation in wrestling ruined, he returned to boxing with dreams of one day fighting for that sport's championship.[44] His first bout was with a bruising thirty-six-year-old journeyman named Andre Anderson on December 23, 1925. Word had circulated prior to the fight that it was to be fixed in favor of Munn. In response, the secretary of the Kansas Athletic Commission, Leslie Edmonds, decided to sit ringside and judge the match's integrity for himself. As he watched Anderson humiliate Munn, knocking him out cold in less than two minutes with just three punches, Edmonds decided that the match had been honest.[45]

Later that evening, Anderson was said to be agitated, expressing fear that his win would carry heavy repercussions for him. His manager recalled him saying, "I'm through throwing fights and laying down every time they want me to."[46] His fears of payback were realized on the evening of March 31, 1926, in a cabaret bar in Cicero, Illinois. Eyewitness accounts differed in the details, but they all agreed that Anderson had been arguing with a squat, hard-eyed machine gunner for the Chicago mob named Leo Mongoven over the bout with Munn. In the heat of the conflict, Anderson was shot, and died the next day.[47] Mongoven fled the bar and avoided arrest until late 1927, though he was never prosecuted for the Anderson murder.[48]

Munn, who was never suspected of having any involvement in the attempted fix, gave up boxing and struggled to revive his wrestling career. One of his final matches came in Boston on May 11, 1928, against another young ex-football player-turned-wrestler named Gus Sonnenberg. Like Munn, Sonnenberg had turned professional as a complete novice yet managed to defeat men with years of experience and training. Munn outweighed Sonnenberg by seventy pounds and stood almost a full foot taller. Nonetheless, Sonnenberg made short work of him, winning the match in less than two minutes. Gus Sonnenberg was action layered over action. He had been stamped from the exact same press that had produced Munn but was something else altogether. It wouldn't take long for him to change wrestling forever.

FIGURE 15. Gus Sonnenberg and Judith Allen in Boston, 1931. Courtesy of the Alton
H. Blackington Collection, Robert S. Cox Special Collections and University Archives
Research Center, UMass Amherst Libraries, University of Massachusetts Amherst.

CHAPTER 14

The Man Who Revolutionized Wrestling

ON SEPTEMBER 14, 1944, the *New York Times* published an article head-lined "The Man Who Revolutionized Wrestling." In it, sports columnist Arthur Daley wrote, "Perhaps no man ever left as profound a mark on a sport as [Gus] Sonnenberg."[1] Sonnenberg had died of leukemia two days earlier after spending almost eight months in a naval hospital in Bethesda, Maryland. He was only forty-six years old. During his short, tumultuous career, Sonnenberg made wrestling move faster than it had ever moved before. He didn't have the faintest whiff of antiquity about him. In 1928, the *Boston Herald* declared him "the prophet of a new and fiery type of wrestling."[2] In his matches, there was no glum tugging, no cumbersome grappling. When Sonnenberg got into a wrestling ring, he broke through walls, scattered the furniture, turned tables over. He was nicknamed "Dynamite" for his explosive presence, but when you saw him rolling over his opponents, you'd have thought he looked more like a Dusenberg screaming ahead at top speed.

Gustave Adolph Sonnenberg was born on March 6, 1898, in Ewen, Michigan, a hardscrabble logging town in the state's Upper Peninsula. His father was sixty when Gus was born, and his mother was at least fifty. As a boy, he studied violin and read poetry. As an adult, he lived fast and hard. He had a head of thick, curly hair he would try to slick back with water, and strong hands like a boxer, with fingernails the size of nickels.[3] He married and divorced twice. In interviews, he could be frank and engaging, speaking in a baritone voice and playing up his pitch-black sense of humor, though it didn't take much for him to start sounding bitter and aggrieved. Fans called him "Sonny," but friends came to refer to him as "Gloomy Gus." He could be moody, with a hair-trigger temper that became more unpredictable the more he drank. A Montreal bar owner who befriended Sonnenberg later in his life remembered an evening when a patron engaged him in a friendly conversation. Before anyone knew what was happening, Sonnenberg lifted the man up and heaved him into a corner. "He just asked me if wrestling was on the level," Sonnenberg said, before breaking into an enormous laugh. "He had a bad habit of ordering a drink and paying for it with a \$20 bill," the bar owner recalled. "Then he'd leave the change on the bar and sit down at a table. I think he was hoping somebody would pick it up so's he could start something."[4]

Just 5' 7" and thickset, Sonnenberg was physically underwhelming. Damon Runyon described him as being "built like a dull, sickening thud."[5] He was naturally aggressive, though, a trait that served him well in his athletic career. He excelled at football in particular, and in 1920, he was named to the All-American team after a standout year at Dartmouth College. He worked hard to support himself through school, washing dishes and pressing suits for his classmates when he wasn't on the field. His days could begin as early as 5 a.m. and would often run past midnight. "I finished delivering clothes at 10:30 or 11 and then went to my little room to study," Sonnenberg later recalled. "Many a night I couldn't get to sleep before 2 a.m."[6] The indignity and resentment he'd felt while doing it all helped fuel him. Teammates remembered him for, among other things, a habit of ripping out hotel room radiators from the floor. "Just one of his playful habits," remembered William "Pudge" Heffelfinger, a star at Yale College in the late 1800s who is considered to be the first professional football player. "Gus cost the Dartmouth Athletic Association plenty of money."[7]

Sonnenberg entered professional football in 1923, eventually moving to Rhode Island to join the Providence Steam Rollers as a tackle and kicker.[8] It was a teammate named John Spellman, who'd won a gold medal in freestyle wrestling at the 1924 Olympics and who wrestled professionally during the off-season, who helped Sonnenberg train for his first match. Spellman also introduced him to Boston promoter Paul Bowser. For years, Bowser had been searching for a wrestler he could develop into a champion. His ideal candidate, instead, all but found him. Bowser and Sonnenberg would spend the next two years together on a coast-to-coast romp that so brazenly blurred fact and fiction that untangling the truth of exactly what happened is impossible.

Gus Sonnenberg made his professional wrestling debut on January 24, 1928, in Providence, beating his opponent in just ninety seconds. From there, Bowser adhered to the same plan Billy Sandow had followed when developing Wayne Munn. Sonnenberg won his matches quickly, wrestling only opponents Bowser felt he could trust. Sonnenberg soon became famous for the way he moved through his opponents, never around them. He ignited when he entered the ring, burning as hot and bright as an arc light. He put his man down without fail, tearing across the ring and hurling himself headfirst at them with a move that came to be called the flying tackle. It was an audacious, winner-take-all proposition; it finished with either Sonnenberg's foe flat on their back or Sonnenberg himself crashing out of the ring. The fans loved it. Sonnenberg was unstoppable, and with each win, his audience grew.[9]

He matured quickly as a performer, communicating to the thousands who paid to see him through his constant motion. If an opponent took him down to the mat, Sonnenberg would kick his legs high and rock on his hips to try to break the hold. If he wanted fans to know he'd hurt his leg, instead of limping imperceptibly he would grab his hamstring and jerk his knee up and down.[10] He won every match Paul Bowser made for him, some thirty-nine in total, leading up to his first match with Strangler Lewis for the heavyweight championship.

Sonnenberg had achieved some measure of real fame for his skill on the football field, but he'd also been shot at and had the windows of his train car smashed by unhappy gamblers. As a wrestler, he was making thousands of dollars for just a few minutes of work each night, performing for crowds that cheered him as a matter of course. "I had a lot of glory in college," he later said, "and I scrubbed a lot of floors to get through school too. A lot of good glory did me. When I saw a chance to get some money, I decided that if I had to choose between shekels and fame, the shekels would have it."[11]

On June 29, 1928, with every seat in the Boston Arena filled and an overflow crowd of people standing rows deep along the fringes, Gus Sonnenberg and Strangler Lewis wrestled for the first time. Sonnenberg appeared, as David Egan wrote the next day in the *Boston Globe*, like "a streak of white cutting the smoke clouds. . . . Thrill follows thrill."[12] In the first fall, he pinned Lewis after thirty-seven minutes of wrestling. During the second, he sailed between the top and middle ropes after

missing Lewis with a flying tackle. Flying over the row of reporters seated ringside, Sonnenberg landed hard on the floor. Initial reports on his
injuries ranged from a concussion to a broken neck to a fractured skull.
All predicted a long recovery period.[13] In a twist of fate possible only
in professional wrestling, Sonnenberg defied every dire prognosis and
was back in action on the football field in time for the Steam Rollers'
1928 season. The team would finish with eight wins and their first NFL
championship. Everything was coming up Gus.

On January 4, 1929, a month after the Steam Rollers' final game of the
season, Sonnenberg and Strangler Lewis met again, this time at the
newly opened Boston Garden. On an otherwise bleak Friday night in
downtown Boston, an enormous crowd of as many as 20,000 people
gathered to watch, including Massachusetts Governor Frank Allen, who
took in the match with friends from a flag-draped box. Thousands more
followed the match on the radio. As a battery of movie cameras set up
at ringside began to whir, Sonnenberg, forever a jangle of energy and
nerves, tugged on the ropes so hard that it looked to some as if he were
trying to pull the ring apart.[14]

Sonnenberg had little to be concerned about. Behind the scenes, Paul
Bowser guaranteed more than $100,000 to Lewis and Billy Sandow for
Lewis's appearance that evening and in two future matches. He had
handed the pair $40,000 in cash prior to the match without asking for
a receipt. Paying in cash instead of by check was a matter of preference,
Bowser later said, though it conveniently left no paper trail. Such arrangements, he later admitted, were "quite ordinary."[15] Sonnenberg won
the match, and Lewis's heavyweight championship, in straight falls. The
audience's reaction was immediate and uproarious. Sonnenberg tried
to make a quick exit from the ring but was stopped halfway down the
aisle by howling fans who shook and hugged him and compelled him to
return to the ring to take a bow.

With his new championship, Sonnenberg set to tearing about the
country, filling arenas everywhere he went—8,000 people in Chicago,
10,000 in Los Angeles, and 15,000 when he returned to Boston. He later
said that he wrestled 113 matches in 1929, which included multiple trips
by Pullman car to perform in California.[16]

Bowser carefully selected Sonnenberg's opponents and preferred
working with promoters who allowed him to do so. He drew considerably

smaller gates in cities like Philadelphia and New York, where promoters Jack Curley and Ray Fabiani were busy grooming stars of their own, against whom Sonnenberg refused to be matched. Curley had tried using him in a main event match in Manhattan against a wrestler named Howard Cantonwine, but the night was a dud. The athletic commissions that governed wrestling in several East Coast states soon grew frustrated with Sonnenberg's insistence on only meeting opponents of his choosing and suspended him from making future appearances.[17] "I didn't care," Sonnenberg later said, "there were other states in the Union."[18]

At home in Massachusetts, Bowser and Sonnenberg had no such problems. The state's commission had no oversight of wrestling and no interest in taking it on. Free to wrestle when, where, and against whom they liked, Sonnenberg and Bowser set their eyes on creating a blockbuster event. Bowser circled July 9, 1929, on his calendar and booked Fenway Park. He had paid Strangler Lewis $100,000, which was contingent on his appearance in three matches, and Bowser intended to make the final one count.

Charles W. Morton, a future editor at *The Atlantic*, was still getting started in Boston as a freelance journalist in early 1929 when he received a call from an editor at the *Herald*. A local woman named Lillian Squires was trying to get started in the wrestling business, Morton was told, and he should talk with her. "It might make an odd sort of story," the editor said. Morton met Squires at her flat in Back Bay the next afternoon. Squires, Morton learned, had been financing the efforts of an aspiring local wrestling promoter who was in competition with Paul Bowser. Bowser, she felt, had conspired with other promoters to stymie their efforts and have their matches belittled in the press. She'd had enough, she told Morton, and was out for revenge.

Seated at her dining room table under a Tiffany glass center light, Squires produced a stack of placards and a pile of newspaper articles advertising appearances by Gus Sonnenberg. She'd tracked Sonnenberg's movements by subscribing to a press-clippings service, asking for any articles about him. She then sent a dollar to the postmaster in towns where Sonnenberg was appearing and asked that, in return, the postmaster send her one of the placards used to promote the match. It became obvious to her, by matching the photographs on the cards with the names underneath them, that Sonnenberg was only wrestling a select group of men, all of whom adopted different identities in each town in which they appeared. A picture of Dan Koloff, a Bulgarian wrestler who was also Sonnenberg's training partner and occasional roommate when traveling, appeared on at least six placards under six different names. Another wrestler, George McLeod, had faced Sonnenberg under at least three different names. "The clips and the placards made the whole arrangement all too clear," Morton later wrote, "including the venality of the sportswriters and editors concerned. It was marvelous to read that Gus was wondering what manner of man his opponent would prove to be, and to read the same story in another paper published a few days earlier or later, the only difference being the opponent's name."[19]

The *Herald* ran Morton's resulting expose in five installments over the week of June 11, 1929. One reproduced a selection of the incriminating placards.[20] Another lamented the Massachusetts Boxing Commission's inability to impose regulations that might protect wrestling fans.[21] "'Championship' wrestling in this country is today the greatest gold-brick industry in the history of modern sport," the paper declared.[22] Morton's work earned him a position at the paper and the ire of the *Herald*'s sports editor, who had been caught by surprise by its publication.[23]

Sonnenberg and Bowser were in Montreal when Morton's story broke. Sonnenberg only learned of it when a bellboy at his hotel handed him a copy of the day's paper.[24] He and Bowser made immediate plans to return to Boston for a conference with Billy Sandow on how to contain the fallout and salvage hope for the Sonnenberg–Lewis match at Fenway, which was less than a month away.[25] Before they left, Sonnenberg fired off a telegram to the *Herald*. "Story now running in your paper attacks my character and reputation," he wrote. "Can explain what I have done since being champion and am ashamed of none."[26] That Friday evening, Sonnenberg appeared on Boston radio station WNAC to defend himself. His address lasted only five minutes, during which he introduced a breathtaking attempt at misdirection.

"Hello, everybody," he began. "Gus Sonnenberg speaking. Talking over the radio gives me as great a thrill as when I apply one of my flying tackles in a wrestling bout. My success with my flying tackle and football rushes has created considerable jealousy among other wrestlers.

This jealousy has been followed by a deep-rooted hatred. They have resorted to all kinds of illegal tactics and evil propaganda in an effort to injure me." His suspensions in New York and Pennsylvania, he said, were part of a campaign organized by Billy Sandow and Strangler Lewis to discredit him. He didn't address the *Herald* articles directly, leaving it unsaid as to whether they were a product, as well, of Sandow and Lewis's alleged campaign. "It has always been my policy to give everything I had in each bout," he continued. "The hundreds of thousands who witnessed the contests I fought know full well that I have always been honest, open, and above board."

His rematch with Strangler Lewis at Fenway Park was still on, he announced, and the matter would be settled there. "I am going to get into the best condition of my career and grind Lewis under the fury of my attack. This time I shall be fighting to prove Gus Sonnenberg is the greatest wrestler in the world, but it will be the old Dartmouth spirit which will enable me to gain the victory. I would like to say more about the attacks upon me, but why dignify a lie about me with an answer? Good night."[27]

Among the people listening at home, who can say how many felt reassured hearing Gus's side of the story and how many were only left shaking their heads, wondering why he'd ever gotten himself involved with the wrestling racket in the first place.

Paul Bowser had 42,813 tickets printed for the Fenway match. If he could sell them all, he estimated that he would bring in $268,000, an absolute windfall for an evening of wrestling.[28] Sonnenberg had been pushing him hard for a guarantee of $75,000 for the evening, but the *Herald* stories complicated everything. Bowser later claimed he'd initially planned to pay Sonnenberg his asking price. Following the articles, though, he came to feel it was far too much money, and he convinced Sonnenberg to settle for a percentage of the gate instead.[29]

On July 9, 1929, at Fenway Park, the Sonnenberg–Lewis match came off as planned. Black clouds had threatened rain throughout the day and only helped to depress the final turnout. The *Boston Globe* reported 25,000 people in attendance, but the crowd was much smaller—not more than 15,000.[30] Sonnenberg defeated Lewis in a convincing manner in three falls, though shouts of "It's in the bag!" could be heard after each one. It could only have been a bitter disappointment. Sonnenberg's final take for the evening amounted to just less than $10,000, well short of what he'd thought he deserved.[31]

Earlier in the day, a group of fans willing to chance the weather had gathered together outside of the gates of Fenway. A reporter from the *Herald*, bemused that anyone had come at all, stopped to listen in on their conversation. It reminded him, he wrote, of an old story about a poker game held deep in the far reaches of cow country. During the game, one of the card players turned to another and asked, "Don't you know that this poker game is not on the up-and-up?" "Sure I do," came the reply, "but it's the only game around here in progress."[32]

The endless insinuations about the integrity of his matches bothered Sonnenberg to no end. "Wrestling is a dirty business," he told *Chicago Tribune* columnist Westbrook Pegler. "I have to work on foul mats that haven't been cleaned or aired for years. You know what goes on in a ring. Did it ever occur to you that after two or three years of regular use, a wrestling mat is not a pleasant mattress to roll around on? I have to meet all kinds of men. Some of them are diseased, with open bruises and cuts. The body contacts are close. A man might pick up anything—skin disease, eye infections, blood diseases. I'm earning all I get."[33]

Sonnenberg was rumored to have contracted the eye disease trachoma and had taken to wearing a pair of glasses with smoked lenses on days when his eyes bothered him.[34] Trachoma spread easily among wrestlers, and a safe and effective treatment for it was still a decade away. Untreated trachoma, or repeated infections, could cause permanent blindness. Strangler Lewis suffered from the disease so severely that it's been said he was forced at times to rely on shouted instructions from ringside to navigate his way through his matches.[35] Wrestlers washed their eyes with antiseptic before and after matches to try to protect themselves. Once infected, however, the only treatment involved destroying the diseased tissue, either by scouring it with corrosive chemicals or by scraping it.[36] "It was awful," remembered wrestler Milo Steinborn, who contracted trachoma in the early 1930s, "the most awful thing I have ever experienced."[37]

Disease was only one of Sonnenberg's worries. On the afternoon of October 22, 1929, he was assaulted in Los Angeles by an aspiring wrestler and full-time bail bondsman named Pete Ladjimi. Sonnenberg had been standing on the corner of Sixth and Broadway, near the Los Angeles Athletic Club downtown, when Ladjimi approached him to discuss a possible match. Sonnenberg referred Ladjimi to promoter Lou Daro and tried to end the conversation. As Sonnenberg turned to go, Ladjimi lowered his head, sprung forward, and rammed Sonnenberg in the chin. Bleeding from his lips and nose, Sonnenberg fell, hit his head hard on the sidewalk, and was knocked unconscious. Ladjimi was arrested for assault and sentenced to thirty days in prison. The incident was reported widely and caused no small measure of embarrassment for Sonnenberg. Jack Curley, who had been in a bitter on-again off-again competition with Paul Bowser for years, took it as an opportunity to gloat. "Can you imagine a heavyweight champion calling a policeman to protect him from assault?" he mockingly asked reporters. "Sonnenberg is a bum. I am fifty-two years old, and I could put him in a waste basket myself." Sonnenberg was forced to show up at the Olympic Auditorium the evening after the attack to wrestle in front of a sellout crowd with a black eye and a split lip.[38]

The next month, the Boston Better Business Bureau produced a scathing report titled "The Sonnenberg Wrestling Racket," which called for legislation to expand the duties of the state's Boxing Commission to include wrestling. "It made me feel cheap," Sonnenberg later said of the time. "Before, I was proud to get around, to be seen. But this made everything altogether different. I didn't feel like being seen anywhere." Audiences began booing him, calling him a fake and a bum. He had trouble eating and sleeping and began to lose weight. In Tulsa, he had rocks thrown at him. In Kansas City, he was hit by a bucket of water thrown from the crowd and knocked unconscious. In Milwaukee, someone pulled an iron leg from a chair and threw it at his head during a match. "[It] went straight through the mat, of course, and made a hole like nobody's business," he said. "It would have killed me if I had stopped it."[39]

By the end of 1929, Gus Sonnenberg had redefined what spectators could expect from a wrestling match. He accelerated the pace and put the emphasis on blunt physicality. Fellow wrestlers copied his style ruthlessly. By 1931, as many as thirty former college athletes would follow his lead and begin wrestling professionally.[40] An evening of matches was no longer considered complete until someone on the card—preferably a former college football player—tore through their opponent with a flying tackle.

For the athletes, the attraction to wrestling was simple. With money scarce, a career in wrestling provided steady work and a modicum of fame with considerably less physical abuse than one would endure in a football career (if a career in football was even an option). "These guys think anybody that weighs 200 pounds can be a wrestler," Jack Curley complained when asked about the influx of college athletes into the professional ranks.[41] What he left unsaid was that most people were becoming more and more convinced that it absolutely was possible for just about anyone to become a star given the right promoter.

To account for the lack of actual wrestling skills among the new recruits, experienced hands were called upon to lose to them night after night. Compliance in making the youngsters look good was an easy way to guarantee a payday, but the money didn't make the experience of doing so any less humiliating. When one unnamed veteran wrestler was asked by a reporter about the state of wrestling, he complained, "Suppose you were in my position. You know I can wrestle. Suppose you were compelled to let one of these football players, knowing nothing about the game, win from you? How would that make you feel? That's exactly the way most of us feel."[42]

For Sonnenberg, success came with hard knocks, but it came all the same. He made $33,000 in 1929 and $66,000 in 1930—this at a time when the world was sinking into an economic depression that only was getting worse with each passing month.[43] Millions were unemployed, and breadlines in major cities could stretch for blocks. For Sonnenberg and Bowser, though, business was good. "I didn't notice any economic depression in wrestling until the summer of 1932," Bowser later said.[44] But it was undeniable that the endless negative press had turned Sonnenberg into a liability. The constant travel and abuse had begun to wear on his body, as well, and he openly talked of retiring and becoming a lawyer or using his wealth to open a home for broken-down wrestlers. On December 10, 1930, in Los Angeles, he lost his championship to a twenty-five-year-old University of Michigan graduate and member of the United States' 1928 Olympic wrestling team, Ed Don George. Though Sonnenberg would remain an attraction for the rest of his career, he would never again match the furious success of his initial championship ride.

Gus Sonnenberg changed professional wrestling forever, but his accomplishments brought him little peace. "When you're at the bottom of the pack, everybody is your friend and your pal," he told writer Gene Kowske. "But the minute you get on top and begin making money, all you get is the royal razz."[45]

FIGURE 16. Jack Pfefer measures the arm span of wrestler Leon Pinetzki. Courtesy of Johnny Griffin.

CHAPTER 15

I Know Where They Grow

JACK CURLEY WOULD never stop loving boxing, even when it barely had any room left for him. He was always happy to hold court with sports-writers and friends and tell them all about the mythical fights he'd witnessed and the legendary fighters he'd known. Given the chance, he'd opine for hours on just who would have beaten whom, had they been matched together in their prime, in a fair fight, on a clear, cool day. He'd lived long enough to see boxing pass from social menace to civic institution. When he was a young promoter, boxers risked jailtime for merely stepping into a prize ring. By the 1920s, they risked fines and suspensions from state commissions for *not* fighting or for being sus-pected of not giving it their all during a bout. Where fights were once held in cow pastures and other hilariously out-of-the-way locations, they were now elaborately promoted and held in specially built arenas. When Curley's friend Jack Dempsey fought Gene Tunney in 1926 in Philadelphia, 120,000 people showed up to watch. Their rematch one year later in Chicago grossed more than $2 million.[1]

Curley had only happened into professional wrestling, if he was be-ing honest, as a sideline, but by 1928, he'd grown to embrace it. He'd become something of a grand old man in the sport, and his name was synonymous with it. Sportswriters loved to needle him and to try to get him to fess up to it all just being a big gag. Curley, though, always found a way to laugh it all off or redirect the conversation, only taking a strong stand when forced. "Wrestling comes first in my affection," he wrote. "There is no accounting for this feeling. Maybe it is because wrestling is the most maligned and the most abused. Maybe it is the feeling of the mother, with a flock of good children, who bestows most favor upon the black sheep of her flock."[2] He knew the sport better than anyone else. Whether he wanted to admit it or not, he was made for it.

Over time, Curley started to wonder whether it was boxing or wrestling that represented the most basic technique for fighting. He'd spent most of his life collecting money from people interested in watching two men punch and pull and choke each other into semiconsciousness. In the first violent encounters among the first men, he asked himself, had a punch been thrown or a wristlock applied? He observed young children fighting and noted that they tended to bite and throw things. He noticed, too, that when a boxer lost his head during a bout, he would take hold of his opponent and try to throw them to the canvas. When wrestlers became enraged during a match, they began to throw punches. The more he considered the question, the further away an answer felt. In time, he learned to let the question lie. He knew he would never resolve it.[3]

"I say that wrestling is not only a business," wrote Los Angeles sportswriter Mark Kelly in 1929, "but an art."[4] Suggesting that professional wrestling was something other than good, honest competition would have offended Jack Curley, the renowned sportsman. But calling it art would have intrigued Jack Curley, the tireless aesthete. He knew that wrestling couldn't hope to match boxing's primordial appeal. As a sport, boxing needed no explanation. Wrestling, though, was a different story. He'd come to think that what people either appreciated or were repulsed by when it came to a pro wrestling show was the strange, engrossing sensation of watching a person squirm and shriek as their body was twisted and tossed in ways no human should be able to bear. "No one is born with a taste for wrestling," he said. "It is a sport, a game that must be cultivated and, let us say, forced on the fellow that patronizes the box office."[5]

But the competition had grown stiffer than ever. Spurred by the success of Gus Sonnenberg, new promoters were getting involved in the business like never before, straining an already shallow pool of top-line talent. Fighting over performers and venues was now commonplace. Like all promoters, Curley had been forced to learn to work with the growing number of state athletic commissions, as they exerted varying degrees of control over who could wrestle whom, as well as when, and where. He'd been called a fake and a conman more times than he could count. And he had taken it all with a smile and a friendly word.

As the 1920s wore on, Curley's financial problems only deepened. In 1928, he experienced his worst year yet, making "way minus, below nothing."[6] The wrestling business in New York looked at times as if it would never recover from the damage it had suffered in the early parts of the decade. Curley had flirted again with managing boxers and had tried but failed to stage a Jack Dempsey fight. He looked into bringing greyhound racing into New York. He imported cyclists from across Europe and staged a six-day bicycle race in the Bronx in January 1929. The event lost close to $15,000, and the cyclists were reduced to threatening lawsuits in order to receive their pay.[7] That same month, Curley's sometimes rival, sometimes business partner Tex Rickard died at the age of fifty-nine due to complications from an infected appendix.[8] In June, Curley's longtime associate, Harry Frazee, with whom he'd worked on the Johnson–Willard bout in Havana, died at only forty-eight.[9] Two months later, one of Curley's closest friends, the sportswriter and fight promoter Otto Floto, died at the age of sixty-six.[10]

Curley was now fifty-two. He'd had his own major health scare in 1928, when an ear abscess had led to an infection in his mastoid bone. He'd had to borrow money from a friend to pay for the multiple operations that were required and was kept out of work for almost seven months.[11] When he ran into reporter Joe Williams in October 1929 outside the Astor Hotel in Times Square, he must have been feeling reflective. He was planning to leave New York, he told Williams, and to retire to a sugar beet farm in Colorado. "This is my last season in the game. I'm getting a little old and tired, and I feel the need of a long rest," Curley sighed. "I don't expect ever to come back. Broadway doesn't seem to mean much to me anymore, and the sport game has sort of gone past me. I don't know how just to explain it."[12]

To prepare for what he thought would be his final year in the sports business, Curley brought in several new faces to help run his wrestling promotion. Rudy Miller, a German-born promoter who booked shows in the Bronx, was made an associate promoter. Toots Mondt, the well-known associate of Strangler Lewis and Billy Sandow, became Curley's partner and his designated business heir.[13]

From Chicago, Curley hired as his "Manager of Foreign Stars" a diminutive thirty-four-year-old Polish immigrant named Jack Pfefer. Born in Warsaw, Pfefer had come to the United States in 1921, at the age of twenty-six, working on a tour with Russian ballerina Anna Pavlova. Wrestling lore has it that he was the company's manager, although by the best available records he was working instead as a porter and stagehand.[14] After a love affair with a young opera singer in San Francisco ended badly, Pfefer vowed to stay a bachelor—a promise he kept.[15] Over time, he developed a single-minded focus on professional wrestling. Though how he first got involved with the business is unknown, he came to specialize in getting coverage for his performers in the numerous foreign-language newspapers that catered to immigrant communities in major American cities.[16]

A mere five feet tall on his best day, jittery, with a prominent nose and a big, conspiratorial smile that took over half his face, Pfefer cut a slight but unforgettable figure.[17] On the streets, he was often seen carrying a fashionable ivory-headed cane and wearing a pinky ring set with a diamond that wrestler Dave Levin remembered as being "half as big as [Pfefer] was. It was as big as a dime, really."[18] Pfefer spoke with a thick, almost affected, accent, and wore his raven-colored hair long. "Like I was a poet," he said. "I don't want to be mistook for a wrestler."[19] He liked to listen to opera to calm his nerves, and in his office, scattered among the framed portraits of wrestlers, he kept signed photographs of opera singers and a death mask of Beethoven.[20] He claimed to sleep only four hours a day and to work the other twenty. Later in his life he favored photos of himself in which he was working two phones at once.[21] "I am the hardest working man on Broadway," he liked to say. "I am what you call Tynamic with a capital T."[22]

He accepted professional wrestling as performance as much as sport. For Jack Pfefer, in fact, it was hardly sport at all. "I'm not an athletic promoter," he would later say. "I'm a theatrical man. Like Ziegfeld, or the Shuberts, maybe."[23] He sensed, too, a deeply sadistic impulse in his adopted country, a taste for blood that he was happy to exploit.[24] In time, he would begin referring to his wrestlers as "freaks," emphasizing their physical abnormalities. With the dime museums that had once been popular in many cities gone, Pfefer openly catered to people's desire to see the unusual up-close. He clearly understood the shock value for American audiences cooked into seeing a 250-pound Russian with a curlicued mustache, like Ivan Poddubny, or a bald, barrel-shaped Hungarian who seemingly lacked a neck, like Ferenc Holubán. He had one of his wrestlers perform in an outfit made of leopard skin while others dressed in colorful clothes from their home country.

Pfefer would come to harbor an antagonistic attitude toward his performers. "I treat them like a father," he said of them, "like a mother beats up her baby."[25] He denigrated them openly, calling them bums and palookas, and was notorious for paying low wages and short-changing performers whenever he could.[26] "They need me, but I don't need them," he declared. "I know where they grow."[27] Later in his life, he would be publicly assaulted by one wrestler, punched out in a locker room by another, and was said to have been dangled out of the window of his office on the tenth floor of the Times building by still another.[28]

Nonetheless, Pfefer was curiously engaging and personable. Despite his public declarations to the contrary, he nurtured a deep love for professional wrestling. "He represented the best and the worst things about wrestling," said Paul Boesch, a longtime wrestler and promoter who began his career working for Pfefer.[29] Over time, Pfefer would amass what he called his "museum collection"—thousands of posters, show bills, newspaper clippings, photos, and correspondence that he stuffed into cardboard boxes. Unlike his contemporaries, he saw wrestling history as something worth preserving.[30]

European wrestlers, "exotics" as they were sometimes called, had always been a significant part of Jack Curley's shows, and his hiring of Pfefer was an acknowledgement of his desire to expand that portion of his business.[31] Importing wrestlers could be an involved business, and it was financially risky. Arrangements needed to be made and honored, usually involving the exchange of dozens of letters and telegrams. Money was needed for photographs, boat and train tickets, passports, and other paperwork. There were government agencies to appease and constantly changing immigration laws and quotas to contend with.[32]

Curley promoted a champion for each of New York City's ethnic groups in the hopes of drawing them out to cheer for their favorite during his weekly shows at Brooklyn's Ridgewood Grove or Manhattan's St. Nicholas Arena. There were Jewish wrestlers (Abe Kaplan and Sammy Stein), Polish wrestlers (Leon Pinetzki), Hungarians (Sandor Szabo), Germans (Hans Steinke and Fritz Kley), and Italians (Renato Gardini and George Calza). Pfefer and Curley used their extensive connections throughout the world to scout new wrestlers and book them on US tours.

The recruits would enter the country through Ellis Island, wrestle around New York for a season, and then be sent to tour the nation before either returning to their native land or staying and building a new life in America. Professional wrestling offered steady work that required no formal education or training and promised consistent, if sometimes unspectacular, pay at a time when both were difficult to come by.[33] "They wrestle when they are told, where they are told, and usually how they are told," wrote sportswriter Frank Menke. "If they don't—well, they soon cease to have rassling jobs. For it's easy to get an ice wagon driver to wrestle for $100 a week but it isn't so easy for an ice wagon driver to get a job wrestling."[34]

One of the most successful non-American wrestlers in the 1920s was, in reality, not foreign-born at all. Reginald Siki was born Reginald Berry in Kansas City, Missouri, on December 28, 1899. Tall and muscular with an infectious smile, he had begun wrestling in 1923 and soon became one of the best-known Black athletes in America. Instead of being listed from Kansas City, promoters claimed he'd been born in Abyssinia, the predecessor of modern-day Ethiopia. They told reporters that his birthname was Dejatch Tedelba, and some of the most outrageous stories about him, such as one from *Ring* magazine, portrayed him as "breaking into cooked food life as a wild, wild tribesman, bedecked in three beads, war paint, a scowl, and a stone hammer."[35] In truth, he studied philosophy and photography, and was a world traveler.

Siki wasn't the first Black professional wrestler in America, but he was the first to sustain a career. Viro Small, the earliest known Black professional wrestler in America, began his career in the 1870s in Vermont. He performed around the Northeast before gaining more prominence in New York, where he performed at the first two locations of Madison Square Garden. A wrestler named Ila Vincent had performed in America in the early 1910s, but after struggling to find opponents, Vincent left to pursue his career in Russia and several European cities.[36]

Siki was a thrilling performer, surprisingly agile given his height. He met with success early in his wrestling career, and there was immediate talk among sportswriters that he could be a challenger for the world heavyweight championship. No such match was ever made, however. Joe Stecher refused to wrestle Siki because he was Black, and Ed Lewis refused to wrestle him without being paid a substantial guarantee. "[Siki] is a giant in size and weight, with what I understand tremendous strength," Lewis said. "I don't propose to take a chance of losing the title without being well paid for it."[37]

After moving to Los Angeles to work for promoter Lou Daro, Siki was cast in multiple films, most famously 1927's *Tarzan and the Golden Lion*. He was said to have lost out on a part in Cecil B. DeMille's biblical epic *The King of Kings* only because DeMille considered him too large.[38] Siki moved to New York in late 1927 to work for Jack Curley and in less than three months was appearing in main-event matches. After less than a year working in the city, he departed New York for unknown reasons, traveling to Europe in the spring of 1928. He would spend the next decade performing throughout Asia, Europe, and the United States.

With his new management team of Jack Pfefer, Toots Mondt, and Rudy Miller in place and ready to take over his business, Jack Curley prepared to walk away. But as 1930 began, he must have sensed an opportunity to turn things around. With the retirement of former champions Jack Dempsey and Gene Tunney, boxing had been left with few marquee names. People, it seemed, were once again turning to wrestling.[39] By March 1930, Curley's wrestling shows were once again drawing sizeable crowds.[40] It was nothing like his wild heyday of the late 1910s, but audiences were coming back to professional wrestling. Curley had even started staging matches at Madison Square Garden again, bringing an end to a six-year period in which the venerated arena hadn't hosted a single night of wrestling.

With the increased gates, however, came increased oversight from William Muldoon and the New York State Athletic Commission. They handed out suspensions to Curley's wrestlers for all kinds of offenses, from failing to appear for a match to unsportsmanlike behavior. The commission also established a working agreement with athletic commissions in other states, so that a suspension in one state could result in a wrestler being barred from working in several others as well.

Curley's group was dealt what they thought constituted an insurmountable setback in April 1930, when Muldoon's Commission declared that an evening of wrestling could only be advertised as an "exhibition" or as a "show"; use of the words "match" or "contest" in promotional material was disallowed without their special advance permission. Commissioner Muldoon offered no public comment on the decision after issuing it, but it was taken as having the dual intent of both protecting the public from dropping a dollar on a less than honest evening of sport and as a final attempt to safeguard his beloved sport of wrestling from those who would drag it into further disrepute.[41]

On the day of the commission's announcement, a crowd of Curley's wrestlers blocked traffic in Union Square for an hour, shaking placards bearing the slogan "Doubting Muldoon" and depicting the commissioner with his foot on the neck of a wrestler while cracking a whip against the back of a promoter.[42] Some writers took the decision as a death knell for wrestling, convinced that divorced from any official acknowledgement that a night at the matches might be on the level, spectators would keep away for good. To others, the idea that the Commission saw the need to act at all was, as one writer put it, "astonishingly ludicrous."[43] If it was impossible to prove matches were dishonest, why impugn the athletes in the first place? If it was all a known fake, why allow it at all?

The Commission's decision would have served as a perfect opportunity for Curley to close the book on his adventures in professional wrestling. However, despite any promises he may have made to turn his business over to his new partners, something made him change his mind. Maybe he was broke and couldn't afford to stop working. Maybe when the time came to say goodbye, he just couldn't bring himself to walk away. Or maybe he had a notion, born of a well-honed instinct for sensing electricity collecting in the air, that something immense was on its way. Whatever it was, he decided that retirement could wait. He would stay on for whatever it was that was coming next.

FIGURE 17. Jim Londos. Courtesy of Steve Yohe.

CHAPTER 16

The Golden Goose

LINES OF PEOPLE began forming outside Madison Square Garden in the early afternoon of January 26, 1931. It was an unusually warm Manhattan Monday but still much too cold for so many people to be queuing up in the elements, three abreast, waiting to watch a wrestling match. The show had been all but sold out for two days, and "Standing Room Only" signs covered the Garden's exterior walls. Those tickets, too, would soon be gone. By fifteen minutes into the evening's first bout, the place would be completely full.[1]

By the time the night was over, more than 22,000 people would click through the gates. Mounted police were needed to keep the crowd from getting trampled at the Eighth Street entrance, with some attendees fainting in the crush to get inside.[2] The event was Jack Curley's third straight packed house at the Garden. Attendance for his show in November 1930 had been a shock at 14,000. December's show at 19,700, with 10,000 turned away? Unheard of. In total, the reported attendance for the four wrestling shows Curley would run at Madison Square Garden between November 17, 1930, and February 23, 1931, was close to 76,000 people. Numbers like this were unfathomable when it came to professional wrestling.[3]

The cause of all the commotion, the man everyone had come out to see, was Jim Londos.

Born Chris Theophelos on January 2, 1894, in Koutsopodi, Greece, Londos had traveled on his own to America as a teenager and settled in San Francisco. He stood out as an amateur wrestler and wrestled in his first professional match in 1914. He adopted his new ring identity the next year, joking that fans were cracking their jaws trying to pronounce his birth name.[4] "[Londos] sounded Greek, even if it wasn't, and the newspaper reporters could spell it without sorting the consonants," he later said.[5] He toured throughout the 1920s, holding his own against the best wrestlers of the decade. Londos was thick with muscles, spoke in a high, soft voice, had black, curly hair, deep brown eyes, a set of straight, clean, white teeth, and a broad chest that shined like freshly polished gold.[6] His relentless touring schedule and fierce work ethic served to slowly build his fanbase and sharpen his performance skills, but when real success came for him, it seemed to hit all at once. Unlike any wrestler before him, Jim Londos actually improved with age.

When he won Jack Curley's version of the heavyweight championship on June 6, 1930, defeating a wrestler named Dick Shikat in Philadelphia, the news garnered almost no attention from the New York media.[7] But within just five months, the press interest in Londos would be insatiable. Everywhere he appeared, box offices were running out of tickets and having to shut down early. When Londos performed in St. Louis in February 1931, the line to see him stretched for three blocks. In Baltimore that March, 2,000 people were turned away at the gate after tickets sold out. In Philadelphia, three days later, the number of people turned away neared 10,000. The size of his crowds and his sudden embrace by the media caught everyone involved in wrestling off guard. Gus Sonnenberg had been a hit, but not like this.[8]

"Jim Londos isn't the greatest wrestler by fifty lengths," wrote Damon Runyon, "but he has more grace, more rhythm, more poetry of motion than any other of my observation."[9] It was impossible to be neutral when watching Londos work. He believed earnestly in the primacy of giving the paying customer a show. A gifted physical performer, he used his body to connect with spectators across vast arenas. He could communicate joy or agony through his pained facial expressions and exuberant leaps. He had a singular talent for slumping his shoulders in exhaustion and gulping for breath. If he was suffering, he reached his arm out to the crowd like he was steadying himself against them. "If this be play-acting, then it is play-acting of the highest order and comes close to being the best entertainment in town," wrote Joel Sayre in his March 1932 profile of Londos for the *New Yorker*. "To cavil at it for being play-acting is to cavil at a Booth or a Barrymore for getting up off the floor and putting on his street clothes after the final curtain has been lowered on *Hamlet*. . . . What a man! What an artist!"[10]

Londos's magnetism was compared with that of boxer Jack Dempsey's more than once, but the element of Dempsey's style that Londos most magnified was the ability to take punishment in the ring and still come out the winner. Dempsey famously said, "A champion is someone who gets up when he can't."[11] Londos enacted that maxim for fans night after night. It was, for many, the core element of his appeal. At just 5'8" and less than two hundred pounds, Londos was forever overmatched and outweighed. Always the underdog, his opponents would chase him around the ring and out onto the floor, wrenching and beating on him mercilessly. They'd trap him on the mat for long stretches, squeezing and pulling on his body while Londos contorted his face in distress. But no matter how much he was forced to endure, he always found a way to make his comeback.[12] Each time he managed to wind his way out of another tight jam, cheers rose, igniting the air.

To finish off his opponents, Londos relied on a novel maneuver called the airplane spin. After threading one arm between his foe's legs and wrapping his other arm around their neck, Londos would lift them up into his arms or onto his shoulders and spin three times in a circle before depositing them forcibly back down to the mat. The maneuver, wrote the *New Yorker*'s A.J. Liebling, was "like the climactic movement of an adagio dance or a hammer throw."[13] And it would have been impossible for Londos to execute without some degree of cooperation from his opponent. That fact was so obvious that, on its face, the move was almost ridiculous. But in practice, with thousands yelling and stamping their feet, mesmerized by the action in the ring, it represented the unusual alchemy of professional wrestling in its purest form: a bell, a referee, and two grown men dressed in their underwear, starkly lit, captivating a crowd by simulating athletic competition.[14]

There was something undeniably compelling in seeing the little guy get kicked around, only to have him find his way back to victory before your very eyes. Jack Curley's good friend, sportswriter Heywood Broun, wrote, "The tragedy of life is not that man loses but that he almost wins."[15] He had been writing about the 1921 heavyweight boxing contest between Georges Carpentier and Jack Dempsey, the fight in which Carpentier had broken his hand hitting Dempsey with an uppercut that had failed to produce a knockout. For Broun in 1921, Carpentier's failure was a beautiful tragedy. But to audiences a decade later who were busy feeling their way through the early days of the Great Depression, with a staggering sixteen percent of the US labor force unemployed and the numbers getting worse every day, there were no beautiful tragedies.[16] There were winners and there were losers, and audiences didn't pay to watch to losers. Jim Londos was as far from being a loser as you could find.

In *Vanity Fair*, when writer Tommy Armour built what he called a sports god from the component parts of the greatest athletes of the era, he gave it the eyes of Babe Ruth, the hands of golfer Bobby Jones, and the physique of Jim Londos. "Londos is unquestionably the ranking candidate for the framework of this assembled job," Armour wrote. "The battering that he gives and takes, night after night of an extremely strenuous schedule, is all the evidence you need."[17] That Londos was included without hesitation among athletes like Ruth and Jones was a ringing endorsement of just how far along he helped bring wrestling in the mind of the public. "Solemnly and with restrained indignation, Londos will tell you that he never faked a match in his life," wrote the *Chicago Tribune's* Wilfrid Smith, "and hearing him, you will believe."[18] "My personal notion, after a season of mild excitement at the ringside, is that the struggle for the main matches is quite an honest thing," wrote the *New Yorker's* Morris Markey in 1931. "Any careful observer will find ample detail to justify such a view, and on the other hand, I do not think even the most careful observer can discover a genuine basis for believing that the matches are fixed."[19]

By then, matches around Manhattan and elsewhere had been goosed with the addition of sound effects and hysterical theatrics.[20] Wrestlers roared in anger, and shrieked and howled like injured animals. Being trained as a wrestler was now less about learning how to properly apply and escape from wristlocks and legholds and more about learning how to pull your punches, how to screw your face up in anguish, how to fall without hurting yourself, and how, in turn, to throw an opponent to the mat without causing an injury. "[This] is done by making his feet hit the mat first with a resounding thud, and not his head," wrote Herman Hickman, who was a standout offensive lineman for the University of Tennessee before beginning his professional career working for Jack Curley in 1932. "Some of the best . . . could appear to be tearing a man's head off with a headlock, all their muscles straining, and yet their opponents could not even feel the pressure of their arms."[21]

Everything about the matches seemed a little different than what people had been used to. A night of wrestling was becoming not all that different from a night at a magic show. Fans entered the arena looking to be dazzled and knocked back on their heels with delight. "With a grimace, a groan, a rolling of the eyes, a squirm and a writhe, they will make you believe they are in extremis," wrote *New York Daily News* sports editor Paul Gallico, who produced brilliant coverage of wrestling for several publications. "They have developed to the nth degree the art of make-believe so that it is no longer make-believe when you see it, but the truth itself."[22]

Credit for all this would reflexively be given to Jack Curley. It was his name, after all, at the top of the show posters and in the news articles. It is certain, though, that Toots Mondt, Jack Pfefer, and others played key roles, as well.[23] They all knew that audiences were paying for suffering as much as they were paying for sport. It was morbid, and it was cynical, but you couldn't argue with the results. If wrestling couldn't always deliver the sport, it would by all means deliver the suffering. In Jim Londos, they'd found a master artisan.

Long gone were the three- and four-hour matches of years past in which wrestlers spent long periods seemingly inert on the mat. Action was what fans came to see, and action was what they now got. Wrestlers flew about the ring. They crashed out of the ropes, falling onto unsuspecting reporters seated ringside or smacking against the floorboards in dangerous head-first dives that could be so upsetting that Paul Gallico labeled them "a form of public suicide."[24]

The rougher style took an undeniable toll on the athletes' bodies. Knees, back, and elbows subject to stress and banging night after night were particularly susceptible to wearing out prematurely.[25] "It's not what we want. It's what the promoter and the public wants," said one unnamed wrestler to *San Francisco Examiner* sportswriter Curley Grieve. "You actually got hurt diving through those ropes. I don't say all the time, but you take a chance. Not so long ago, I thought I broke a leg. And let me tell you it wasn't until 24 hours later that I could get up and walk. . . . What are you going to do? You have to eat, and you don't eat if you don't do as you're told."[26]

Chicago Tribune sportswriter Westbrook Pegler went the furthest with his frigid assessment of just why fans were suddenly flocking to matches in record numbers. "Many a night at the ringside I have heard laymen sitting in the forward rows explain to their ladies that the punishment which wrestlers inflict on one another really does not hurt them as they are used to it and cannot feel, anyway," Pegler wrote.[27] That wrestlers possessed some inborn invulnerability to pain, a not uncommon belief at the time, made watching the violence they inflicted on each other nothing more than a victimless crime. What these audiences were paying for, Pegler decided, what they really wanted to see, was "a pleasant illusion that they were witnessing something very like a slaughter."[28]

FIGURE 18. Marquee announcing an appearance by Jim Londos in Chicago, October 1931. Courtesy of Steve Yohe.

If I Were to Tell You the Real Inside about Wrestling, I Probably Would Spend the Night in the Tombs Instead of at Home

FOR JACK CURLEY, success was coming upon success. A long way from his notions of retirement, 1931 was looking like it would be one of his best years yet. When asked to comment on it all, though, Curley chose to play it cool. "It has always been an in-and-out game," he told a reporter. "About every five or six years, wrestling comes back and goes big for a while. This year isn't anything to get excited about. . . . You take it as it comes."[1] He used his unexpected prosperity as an opportunity to wander in new directions, leaving it to Toots Mondt to run much of the daily operations of his wrestling office. Curley looked into promoting speed boat competitions and auto racing, and he organized an all-female boxing show.[2] He seized on the dance marathon craze of the early 1930s in which contestants would stay in near-constant motion for weeks at a time, staging several such endurance contests around New York and Connecticut.[3] What caught his attention the most, though, was tennis.

During the Golden Age of Sports, Bill Tilden's name was synonymous with amateur tennis around the world. He won Wimbledon three times, the US Open seven times, and the French Open twice. These major events were closed to professional players, and Tilden had declared unequivocally that he would never leave the amateur ranks. It was a headline-grabbing event, then, in December of 1930, when he announced that not only would he be turning pro, but that he planned to do so under the management of Jack Curley.[4] The mention of Curley's name in proximity to Tilden's provoked anxiety among purists who worried that Curley would convince him to manipulate his matches in the interest of generating excitement. Stoking the flames, Curley told one writer, "Tennis is just wrestling in white pants."[5]

Curley booked Tilden on a tour that stretched across the United States, Europe, and Australia. He did everything he could to agitate for provocative headlines that he hoped would sell tickets, hinting at other amateurs he was looking to lure into turning professional and talking up supposed rivalries between players on the tour.[6] Tilden drove Curley mad, however, through his constant winning. Not only was he victorious in every match he played, he rarely even lost a set. By May 1931, Tilden's appearances were said to be drawing poorly, precisely because the outcomes had become predictable.[7] Professional tennis, it turned out, was far from being just wrestling in a different set of clothing—at least as Bill Tilden played it.

Later that year, Jack Curley and Toots Mondt found themselves staring down a similar predicament with Jim Londos. A cartoon that had run in newspapers across the country depicted Curley as a ringmaster leading a line of tamed elephants, the lead pachyderm labeled "Those Wrestlers."[8] It was the way writers imagined that the wrestling racket operated, but if Curley ever had that kind of control over his athletes, Jim Londos was proving to be much harder to pull along.

Londos was all but living in a Pullman car, working at a murderous pace, and attracting audiences that were jaw-dropping in size everywhere he went. In 1931 alone, he performed in front of 10,000 or more people on thirty-one occasions, including one match in front of 30,000 people in New York's Yankee Stadium that June.[9] And though the money valve was opened at full throttle, less cash was finding its way to him than he would have liked. His contract called for a full forty percent of his pay for an evening's work to go to Curley's New York booking office. Another forty-two percent of it was divided among the other promoters and wrestlers who played a role in supporting him. After these deductions, Londos was left taking home just eighteen percent of his overall earnings.[10]

Londos had been in professional wrestling for almost twenty years. He'd wrestled in tank towns, dealt with gamblers and swindlers, and been stretched, twisted, and beaten up. He understood the wrestling business and the men who ran it, and he trusted very few, preferring instead to work within a small network of associates.[11] A more than capable grappler, he nonetheless refused to have his opponents dictated to him and he was unwilling to lose on demand. "No one can tell Jim what to do and where to go," Philadelphia promoter Ray Fabiani told a colleague.[12]

Londos's newfound stature put Curley, Mondt, and Jack Pfefer in a difficult position. They could effectively allow themselves to become Londos's employees, or they could tear down their star attraction. Forcing the issue was a claim from Pfefer that he'd discovered a new managerial contract between Londos and a Chicago-based promoter named Ed White on file at the offices of the New York State Athletic Commission. The contract, Pfefer said, cut Curley, Mondt, and himself out of any further guaranteed percentage of Londos's income.[13]

Jim Londos was undeniably special. On nights he was not scheduled to appear, the attendance for wrestling shows at Madison Square Garden was down by better than two-thirds. He'd not only endeared himself to fans and writers, but he'd also won over tens of thousands of people who would have never otherwise dreamed of buying a ticket to a wrestling show. Curley may have controlled wrestling in New York, but without Jim Londos, he risked finding out that his monopoly was worthless.

As the Great Depression bore on, Americans went mad for wrestling. Promoters raced to keep up with the demand for matches by expanding beyond their home bases and into new cities and towns. Jack Curley maintained a loop that included not just Manhattan, Brooklyn, and Harlem but a number of cities in New Jersey, Massachusetts, and Connecticut. In California alone, a wrestler working for promoter Lou Daro could stay busy for months. St. Louis promoter Tom Packs organized a circuit of eighteen cities in eight states running from Texas to Georgia and guaranteed wrestlers a lump sum payment to work it. A top-name wrestler working three nights a week could complete Packs's run in just more than a month and pocket $10,000 for their efforts.[14]

A wrestler's engagements were handled through booking offices, of which Curley's Manhattan office was by far the largest. Promoters in smaller towns looking to put on a show would contact a booking office to obtain talent. As one booking agent explained:

Let's say a fellow comes in from Zenithville and tells me that he wants some talent for a show. Well, a $1,000 house is about as small as you can fool with. I tell the fellow that my talent will cost $500. For that, I send him a complete card. The boys split $400 between themselves, and the office gets $100. The local promoter gets $500. His expenses are, say $200. At that rate, he can make $15,000 or $20,000 a year. Where else can he make it? And he takes no gamble. If the first show is a flop, we cut our prices or give him the talent for only their railroad expenses. The talent is willing.[15]

For travel, wrestlers hopped trains when they could and carpooled when they couldn't. A circuit comprised of towns that could only be reached by automobile came to be known as a gasoline circuit. Wrestlers working one would gather at designated spots after the evening's matches were complete, sometimes meeting on the edges of town to avoid being seen cramming into a car with their opponents from earlier that night. Once together, they would drive nonstop if necessary to make it to the next engagement, trading off shifts at the wheel, playing cards, and sharing stories to keep each other from falling asleep. Upon arriving at the next booking, they would split up and check into their separate hotels to sleep, relax, and prepare for that evening's event. After it was all over, if the schedule demanded it, they would repeat the routine.[16]

For promoters interested in empire building, expansion could be expensive. When Jack Curley began sending wrestlers to Baltimore, he was said to have spent $28,000 before seeing a profit at his shows.[17] Once established in a new area, promoters did all they could to keep rivals out. They began forming tenuous talent- and profit-sharing partnerships with other promoters. The factions fought each other deliberately and ruthlessly, encroaching into each other's cities and venues and luring away each other's wrestlers whenever they could.[18] "Their wars over territory [were] as jealously and bitterly contested, short of the killings, as any beer monopoly during the sainted days of prohibition," wrote Paul Gallico.[19]

The unfolding palace intrigue was fodder for sportswriters looking to fill inches in their columns, and the creeping disorder did little to put fans off from coming to the shows. Attendance was up everywhere, and for some, being a wrestling fan was as much about guessing at the intentions of these warring promoters as it was about watching the matches. Some came to believe that everything that happened in or around a wrestling ring was planned from top to bottom. What might have looked like happenstance to most people was, to the true wrestling fan, part of some larger plot to put one over on the hayseeds.

Hollywood studios took notice of wrestling's popularity, as well as its behind-the-curtain drama, and released multiple films in 1932 depicting the chaotic scene. In one titled *Madison Square Garden*, an honest and aging fight manager from California, played by William Collier, tries to break a young wrestler into the New York sports scene, only to become embroiled in a battle against racketeers and gangsters. In director John Ford's *Flesh*, a naive German wrestler named Polakai, played by Wallace Beery, moves to America to compete for the world championship. To find work, he's forced to compromise his integrity and agrees to take part in fixed matches. "You're going to wrestle for me, you're going to win when I tell you to win and you're going to lose when I tell you to lose," Polakai is told by Joe Willard, the fictional head of wrestling in New York. "Clear enough?"[20]

Deception, released in April, hit closest to home. Written by Nat Pendleton, a one-time star for Jack Curley who had abandoned wrestling in the mid-1920s, *Deception* was a *film a clef* centered on a smooth-talking, crooked sports promoter named Jim Hurley, played by Leo Carrillo, who takes over the career of a promising college football star named Bucky O'Neill, played by Pendleton. After a series of early professional wins, O'Neill becomes disillusioned when he discovers that Hurley arranged for those victories. When O'Neill tries to go straight, Hurley plots to have him killed. The film featured multiple wresters who had worked closely with Jack Curley over the years, including Jim Londos. Pendleton's thinly veiled allusions to Curley in the character of Hurley were lost on no one and were said to have made Curley furious.[21]

Curley's relationship with Jim Londos was falling to pieces, and tension mounted in January 1932 when rumors circulated that Londos's long-time rival, Strangler Lewis, had signed with Curley's group.[22] A Londos versus Lewis match figured to be a blockbuster, but animosity between the two men was said to run deep. Even later in his life, Lewis would refuse to refer to Londos by name, calling him instead "that yellow Greek sonuvabitch." It was widely assumed that convincing the two men to work together in the ring would be challenging—if not impossible.[23]

Lewis's move to the Northeast couldn't have come at a better time for him. In December 1931, he had gathered reporters together at Los Angeles's Biltmore Hotel for a press conference and formally announced his break from his longtime manager Billy Sandow.[24] "We didn't have

any quarrel," he told them. "We just quit."[25] He'd had a brief run as Paul
Bowser's heavyweight champion in April of that year, but after losing
the championship in early May to a Canadian wrestler named Henri
DeGlane in a bizarre match in Montreal in which DeGlane had accused
Lewis of biting him on the wrist, he'd been reduced to spending more of
his time running his two Los Angeles-area restaurants than performing
in the ring.[26] Signing with Curley and Mondt would mean not only a
busier work schedule but also a chance to be a star one last time in the
biggest media market in the nation.

Lewis's alignment with the Curley organization put immense pressure on Londos and raised problems for him with the New York State
Athletic Commission, which considered Lewis a logical contender for
Londos's championship and soon began demanding the two wrestle. As
fears mounted that Londos would stop working with Curley altogether,
Curley and Mondt went to him in March in the hope that he would agree
to lose his championship. As a compromise, they proposed that the man
to replace him as title holder would not be Strangler Lewis, their first
choice, but Dick Shikat, the thirty-five-year-old former German naval
officer whom Londos had defeated for the title eighteen months earlier.
"It belongs to Dick by rights, anyway," Mondt told Londos. "He only lent
it to you."[27]

Born on January 11, 1897, in Prussia, Shikat was a skilled Greco-
Roman wrestler who had arrived in America in 1923. He'd labored in
San Francisco before settling in Philadelphia, where he had worked for
Toots Mondt and Ray Fabiani. Shikat split the difference between the
burly, top-heavy tusslers of the past and the emerging generation of
college boys and musclemen who were attracting new fans. He was both
convincing as a wrestler and not above putting on a show. He played
to the crowd, cowering from his opponent in the corner of the ring or
covering his face in fear. "Doesn't THAT get the mob roaring at him!"
wrote sportswriter Murray Robinson.[28]

Curley publicized a match between Londos and Shikat for the evening
of April 4, 1932, at Madison Square Garden, but Londos never appeared
for it.[29] "Our patrons will probably wonder why Jim Londos is not on this
card," Curley wrote in that evening's program. "We made every effort to
sign Londos, but we must admit that he was the unwilling party to enter
into a match with Shikat, while on the other hand, Shikat cheerfully
consented and signed the articles."[30] It was the clearest signal yet that

Curley's once cozy relationship with Londos had frayed. Their fragile congeniality, which had helped enable wrestling to achieve such extraordinary popularity, was gone.[31]

When Curley attended an amateur boxing show at the Friars Club of New York later that month, the rumors of conflict within his ranks were all anyone wanted to talk about. When one of the club members turned to Curley and said, "Tell us the inside about wrestling," Curley smiled broadly and responded, "If I were to tell you the real inside about wrestling, I probably would spend the night in the Tombs instead of at home."[32]

In preparation for the fallout, alliances were hastily reshuffled. Curley settled his differences with Boston's Paul Bowser to solidify a powerful circuit in the northern portion of the East Coast. In late September, with the pressure on Londos to wrestle Strangler Lewis reaching a fever pitch, Curley went to the New York State Athletic Commission and had Londos stripped of his championship recognition in the state.[33] By then, Londos was well on his way to launching a new wrestling group with himself at the center. He would work on his own terms or not at all. He'd been named the heavyweight champion of an organization that called itself the National Wrestling Association, which was comprised of the athletic commissioners of more than a dozen states.[34] With a recognized championship claim, Londos concentrated on working a supportive circuit of towns in partnership with promoters Tom Packs, Ray Fabiani, and others. It ran from Philadelphia to Los Angeles, but the group soon made plans to expand, including into New York—into direct competition with Curley.[35]

No one was quite sure exactly what a full-blown war in professional wrestling would look like, but they were about to find out.

FIGURE 19. Jim Browning applies pressure to a leglock in a match against Strangler Lewis in Chicago, April 11, 1933. Courtesy of Steve Yohe.

CHAPTER 18

Flipflops and Acrobatics and All That Fake Stuff

AFTER REIGNING AS the king of the wrestling jungle for more than a decade, Strangler Lewis had grown comfortable in his middle age. On June 30, 1932, Lewis turned forty-two. He was on his third marriage, his hair had thinned, and he'd let his once-imposing physique go to seed. He looked, as one particularly ungenerous writer described him, "sedate, [and] very, very fat where it does not help."[1] Lewis's physical appearance was an unmistakable reminder to fans of just how much of an anachronism he'd become. Wrestlers were now younger, faster, and took bigger chances with their bodies in their attempts to entertain spectators. Lewis had ushered this new era in, but now, though still a dangerous grappler, he appeared more than anything else to be a hold-over from a more ponderous, deliberate time. Nonetheless, earlier in the year, in a curious move, he'd been hired by Jack Curley and Toots Mondt to replace Jim Londos as their star attraction. They were betting that fans had grown tired of showy theatrics and were ready for something rougher and more convincing. If anyone could make people believe in the honesty of wrestling again, they wagered, it was Strangler Lewis.

On October 10, 1932, Lewis wrestled in Madison Square Garden against a rugged and unrelenting wrestler named Jack Sherry in a match to name a new heavyweight champion in New York. Curley and Mondt sold the contest to fans as what was called a "shooting match," one that was guaranteed to involve an honest effort to win between the contestants. Such were Lewis's and Sherry's reputations that even William Muldoon, now eighty-eight, secured a seat at ringside to watch them go head-to-head. Shooting matches were fascinating to wrestlers but tended to be unrelentingly dull in practice for those spectators not schooled in the finer points of the sport. Just 5,000 people came out to watch, leaving the massive Garden almost three-quarters empty.

While Lewis and Sherry tugged and pulled and jockeyed for leverage, their heavy perspiration collecting in pools on the canvas, Muldoon, wearing a bulky overcoat and slouch hat and leaning on a cane, sat expressionless and focused on the ring. The sparse crowd, irritated by the match's lack of action, soon grew restless and began to hoot and jeer in disapproval. An irritated Muldoon, his blue eyes watery, turned to the reporter seated next to him and shook his head sadly. "This is real wrestling," Muldoon told him. "They don't want real wrestling here. They want flipflops and acrobatics and all that fake stuff."[2] Lewis finally pinned Sherry after ninety minutes to take over as Curley's champion. His win kicked off what would be the wildest fourteen months in professional wrestling history.

In December, Lewis wrestled in another main event in Madison Square Garden, this time against a wrestler named Ray Steele. By most accounts, Steele was one of the most talented and potent wrestlers of the era. He was friendly and well-liked outside of the ring, as well as amenable to working with less skilled opponents to entertain an audience. "Kid," he told one young wrestler, "you may have the aptitude to become a great wrestler, but if you don't learn to make money at it . . . well, then it's only a hobby."[3] Steele was well-known to fans as an associate of Jim Londos. The pair had worked together in numerous matches across the country, and Steele was said to be loyal to Londos in his skirmish with Jack Curley. Given Steele's close relationship with Lewis's archrival, many in attendance expected a rowdy evening. They wouldn't leave disappointed.

During the match, Lewis and Steele moved cautiously, hesitant to engage. After thirty minutes of uninspired maneuvering, the match became unhinged. Steele let loose, hitting Lewis in the face multiple times with his forearm and elbow. When the referee disqualified him, ending the match on a foul instead of allowing the two men to fight to a conclusive finish, the crowd flew into a collective rage. From the Garden's upper levels, apple cores, fountain pens, and smoldering cigarette butts came flying down into the ring as well as onto the spectators seated around it. At least one woman fainted, while as many as thirty separate fights broke out in the crowd. Standing by the press table, Jack Curley was punched and knocked down by a wrestler named Tom Marvin. Police and ushers responded in an instant, downing Marvin with a blow to his temple before kicking him bloody.[4]

Fearing that the fighting would continue outside as fans were driven from the building, twenty-five additional policemen were summoned from nearby stations to keep order on the street. Steele and several others drew suspensions from a not-at-all pleased New York State Athletic Commission the next day. "Wrestling was dull. Now it's dangerous," wrote the Associated Press' Jimmy Powers, who covered the match. "The customers welcome a riot confined to the principals but don't care to indulge in one personally."[5]

Three months earlier, in September 1932, Connecticut State Athletic Commissioner Tom Donohue, well known in the state for his fairness in overseeing boxing and wrestling, sat down for an interview with Albert Keane, sports editor for the *Hartford Courant*, just before leaving to catch a train to Baltimore. "I am working on the strangest story in my experience," he said to Keane, "but it is unsupported by any fact."[6] The story he told involved panicked phone calls Donohue had received from his deputy commissioner on the evening of September 12, 1932, concerning that evening's scheduled wrestling match between Jim Londos and a red-haired journeyman wrestler named Pat O'Shocker. Londos was refusing to appear, Donohue was told, insisting that he'd been tipped off that the match was fixed against him.

Londos's information had come from O'Shocker himself, who claimed to have been approached by Toots Mondt and another man offering him $25,000 to sign a five-year management contract with them. The referee for O'Shocker's match with Londos had been paid off, Mondt was to have assured him, and would declare O'Shocker the winner and award him Londos's championship belt. All O'Shocker needed to do was wrestle as he normally would and let the referee take care of the rest. He remembered being told, "Pat, here's a chance for you to fall into a gold mine."[7] O'Shocker accepted the deal initially but, feeling regretful, decided to contact Londos to warn him. Knowing he would be blacklisted by Mondt and Curley for reneging on the deal, he asked Londos to promise he would offer him future work.

Even with O'Shocker pledging not to follow through on the arrangement, Londos insisted on a new referee for the match, knowing that it
couldn't be guaranteed that the appointed one would not find a reason
to award O'Shocker a victory anyway. "We are not going into the ring
because we are certain that if we do, an attempt will be made to steal
the title," Londos's manager, Ed White, told Donohue. Donohue flatly
rejected the request and responded that if Londos refused to appear,
he would likely be banned from wrestling in Connecticut, as well as in
other states. Left with little choice, Londos followed through with the
match. He beat O'Shocker in a disappointing bout that lasted just twenty
minutes. When questioned afterward about O'Shocker's claims, Toots
Mondt denied them. "I wasn't even in New Haven the night the bout was
held," he told a reporter. "I was never mixed up with anything shady in
wrestling and never intend to be."[8]

The threat of a double cross, the wrestling world's equivalent of foul
play, had dogged Londos since his break with Jack Curley's organization.
He'd been fortunate that O'Shocker had had a change of heart before
their match began, but there was no way he could guarantee that his luck
would continue. If a rival wrestler managed to surprise him and steal
his championship, it would push his new business venture into bank-
ruptcy. All it would take was the right offer to reach the right referee or
opponent and everything Londos had worked to build would come to an
inglorious end.

His good fortune ran out seven months after New Haven, on April 7,
1933, at Chicago Stadium in a match against one of wrestling's brightest
young stars, Joe Savoldi. A twenty-five-year-old Italian immigrant whose
5'11" frame was a mass of muscles topped by a head full of rich black
curls, Savoldi had been a three-sport standout in high school before being recruited to Notre Dame by legendary football coach Knute Rockne.
After three years of college football, Savoldi signed with the National
Football League's Chicago Bears in late 1930. Savoldi's inflated salary
and personal fame earned him the ire of his teammates, and in 1931,
despite being the second-highest paid player in professional football,
he accepted an offer from Billy Sandow to jump into wrestling. Young,
impossibly handsome, accustomed to winning, and the possessor of a
sly smile and stunning resume, Savoldi was a promoter's dream.[9]

Londos–Savoldi should have been a routine affair—forty or fifty minutes of drama capped by a thrilling Jim Londos come-from-behind victory. Instead, twenty-five minutes in, things became strange. With both men down on the mat, Londos took hold of Savoldi's arm and bent it at the elbow. He wrapped his legs around the bent arm to hold it in place and began pulling, a hold he called the Japanese jackknife. Instead of submitting, Savoldi stood up, rolled Londos onto his head, and forced his shoulders down against the mat. The referee, Bob Managoff, tapped Savoldi on the shoulder, a signal to break the hold. Savoldi stepped back to his corner of the ring and, by all indications, appeared ready to continue the bout. Instead, Managoff walked over to him and raised his hand in victory.[10] Shockwaves reverberated across the arena's 7,000 spectators. Joe Savoldi had just defeated the unbeatable Jim Londos. As the crowd broke into a long cheer for Savoldi and the realization settled in that Managoff had just signaled his first defeat in more than three years, Londos looked around the ring in confusion. "Savoldi appeared to be the most surprised man in the stadium," wrote the *Chicago Tribune*'s George Strickler, who'd watched from ringside. "Unless it was Londos."

Afterward, fans expressed a tangle of conflicting opinions on what had just occurred. "Many felt that Savoldi had double crossed his opponent; others felt it was a gambling coup," wrote Strickler. "Not a few predicted there now would be a rematch at Soldier's Field before a larger gate. There was no evidence to prove any of these assertions. Wrestling is that way."[11] Londos would protest bitterly following the match, but Managoff's decision was upheld by the Illinois Athletic Association. "Londos's complaint should have been carried by papers in the comic sections," Jack Curley joked to reporters when asked to comment.[12]

Bob Managoff, himself a former wrestler, worked two jobs to support a wife and four children, in addition to his officiating work. His pay for the Londos–Savoldi match had been $50. "Londos's shoulders were pinned to the mat," he said afterwards. "He was down, and I called it as I saw it."[13] "It will be easy to tell whether the match was a frame-up," commented Missouri Athletic Commissioner Seneca Taylor when asked for his take on the controversial outcome. "If Savoldi jumps the Londos–[Tom] Packs crowd and starts wrestling for one of the groups working in opposition to that faction, everyone will know the bout was not on the level."[14]

Before the month was out, Savoldi did exactly that, leaving Chicago and going to work for Jack Curley in New York. A ham-handed attempt at retribution aimed at Savoldi was made two months later, on June 26, by Londos's allies in Manhattan. Savoldi was working in what should have been a mundane Monday night match against a wrestler named Sol Slagel, a double-jointed contortionist whose unusual flexibility had earned him a role in Curley's group. After only twenty minutes of wrestling, Slagel began trying to strangle Savoldi and force him down to the mat. Bewildered spectators at ringside overheard a disoriented Savoldi telling his manager, "Stop the bout. He'll throw me in a minute if you don't."[15] After repeated warnings from the referee, Slagel was disqualified. When Savoldi left the ring, a third wrestler entered and raised Slagel's hand in victory. A photographer planted at ringside snapped pictures of Slagel's raised hand and copies of the photograph were distributed to the local press with a caption declaring that it showed Slagel being awarded victory over Curley's new attraction.[16]

While some fans took a dark type of pleasure in the back and forth between the warring groups, for casual fans, the crooked matches, vengeful promoters, and shadowy double deals were starting to feel out of control and did nothing to bolster their confidence that wrestling matches had even a whiff of integrity. It was getting easy to feel that the only honest competition was in the action that took place far from the wrestling ring, in the closed-door meetings where plans were made and deals were struck. "A nationwide probe of wrestling should be started immediately," wrote respected syndicated columnist Sid Keener. "Honest matchmakers and performers deserve that recognition. If there are other promoters, matchmakers, officials, impresarios, referees, and what not who are trying to put over a *coup de fix*, why, then hunt them down and run them out of the sport."[17]

Since being recruited to New York by Mondt and Curley, Strangler Lewis had headlined in Madison Square Garden seven times. It was impossible to deny that his best days were long behind him. Even on his best nights, he was only drawing a fraction of the audience that had once overrun the ticket windows to see Jim Londos. After striking a deal that was said to have paid him $42,000, Lewis agreed to lose his claim to the New York heavyweight championship and step aside. "He had been a financial as well as an artistic failure," lamented one sportswriter. "Wrestling could excuse the latter, never the first."[18]

His successor was Jim Browning, who pinned Lewis clean in the middle of the ring in front of 7,000 people at Madison Square Garden on February 20, 1933. Browning was 6'2" and rugged, a former oilfield and railroad line worker with a prominent pair of cauliflower ears sprouting from his head and a chest like a wine cask.[19] He was a better than competent wrestler with more than a decade of ring experience. With Browning, Curley was keeping himself firmly straddled between the past and the future. There wasn't another wrestler working who could take Browning in an honest match, but his ability to captivate an audience was uneven at best. "As colorless as a jammed coalbin," was one New York writer's unforgiving take on Curley's new titleholder.[20]

On nights when the turnout for one of Curley's wrestling shows at the Garden was worse than usual, spectators in the arena's vast seating bowl would sit quietly, their hands either in their laps or occupied with shelling peanuts. When someone did shout down at the wrestlers, their voice would ring out clear across the empty arena. In June 1933, Browning wrestled a particularly grim match with Joe Savoldi on a miserable night at Yankee Stadium. "It was raining so hard the crowd was almost invisible," Jack Pfefer would remember.[21] The event was intended to be the highlight of the summer. Instead, only 6,000 people attended. The yawning stretches of vacant seats could only have served as a taunting reminder to Curley of the heady days of just two years past when Jim Londos had almost filled the place.

By the summer of 1933, Jack Pfefer was ready to make his move. He'd been working for Jack Curley for five years, during which time he'd developed his own connections as well as his own ideas on how professional wrestling should operate. He was said to have access to significant personal savings, which he would use to broker deals and sometimes lend to other promoters who had run short on cash.[22] It was his money, some suspected, that had been used to fund the pay-offs that had ensured Joe Savoldi's victory over Jim Londos in Chicago.[23] He'd never gotten the credit he deserved for resuscitating the wrestling business in New York, Pfefer felt, and he was forever in Curley's substantial shadow.[24] Though he deeply admired the man, it was time for Jack Pfefer's name to appear on top. "When I came on the scene, the wrestling business was dead like a cemetery," he would brag to reporters. "Jack Curley's office was a cemetery. With me, it is an art to make things boom."[25]

When Pfefer was approached by Jim Londos's manager, Ed White, with an opportunity to work together instead of in opposition to each other, he took it. "You have the Coliseum and Ridgewood Grove, and I can get three days at the Garden, independent of Curley," Pfefer remembered White telling him, "So why don't you give him the air and come with us?"[26] In August 1933, along with Rudy Miller, Pfefer opened an independent office to stage wrestling shows that would directly compete with Curley's. For a $5,000 deposit, paid with $4,500 in cash along with Miller's diamond ring, Miller and Pfefer were given the exclusive rights to book Londos in New York.[27] Pfefer's ultimate hope was to take over staging shows at Madison Square Garden when Curley's contract to promote wrestling there expired at the end of the year. "I did plenty for wrestling around here," Pfefer told a reporter. "Wrestling is a big enough business for more than one man to control."[28]

His day had finally come. Pfefer took to embracing the nickname "The Little Napoleon of Wrestling" and had it printed on his promotional materials.[29] On show nights, he would don a tuxedo and a black slouch hat and patrol the area around ringside holding a black ebony cane.[30] Twelve years after arriving in America at the bottom of the entertainment business, he was ready to remake himself into the king of New York wrestling. Publicly, Curley was philosophical about his former partner's career move, but privately, it could only have rankled him. "I have never broken in an assistant who did not soon feel he was too big for the job and presto, pulled the strings to get rid of me," Curley wrote. "I have long ceased blaming the individual for such action. There must be something primitive that causes such reaction."[31]

Come autumn 1933, the disorder of professional wrestling was deemed untenable. Conflict between promoters and performers, along with variable oversight by state legislatures and athletic commissions, had created a wildly disjointed state of affairs, with multiple champions and multiple business interests competing to attract an increasingly disinterested public. "The idea of having one champion in New York and another in Baltimore has not served to help the game," said Ed Contos, a promoter in Maryland who had worked with both Londos and Curley. "The time is ripe to bury the hatchet."[32]

Though wrestling remained popular, gates were suffering everywhere.[33] In New York, gross receipts were down by more than two-thirds for 1932 compared to 1930, when Jim Londos first emerged as the talk of the town.[34] Soon, stories of wrestlers being paid just $4 for an evening's work—when they were paid at all—began appearing. "If you encounter a heavy hulk of humanity on a street corner, starving, ten-to-one he's a wrestler who can't get work," wrote the *New York Daily Mirror*'s Dan Parker. "The situation is terrible and there's no hope of relief from the [National Recovery Administration.]"[35]

Meanwhile, Jack Pfefer's hopes of knocking the Curley organization from its perch atop the city's hierarchy were fading almost as quickly as they had taken shape. On a good night, with Londos in his main event, one of Pfefer's shows might bring in $3,000. On nights when Londos was not appearing, the take could be less than half that amount. Good money for some, perhaps, but for Pfefer's new partners, the numbers simply weren't big enough.

In August, Curley had been threatened with drastic action by an aggravated New York State Athletic Commission if he didn't begin working more closely with his competitors to stage higher quality shows.[36] It was all too low-rent, and the unceasing disputes and disagreements had caused enough damage. Everyone had glimpsed what kind of success was possible with the right attraction working a stable string of cities against a renewable well of opponents. Done correctly, professional wrestling could be highly profitable for everyone. Even though it would mean swallowing their pride and finding a way past the old jealousies and bruised feelings, by November 1933, the major forces in wrestling were ready to do whatever it would take to bring back the crowds.

News of a peace accord between Jack Curley, Paul Bowser, Tom Packs, Ray Fabiani, and Ed White began appearing in the New York press on December 3, 1933, four days after they signed their agreement at Manhattan's Hotel Pennsylvania. The wrestling war was officially over just in time for the 1934 season of matches to kick off.[37]

For agreeing to join the new group, the promoters secretly promised Jim Londos victories in the coming year over other prominent wrestlers, including Joe Savoldi, Jim Browning, and, most importantly for him, Strangler Lewis. To guarantee cooperation, Londos demanded and received $50,000 in cash to hold as a forfeit should he unexpectedly lose a match. What this all meant for fans was that matchups that would have been impossible before were now on the horizon. After two years of depressed returns at the ticket office, big crowds were expected to return.[38]

Not revealed in any of the coverage was that the agreement called for a ten-year profit-sharing arrangement that remade all existing contracts between individual wrestlers and promoters into the joint assets of the group. It divided the country up into formal fiefdoms: Curley and Mondt in New York, Fabiani in Philadelphia, Bowser in Boston, White in Chicago, and Packs in St. Louis. The partners agreed to focus their efforts solely on promoting wrestling, as well as to open their books to audits every two months. Performers were to be shared and resources pooled. The arrangement gave the group a near monopoly on talent and arenas that reached across the United States and into Canada. Its purpose, one wrestler later remarked, "was to control the sport of wrestling."[39] While fans were pleased, the sportswriters who had reveled in the backbiting and infighting of the past year predicted that the new agreement would ruin the drama that made wrestling such fun for them to follow. "It looks to me that with the rasslers in accord a good deal of the sport goes out of the game," wrote Paul Gallico. "The only true competition that existed was between the promoters. If they quit crossing and cheating one another, I do not know what we are going to do for pleasure."[40]

Excluded from the new deal were Jack Pfefer and Rudy Miller. They had branched out on their own just four months prior but left without access to their major stars or main venues, they were facing the prospect of being all but forced out of business. Pfefer's suspicion that things were not well had been raised over several weeks of conflicting communications with Ed White and Jim Londos. His worst fears were confirmed on the evening of December 15 in Philadelphia, when Ed White formally delivered the news that he and Miller were being cut out. Pfefer would forever remember it as the evening he was double-crossed.[41]

His anger settled most narrowly on Jim Londos, whom he blamed for his professional exile. Pfefer soon took to openly disparaging Londos in the press, and at one point circulated a story that he had died.[42] Confronting Londos at New York's Hotel St. Moritz one morning, Pfefer shouted, "I'll drink your blood, you lousy Greek bum."[43] But shouting empty threats wouldn't be enough for Jack Pfefer. He would show them, he quickly decided, that they'd picked the wrong partner to high hat. "They should squeeze me out!" he later said. "Not when I got one breath in me they should squeeze me out."[44]

FIGURE 20. Attendants wait on Lord Patrick Lansdowne Finnegan. Reproduced from the original held by the Department of Special Collections of the Hesburgh Libraries, the University of Notre Dame.

CHAPTER 19

Teaching Atheism to Babies

JACK PFEFER ONLY needed a few days to decide on his plan for re-venge. He turned to sportswriter Dan Parker, a featured columnist with William Randolph Hearst's *Daily Mirror*. Born July 1, 1893, in Waterbury, Connecticut, Parker joined the *Mirror* upon its founding in 1924. Standing 6'4" and weighing close to 240 pounds, he was often larger than the athletes he covered. His columns could be lighthearted one day and earnest the next, and he took a particular interest in root-ing out corruption and fraud in sports. His one-time coworker Damon Runyon called him "the most constantly brilliant of all sportswriters."[1] Parker begrudgingly tolerated professional wrestling and could some-times even find enjoyment in the colorful characters it produced. He was also keenly aware of the business machinations that kept the turn-stiles spinning. "I hold no brief for the wrestling racket," he once wrote. "It's phony from top to bottom."

Parker particularly delighted in using his column to guess the re-sults of wrestling shows in advance. "He must have had a pipeline into our booking office, because he kept picking the wrestling winners on the nose," wrote one New York-based wrestler. "The average wrestler didn't have to go by the office in Times Square to get the script for the evening's show. He could read it in Dan Parker's column."[2] While Parker did nurture relationships with athletes and promoters to whom he could turn for inside information, one apocryphal tale had him re-lying on a much more trustworthy source for picking his winners and losers: It was said he had found the printer responsible for making up the advertisements for wrestling shows. By taking a peek at the posters for upcoming weeks, he could suss out likely match outcomes for the current week based on who would be receiving featured billing in the shows to come.[3]

Pfefer and Parker met for a lengthy interview just days after word broke of the peace agreement between Jack Curley, Boston promoter Paul Bowser, and others. As he spoke, Pfefer unraveled what Parker described as "stories of double-crossing, title-bartering, partnerships between contestants in supposed shooting matches, and other revelations of what goes on behind the scenes."[4] Pfefer also authored three articles that ran in the *Mirror* over the last week of December 1933. "How did Jim Londos, an ordinary wrestler who has been thrown scores of times, win the world's championship?" he began. "I know how, because I was a party to the deal, and I will tell you." Pfefer revealed the $50,000 payment Londos had demanded from promoters to protect himself from double crosses, as well as the $42,000 deposit Jim Browning had posted when he won the championship from Strangler Lewis in 1933 as a guarantee he would lose it back when asked.[5] He exposed the payment made to Joe Savoldi to cross Jim Londos when the pair wrestled in Chicago in 1933. He also outlined the deal struck between promoters to split Londos's earnings among themselves when they made him the heavyweight champion back in 1930. "When another wrestling promoter is present," Pfefer later wrote, "I never take any precautions except to have the pocket containing my bankroll sewed up with strong thread."[6]

His most damaging revelation was a seemingly minor one. Pfefer claimed that even the handful of matches Jack Curley had received permission from the athletic commission to advertise as "shooting matches," those that paying audiences could assume were genuinely competitive, had all the same been plotted out in advance. It had been almost four years since the commission had declared that all wrestling bouts, with the exception of shooting matches, had to be referred to as exhibitions. That an exhibition might be prearranged was hardly news. Still, if Pfefer could prove that Curley and others had manipulated even those small number of matches they had sold to the public as legitimate, it risked presenting too serious a situation for the Commission to ignore.

Curley's initial response to the articles was to dismiss them as "sour grapes," but he issued a firmer denial two days later. "There is nothing to his squawk but a lot of lies," he wrote in a rejoinder piece published by the *Mirror*.[7] It all left the New York State Athletic Commission in an awkward spot. They had been formed with the mission of guaranteeing fair, clean sports. Curley and his partners' arrangements stood to make a mockery of their authority. Still, Curley had cultivated a close relationship with a number of elected officials. He donated thousands of dollars to depression-racked charities, most notably the Hearst Free Milk Fund for Babies, and his wrestling shows were generating much-needed tax revenue for the state.[8] It is likely that no one in a position of power was eager to see them shut down.

On January 2, 1934, at the Commission's offices at 155 Worth Street, Pfefer appeared to tell his story under oath, while an uninvited Jack Curley sat listening in from the gallery. Pfefer's testimony was powerful enough to spur the Commission to issue subpoenas for Curley, Toots Mondt, Dick Shikat, Strangler Lewis, Ed White, Jim Londos, Tom Packs, and Pfefer's partner Rudy Miller to appear for testimony the next week under the threat of being banned from future appearances in New York. "I will ruin them," Pfefer promised upon leaving.[9]

Despite blustery statements to the press from commissioners, little actual action was anticipated. Dan Parker himself admitted to finding Pfefer's revelations to be more of a compelling glimpse behind the curtain than a damning exposé. "That fellow seems to be trying to wreck the wrestling business," a confident Curley told reporters. "But he won't be able to do it. Wrestling has been the same for the last thirty years, perhaps for the last three thousand years, for all I know."[10] Pfefer himself may have had low expectations for what actions the New York Commission would ultimately take, though he must have understood that by capturing the attention of the New York press, his story would find its way to other states and cause collateral damage along the way.

On January 9, the group subpoenaed by the commission appeared to respond to Pfefer's accusations. Curley and some of the others had gathered days earlier at Boston's Hotel Manger to settle on a strategy, and for two hours, under questioning from commissioners, they repeatedly denied fixing matches and buying and selling championships. St. Louis promoter Tom Packs even responded with a pained expression when asked directly if wrestling was honest. "Of course she's on the level," he replied.

Pfefer's case was undone even further by the actions of his one-time partner, Rudy Miller, whom Pfefer had expected to corroborate his story. Unbeknownst to Pfefer, though, Miller had met with Jack Curley before the hearing and signed an affidavit denying any knowledge related to the allegations.[11] What exactly prompted Miller to abandon Pfefer is unknown, but later that same month, Miller was featuring Curley's wrestlers at his weekly shows in Brooklyn. With his star witness gone, Pfefer's case was a bust. The commission closed the hearing with a promise to keep the charges on file and issue a decision at another time.[12]

"That's that," Pfefer told reporters.[13]

The commission's formal response, issued on January 24, 1934, absolved Curley and his colleagues of any wrongdoing and promised only modest tweaks to the oversight of wrestling. "We don't allow wrestling to be called matches," Commissioner John J. Phelan said. "I don't see how any fixing can be done any more than in a vaudeville juggler's act."[14] The show was over. Pfefer had played his strongest hand against the new alliance of promoters and lost.

Later that evening in Los Angeles, a crowd of 6,000 people gathered inside the Olympic Auditorium to watch Jim Browning defend his heavyweight championship against Joe Savoldi in a match for promoter Lou Daro. If the New York Commission expected crowds to now regard wrestling as if it were a circus act or to take it as all just in good fun, the message had not yet made its way across the country. Browning and Savoldi got started late, and the pair had only wrestled for thirty-five minutes when the referee declared the match a draw, citing the state's 11:15 p.m. curfew. What started as a roar of disapproval from the audience escalated into pandemonium as Browning and Savoldi departed the ring for the dressing room. Rigged or not, attendees had paid honest money to see one man win and one man lose, and they were determined to get what they'd come for.

The crowd hurled papers, peanuts, cigars, and cigarettes into the ring before tearing down the arena's railings and drapery and ripping up entire rows of seats. Savoldi and Browning had both dressed to leave but changed back into their tights when word was received that the California Athletic Commission had hurriedly agreed to lift the curfew and allow the match to continue. The wrestlers returned to the debris-strewn mat and wrestled for another thirty minutes. When Savoldi crashed to the mat after missing a dropkick, Browning pinned him. With a winner declared, the crowd dispersed peacefully. The night was saved.[15]

"Perhaps the Los Angeles fans are confused," wrote the United Press's Henry Farrell in response to the chaotic evening. "They take their exhibitions too much to heart."[16]

With Jack Pfefer rebuked and peace restored to the business of wrestling, the work of rebuilding its following could begin in earnest. Plans were made for booking the high-profile matches between the major stars that fans across the country most wanted to see. On the edges of the industry, new stars began drawing crowds of their own by adopting characters and pushing wrestling in an all-new direction that had little to do with sport and everything to do with entertainment.

In the Midwest, an accomplished grappler from Springfield, Ohio, named Wilbur Finran, tired of working to empty houses, began calling himself Lord Patrick Lansdowne Finnegan. Once settled on the character of Lord Lansdowne, Finran himself all but evaporated.[17] He took to wearing a monocle and a scarlet-lined black satin cape. Unlike his peers, who frequently posed shirtless, Finran dressed in a tuxedo, or sometimes sandals and gladiator armor, for his publicity photos. Courting the press while never breaking character, he introduced himself to reporters as a representative of the fictional House of Barrington. He owned so many clothes, he would brag, that he never wore the same suit twice in a month.[18]

For match nights, he hired a handsomely dressed valet who would watch, stone-faced and stiff-backed, as Finran paraded about the ring, chin high, nose in the air, monocle in his eye. If a mat was deemed too filthy, he would demand it be disinfected with a prop spray gun. If he decided he wasn't quite ready to begin wrestling, he would make his opponent and the audience wait while he performed his warm-ups.[19] "Lansdowne had the people booing him before he even got in the ring," remembered wrestler Frankie Cain, who saw Finran perform. "He had that excitement." [20] Finran relocated to Los Angeles, briefly, but mostly stayed close to Ohio. He retired from performing for good in 1950, and never discussed the inspiration for Lord Lansdowne. He was diagnosed with amyotrophic lateral sclerosis soon after and died at his home in Columbus on November 29, 1959, at the age of fifty-four, after a long illness. The character he created and the class tension he knowingly exploited would be copied and riffed on by countless wrestlers for decades to come.

Another influential wrestler out of Ohio was Julius Woronick, who dressed in matching fire-red boots, shirt, tights, and cape to become the Great Mephisto. He mesmerized spectators, moving with the finesse of a ballet dancer. Some who saw him judged him to be the finest in-ring performer of the twentieth century. He'd been raised in flames. As a child, Woronick claimed that his parents had put him to work in a circus where he was dressed in an asbestos-lined suit, doused with gasoline, and lit ablaze before diving from a fifty-foot-high platform into a pool of water. A severe alcoholic, he died in 1968 at the age of fifty-seven.[21]

The most successful of this new wave of showmen was a wrestler named Man Mountain Dean. Born Frank Leavitt in the Hell's Kitchen neighborhood of New York in 1891, he was a journeyman performer for much of his career. An injury had almost forced him to retire in the 1920s, but at the encouragement of his wife, he grew out his beard, declared himself to be a hillbilly from Georgia, adopted his new ring name, and returned to work. After working on the East Coast for Jack Curley and Paul Bowser in the spring of 1934, Dean moved to Los Angeles. Appearing weekly at The Olympic for Lou Daro, he became an immediate sensation.

In matches that lasted just a few minutes, he leapt onto prone opponents, seeming to crush them under his 300-pound frame. In August 1934, only weeks after his arrival on the West Coast, 7,000 people were said to have been turned away from one of his sell-out appearances.[22] In October, at the age of forty-three, after struggling through an almost thirty-year career full of low-paying matches, Dean wrestled in the biggest event of his life against Jim Londos in front of 23,000 people at Los Angeles's Wrigley Field. "When I was a fine wrestler, I almost starved to death," he told an Associated Press reporter. "Then I lost my holds, grew whiskers, and look at me today."[23]

Publicly, Dean boasted of out-earning Jack Dempsey and Babe Ruth; privately, he complained of low paydays and failing health, in particular leg ulcers that left him confined to bed for weeks at a time. Dean retired for good in the late 1930s, turned to acting in film, and tried unsuccessfully to begin a career in politics. In his early fifties, he enlisted in the Army at the outbreak of World War II and went to work training recruits at Maryland's Camp Ritchie. He died unexpectedly from a suspected heart attack on May 29, 1953, while working in his yard in Norcross, Georgia.[24] In tribute to his distinguished military career in both World Wars, he was buried with full military rites in the Marietta National Cemetery. "I am done with the game I gave nearly thirty years to," he'd written to Jack Pfefer in 1938, just after his retirement. "Bad eyes, broken legs and bones; that and a few bucks is all one makes out of it. It's also true I made some, but the big shots made twice as much out of me."[25]

On April 22, 1934, an odd mix of five hundred athletes, artists, writers, and politicians gathered in the Grand Ballroom of New York's Hotel Astor. Under the gold and ivory domed ceiling, Jim Londos and Strangler Lewis shared the dais with Yankees owner Jacob Ruppert, New Jersey Senator Emerson Richards, and Postmaster General of the United States James Farley. The occasion was a celebration of Jack Curley's forty years in sports. When Curley's turn to speak came, however, he was overcome with emotion, leaving the podium with nothing more than a "Thank you." He'd planned to acknowledge more than a dozen fellow wrestling promoters. He'd written in his prepared remarks that each "deserve more credit than I for the tremendous strides which wrestling has taken in the past ten years." He told his friend Nat Fleischer afterwards, "I'd had a good speech prepared and rehearsed. I just couldn't remember anything I wanted to say. Too excited. Too thrilled by the wonderful testimonial of my friends."[26]

Counted among those friends was Toots Mondt, whose role in the Curley organization had continued to expand. Mondt knew wrestling inside and out, but unlike Curley—unlike almost all the other promoters he did business with—Mondt had actually been a wrestler. He'd worked sideshows and circus tents and scrapped with farmers and factory workers at all-comer shows. He knew what it meant to sacrifice your body to make a living, to rub your skin raw on a germ-infested canvas for almost no pay. He'd dealt with crooked promoters and double-dealing managers. He preferred his current view just fine, and he wasn't going back.

In June, Curley invited Mondt to speak at a party he'd organized at a golf club just outside of Great Neck. For the occasion, Mondt pulled out a story he liked to tell about a washed-up wrestler reduced to impersonating a gorilla for $3 a day at the city zoo. "The wrestler jumped at the chance and did a good job of impersonating the gorilla," he joked, "but a tiger, pacing up and down in an adjoining cage, got on his nerves." Weighing his options, the wrestler decides to try to kill it. "He watched his chance," Mondt continued, "opened the cage door quietly, sneaked up on the tiger, and parked a haymaker on its nose. 'Hey, you so-and-so!' yelled the tiger, which happened to be a phony. 'Lay off that stuff! You ain't the only broken-down wrestler working in this zoo!'"[27]

Jim Londos would be damned if he were going to end up a broken-down old wrestler scrounging for work. He'd be damned, in fact, if he'd end up a broken-down old wrestler at all. He was buying up land in Southern California that he dreamed of turning into a working farm. He had sailed home to his native Greece and performed for a crowd of more than 80,000 people at Athens's two-thousand-year-old Panathenaic Stadium on October 22, 1933. He'd taken on the most powerful businessmen in wrestling and all but bent them to his will. An undersized, unheralded Greek immigrant had become more famous and performed in front of more people in more countries than even the great Frank Gotch. Londos had gone from sleeping on floors and struggling to survive in his new homeland to representing the kind of outrageous success that America stood to offer.

If fans had been dismayed by Jack Pfefer's revelations about Londos and the integrity of his matches, they didn't show it. "Whatever wrestling may or may not be today," wrote John Wray, sports editor for the *St. Louis Post-Dispatch*, "it is what the public asked for."[28] With the chaos of the wrestling war over, people were again eager to see Londos in matchups they had long assumed would never happen. In early 1934 alone, 15,000 watched him defeat Gus Sonnenberg in St. Louis; 20,000 saw him avenge himself on Joe Savoldi in Chicago; and a total of 32,000 turned out for two Londos matches in Detroit against former great Joe Stecher.[29] "I know you newspaper men and thousands of others think professional wrestling is phony, but it isn't as phony as you believe," Jack Curley had told a room full of sportswriters that January. "The best man always wins, so what's phony about that? . . . You boys can flay and kid the wrestlers all you want, but that won't stop the public from turning out to see them because they give the spectators action and thrills."[30]

Londos's victory tour continued with a win over Jim Browning before a New York crowd of 25,000 on June 25, 1934. That win reduced the number of heavyweight championship claims in the new organization from three to two: Londos and the Paul Bowser-affiliated wrestler Ed Don George. George's championship claim, however, came with complications. The claim Londos won from Browning had been pulled from thin air after he and Jack Curley had initially split in 1932. Bowser, however, had originally purchased George's claim from Strangler Lewis and Billy Sandow for $100,000 back in 1929. It had first gone to Gus Sonnenberg, who then passed it to George. Convincing Bowser to liquidate it would not be easy. Londos and George drew a crowd of 30,000 people to Fenway Park for their first match, which ended without a clear winner at 2:30 in the morning. Its lack of resolution was a signal that no one was ready to fully settle on a single champion quite yet. Londos and George met again two weeks later in Buffalo with a similarly unsatisfying outcome.

The victory Londos most wanted, anyway, wasn't over Ed Don George but over his old rival Strangler Lewis. Lewis was not only considered a superior wrestler to Londos but had a significant size advantage. He had never lost to Londos in any of their previous matches—a fact he loved to remind people of—and Londos was said to have explicitly included a victory over Lewis as part of his agreement to work with Curley and his partners once again. On September 20, 1934, at Wrigley Field in Chicago, Londos would get the win that he'd been wanting for years.[31]

Despite ominous clouds and a forecast of rain, thousands gathered hours prior to the start of the match. Another 10,000 fans who had waited to buy tickets threatened to push through the park's admission gates close to match time.[32] The *Chicago Tribune* had featured articles on Londos and Lewis daily in the three weeks preceding the match, and both men had appeared at the offices of the Illinois Athletic Commission to sign affidavits guaranteeing they would wrestle honestly.[33]

Chicago was an important city for promoters, and Illinois commissioners were notoriously tough on professional wrestling, having already proven that they would cancel shows or suspend wrestling altogether for periods of time if they felt that paying audiences had been hoodwinked by a dishonest match. This put Lewis and Londos in a delicate spot and made it all the more critical that they put on a convincing show.[34] Accordingly, their match was slow-moving, and free of the pratfalls, grimacing, and violent action that had come to define the modern era. There were no dropkicks, airplane spins, or desperate pleas to the audience. Both men wrestled barefoot, as if they were nodding to some ancient time. It was near a full twenty minutes before either was even taken down to the mat. After forty minutes, in an attempt to break out of Lewis's headlock, Londos grabbed onto Lewis's left leg and lifted it off the mat. Both men tumbled through the ring ropes, almost taking the referee with them. After they reentered the ring, Londos picked Lewis up off of his feet again, and, holding the giant Strangler in his arms, fell forward. Lewis landed hard on his left side. Londos knit his arms under Lewis's shoulders and neck and rolled him flat against the mat. Londos pushed himself onto the balls of his feet for leverage, and at forty-nine minutes and twenty-seven seconds, the referee slapped him on the shoulders, declaring him the winner.[35]

It was a clean pin, dead in the middle of the ring. There was no controversy and no excuses offered. The match may not have been terribly exciting, but the outcome could not have been clearer. Jim Londos was on top of the wrestling world, and not even the once-great Strangler Lewis could knock him down. "What [the audience] saw," wrote the reporter from *Time* on hand to cover the match, "was a bout which upheld the tradition that, in wrestling, excitement decreases in direct ratio to the honesty of the contestants."[36]

The evening's final tally of 35,265 attendees set a new record for the largest crowd to ever to watch a professional wrestling match in America.[37] From his ringside seat, Jack Curley's mind must have drifted back to twenty-three years earlier. The 1911 match he'd put on in the same city between Frank Gotch and George Hackenschmidt had held wrestling's previous attendance record. After that contest ended, Curley had all but been chased out of town for trying to put one over on a paying audience. Now, everything was different.

Whether the audience had changed professional wrestling or professional wrestling had changed the audience, no one could say for sure. "The majority of those who go to see the big bouts take their seats cynically and leave cynically—but while they are in their seats they have the time of their lives," wrote the *Washington Post*'s William Gilman.[38] The topic of just what it was that all those people who paid all that money to watch the matches really wanted was very much on the mind of writer Alva Johnston when he sat down for a lengthy interview with Jack Curley that would run as a three-part profile in the *New Yorker* titled "Cauliflowers and Pachyderms." Johnston had won a Pulitzer Prize in 1922 for his work covering the American Association for the

Advancement of Science in the *New York Times* and had profiled Albert Einstein in 1933. [39] He held a place in his heart, as well, for the colorful personalities responsible for building America's growing sports and entertainment industrial complex. Far from seeing Curley as ridiculous, Johnston was fascinated by him.

Over the length of the interview, Curley unspooled the story of his life, from growing up in Alsace to stealing his way out of San Francisco to see the World's Fair, to Havana with Jack Johnson and Jess Willard, and finally to New York, where he ruled over the much-derided world of professional wrestling. To Johnston, Jack Curley was something of a recognized authority on successfully fooling the public, even if it may not have been his intention. Unlike P. T. Barnum, whose curiosities and oddities had preyed on a previous generation's credulity, Johnston saw Curley as profiting from a new generation's skepticism. "There is a common belief that wrestling matches are fixed," Johnston wrote. "This adds greatly to the interest and partly accounts for the popularity of the sport. Betting men enjoy the added element of uncertainty; cynics appreciate the ugly rumors. . . . The subject of fixing is always interesting; the question is not only whether a match has been fixed but whether it has been fixed securely, and whether somebody may not come along at the last minute and fix it the other way. Then, too, running like an unknown X through all calculations is the possibility that the thing may be on the level."[40]

Unlike his contemporaries in other sports, if an event carried Jack Curley's name, the question of its honesty always seemed to be an open one. The shows that had brought him the most fame were openly suspected of having been rigged, accusations he had flatly denied. Even when questioned under oath in a New York courtroom about the honesty of his promotions, he responded that every event he'd ever had a hand in had been honest—"and that will cover it all."[41] Still, no one listened. "Curley has no complaint against the cynicism of his patrons," Johnston wrote. "It would be blasphemy, it would be like teaching atheism to babies, to attempt to strip wrestling fans of their simple faith that all bouts are prearranged."[42]

FIGURE 21. Dick Shikat tortures Danno O'Mahony, New York, New York, March 2, 1936. Courtesy of Steve Yohe.

CHAPTER 20

The Upset of the Century

IT WAS DECEMBER 1934, when Danno O'Mahony, twenty-two, fresh-faced and strong, stepped off the *SS Bremen* and onto American soil for the first time. His life had been turned upside down twice in the previous two years—first, by the death of his mother and then by an offer from Paul Bowser to leave Ireland and become a professional wrestler. It didn't matter to Bowser that O'Mahony had little real wrestling experience. Bowser would see to it that he would be trained by the best. If all went as Bowser hoped it would, he'd have O'Mahony working in rings all over the United States throughout 1935. It was an offer that would have been hard to refuse. By accepting it, O'Mahony unknowingly kicked off a chain of events that changed professional wrestling forever.

Danno O'Mahony was born on September 29, 1912, near Ballydehob, a small coastal village in Cork, Ireland. In 1933, he joined the Irish army, where his skill at the hammer throw brought him to the attention of Patrick O'Callaghan, Ireland's two-time Olympic gold medalist in the sport. O'Callaghan had become a national hero after the 1928 Games, where he'd been the first Irish athlete to accept a medal under the country's new tricolor flag. O'Callaghan recommended O'Mahony to one of Paul Bowser's talent scouts. Boston's large Irish population hadn't had a sports champion they could take to heart since John L. Sullivan had ruled boxing fifty years earlier. Bowser was hopeful that a new recruit, this time in professional wrestling, could capture the town's imagination and rebuild his sagging attendance numbers. Danno O'Mahony would be his man.[1]

O'Mahony was tall and powerful but struggled in his training matches. "I felt him out, took him down, stuck on a hammerlock and crotch hold and rolled him over. It was easy," remembered Charles Smith, who wrestled an early match with O'Mahony in London.[2] "I expected to see a Hercules," said Strangler Lewis of his first meeting with O'Mahony, "but when this fellow slouched into the ring and onto the mat, I was afraid to clamp a hold on to him for fear every bone in his body would break."[3]

Despite O'Mahony's inexperience, three weeks after his arrival in America, Bowser slotted him into the main event for a show at the Boston Garden on January 4, 1935. Bowser hired a group of musicians to play a medley of Irish tunes and outfitted O'Mahony in green trunks, a plush green robe with "Ireland" stitched across the back, and a pair of green socks that showed above his ring shoes. When O'Mahony stepped out of the dressing room, he was met with a rousing reception from the 14,000 fans who had stayed late on a Saturday evening to witness his American debut. He did not disappoint. He beat his opponent, a wild and unpredictable wrestler named Ernie Dusek, in thirty minutes. Two weeks later, an even larger crowd poured into the Garden to see O'Mahony defeat Ernie's brother, Rudy. A month later, O'Mahony had yet another win in front of yet another full house. He was making it all look rather easy.

To solidify his standing among locals, O'Mahony made the rounds of Boston's Irish athletic clubs and men's organizations, while Bowser's press agents went to work building his reputation nationally. In short order, O'Mahony gained more than fifty consecutive wins, including ones over prominent names like Gus Sonnenberg, Ray Steele, Henri DeGlane, and Man Mountain Dean. Bowser booked him into all of the major wrestling markets from New York to California. In a show of the collegial spirit now prevailing among promoters, Jack Curley went on the record calling O'Mahony a greater natural wrestler than even the legendary Joe Stecher.[4]

O'Mahony's rapid ascent through the wrestling ranks in 1935 tracked closely to developments in boxing, in which a seemingly unexceptional Irish fighter from North Bergen, New Jersey, named James Braddock, had ridden a series of underdog wins to a bout with the reigning heavyweight champion, Max Baer. Braddock had initially failed to connect with fans and was considered by many to be too old to have a serious chance of defeating Baer. This all changed when newspaper writers took hold of Braddock's hard-luck story of having lost it all in the Great Depression. Writers detailed how he'd been on relief and how he struggled to support a wife and three children while simultaneously rebuilding his boxing career against opponents who were younger, stronger, and faster. The stories rallied the public to his side. The *Daily News'* Jack Miley called him "an underdog of underdogs." Damon Runyon christened him the "Cinderella Man." On June 13, 1935, Braddock defeated Baer in one of boxing's most unexpected and welcomed upsets to become heavyweight champion.[5]

Braddock was a sports hero perfectly pitched for his time, and his success, almost too great to believe, was cheered by millions. Danno O'Mahony, foreign-born and working in an industry that had been laid bare by years of revelations about backroom deals between conniving promoters, was met with an entirely different level of scrutiny. It didn't stop crowds from flocking to his matches.

On June 27, 1935, exactly two weeks after James Braddock had capped his own impossible ascent, O'Mahony defeated Jim Londos at Fenway Park in front of 25,000 people. It was Londos's first clean loss since the 1920s, and it gave O'Mahony a right to one of professional wrestling's two heavyweight championships. Londos graciously accepted his defeat and offered no excuses. Behind the scenes, he was said to have collected the $50,000 promised to him for turning over his title before leaving the country for an extended European vacation. "[O'Mahony] beat Londos, and there's no doubt he believed he had done so fair and square," said Charles Smith, O'Mahony's training partner from London. "There is also every reason to believe he thought he could do the same to anyone. Danno was a decent kid and it never occurred to him at the time that he was anything but a first class matman."[6]

Four weeks later, on July 31, O'Mahony was matched against Ed Don George at Braves Field in Boston. The winner was to be named wrestling's first unified heavyweight champion in more than a decade. Paul Bowser poured his resources into making sure the match would be a success, going as far as to hire James Braddock himself, at the peak of his boxing fame, to referee. Interest in the match was so high that two hours before the main event was to begin, the flow of cars traveling to Braves Field through Kenmore Square grew so heavy that it came to a dead stop. With traffic stalled, thousands of motorists abandoned their cars and walked the final mile for fear of missing the bout. For the remainder of the evening, Commonwealth Avenue and its side streets were jammed with empty cars, people having parked on lawns and in front of hydrants, shops, and garages.[7]

The O'Mahony–George match got underway just after 10 p.m., and it was a thriller. O'Mahony was met with a howl from the packed stadium, photographers crowding into the ring to take his picture.[8] It ended after ninety minutes, with O'Mahony tossing George out of the ring and being declared the new undisputed champion. Afterwards, it took almost a hundred police officers—with dozens having been hastily mobilized during the match—to untangle the mess of cars that resulted from some 20,000 drivers trying to leave the stadium all at once. It was close to 2 a.m. before traffic flowed normally again.[9] The final attendance of close to 40,000 people—bigger than the crowd that had seen James Braddock defeat Max Baer—was even larger than Paul Bowser could have hoped for.[10]

Danno O'Mahony had become an unqualified sensation. He celebrated his twenty-third birthday that September on a train speeding toward Canada. "I could be drunk every day and every night at no expense to myself with the friends I've made," O'Mahony told one reporter. "I win every time out, and I've never been asked to lay down."[11] He'd been in America fewer than twelve months and had already achieved a kind of success he couldn't have imagined possible back in tiny Ballydehob. It was a fast-moving roller coaster he'd strapped himself to, with Bowser putting him to work everywhere he could. In photos from the time, O'Mahony alternates between looking overjoyed by his sudden fame, an impossibly broad smile pasted to his face, and appearing positively shell-shocked, his eyes wide as if he's nearing panic.

Animosity from fellow wrestlers toward O'Mahony began building as it became clear just how much promoters were favoring him over other talent. Despite his height and smooth muscles, O'Mahony often looked unconvincing next to more seasoned and grizzled opponents. His soft skin and lean body just didn't make sense after a hard-driving dynamo like Gus Sonnenberg or the physical genius of Jim Londos. "He isn't strong," wrote Henry McLemore of the United Press. "His arms and chest and legs are those of a youngster who is still years shy of development."[12]

For some of his opponents, O'Mahony's success was nothing less than an insult, and they took any chance they could find to try to make him look weak. During a match in New York, after O'Mahony accidentally bloodied Dick Shikat's nose with an errant elbow to the face, Shikat strangled and kicked him before finally kneeing him in the groin. In Philadelphia, a riot ensued when O'Mahony's match with a wrestler named Sergei Kalmikoff ended after just three minutes. As chaos broke out around the arena, Kalmikoff straddled a prone O'Mahony and punched him wildly. In Holyoke, Massachusetts, O'Mahony was said to have been carried unconscious from the ring after a bout with a wrestler named Yvon Robert.[13]

His most disastrous run-ins, however, occurred during a four-night swing through Texas and Louisiana in February 1936. In cities across Texas, promoters who operated largely independent of the East Coast alliance staged a rawer, more violent style of action. O'Mahony was ill-prepared for it, narrowly surviving matches in Shreveport and Houston, during which opponents aggressively attacked him. By the time he reached Galveston on February 9, 1936, O'Mahony and his manager, Jack McGrath, had had enough. When they learned that O'Mahony's opponent for the evening, a wrestler named Juan Humberto, intended to deviate from plans and take O'Mahony's championship, they decided to leave the arena before the match could begin.[14]

O'Mahony was working at a pace that killed, but Paul Bowser was intent on keeping his young champion's calendar full. During one particularly brutal stretch that February, O'Mahony worked ten straight one-nighters, facing a different opponent in a different city each night in a run of more than 5,000 miles. Just as that grueling tour ended, a new one was scheduled to kick off at the beginning of March. He'd seen more of the country than most Americans ever would. Success had come at him like a rushing wall of water. How much longer he could keep himself from being pulled under it was anyone's guess.

Danno O'Mahony arrived in Manhattan on the morning of Monday, March 2, 1936. It was the beginning of another four-night slate of matches, and he was due later that day at Madison Square Garden, where Jack Curley had him booked in the evening's main event. It would be O'Mahony's tenth match in New York since arriving in America thirteen months prior.

O'Mahony's opponent for the evening was the one-time heavyweight champion Dick Shikat. Since his title run ended in 1930 after his loss to Jim Londos, Shikat had worked himself into an awkward position. His relationship with promoters in the East had soured several years back over their broken promises to one day make him their heavyweight champion for a second time. The honor, instead, had gone to Strangler Lewis, then to Jim Browning, then back to Jim Londos, and finally to

O'Mahony. Shikat was thirty-nine and now much too old to be chosen. On top of it all, he had had a falling out with his manager, Toots Mondt, who was said to owe him $15,000. The dispute had culminated in a spectacular fistfight between the two in a New York hotel room in December 1933, which Mondt was said to have won.[15]

To help calm the situation, Paul Bowser had acquired Shikat's contract and made a promise to repay the money Mondt owed him, which Bowser had so far failed to do. In a move meant to obscure Bowser's managerial relationship with Shikat, should the contract ever be made public, Bowser had listed an employee named Joe Alvarez as Shikat's manager on the paperwork, instead of himself. It "would not look right to the patrons of the wrestling game" for Bowser to be managing wrestlers who were matched against each other, Shikat remembered being told.[16] It was all a complicated bit of contractual smoke and mirrors which, according to Shikat, was now standard operating procedure in wrestling.

On the evening of March 2, 1936, as Shikat would later recount, he was waiting in his dressing room for his match with O'Mahony to begin when Jack Curley, accompanied by the wrestler Rudy Dusek, came to talk with him. They told Shikat that he was to wrestle with O'Mahony for forty-five or fifty minutes and then he was to "lay down."[17] The visit made the point all too clear. When Shikat climbed into the ring in front of 8,000 people, it wouldn't be as a serious contender. It would be as an over-the-hill wrestler with a diminishing set of options.

At ringside, sportswriter Dan Parker took his seat. Looking around, what most caught his attention were the cameras. There was one there from every major newsreel company, he noticed—an unusual sight for a typical night of wrestling. If this had been a heavyweight championship title defense in boxing, the cameras wouldn't have seemed odd at all. But in wrestling, the champion defended his title almost every other night. Only the noteworthy matches that had benefitted from months of advance press tended to be filmed. "Usually, the newsreels pass up the burpers," Parker later wrote, "except for freak shots."[18] They'd been invited to attend this evening's match, he would later learn, on a tip that something significant might take place.

The Shikat–O'Mahony match commenced at 9:29 p.m. The first fifteen minutes were tame. "[It was] one of the crudest, dullest matches ever offered," Parker remarked. Then, things shifted. Shikat began to tear violently into O'Mahony, wrapping his arm around O'Mahony's head and heaving him over his hips and down to the mat. He grabbed onto O'Mahony's arm before suddenly thinking the better of it and deciding to let it go. After both men got back to their feet, Shikat took O'Mahony down again, this time applying a series of toe holds before grabbing O'Mahony's left wrist with both hands and bending it behind his back. O'Mahony, overcome with pain, buried his face in the mat. Shikat then rolled O'Mahony onto his back, trapping his right arm underneath him and locking it into a hammerlock. Hammerlocks hyperextend the arm, pulling it away from the body in a direction where there's no range of motion. They aren't terribly exciting to look at, but when applied correctly by an experienced hand like Shikat, they are cruelly effective. The Madison Square Garden crowd snapped to attention. They'd sat through countless matches full of theatrical ache and agony, but they sensed instinctively that something different was happening now. Professional wrestling, the contrived, mindless sideshow of sports, had become suddenly, unbearably real.[19]

According to Parker, O'Mahony said something to Shikat which sounded like a plea for him to take it easy.[20] Shikat answered by threatening instead to break O'Mahony's arm if he didn't submit. Parker remembered hearing O'Mahony crying out to have the match stopped, "before he kills me dead."[21] "He's killing me. Stop him, stop him," another wrestler remembered hearing O'Mahony shout.[22] After just under nineteen minutes of wrestling, the referee called the match. With O'Mahony lying there, collapsed in the center of the ring, Dick Shikat was declared the new heavyweight champion of professional wrestling. "Make no mistake about that boy," Shikat told a *New York Times* reporter back in his dressing room after the match, "he's a pretty good wrestler."[23]

The result caught the audience off guard. A stunned Dan Parker turned in his seat to Jack Curley, looking to get an immediate reaction to the unexpected outcome. If Curley was surprised by Shikat's actions, he didn't make it apparent. Knowing that his response would undoubtedly wind up in Parker's column the next day, Curley responded evenly, calling it "the upset of the century."[24]

O'Mahony's loss was front-page news in Boston, and Paul Bowser went to work immediately to contain the fallout. O'Mahony was ill and overworked, Bowser told reporters, and had simply come apart during the match.[25] O'Mahony stated that he had never actually submitted. Jack McGrath, his manager, declared the referee's decision to end the bout "a raw deal." McGrath told *Boston Globe* reporter Hy Hurwitz, "They couldn't beat him any other way, so they stole the title." "Just who the 'they' McGrath referred to," wrote Hurwitz of the conversation, "was not explained."[26]

Dick Shikat went to Jack Curley's office the day after the match to discuss the outcome with Curley, Paul Bowser, and Ray Fabiani. Having just crossed the most powerful men in professional wrestling, he could hardly have known what to expect. They offered to return any money owed to Shikat as well as pay him an additional $25,000 if he would return the title. They gave Shikat the choice of either losing it back to O'Mahony or losing it to another wrestler of their choosing.[27] Shikat declined, and instead declared the title for sale to the highest bidder. "My title is on the auction block," he told them. "I'm going to get as much for it as possible."[28]

"How sharper than a serpent's tooth it is, to have a thankless wrestler," Curley later said of Shikat's actions. "I feel terrible about it. I would like to see Dick Shikat stand up and look me in the eyes and say I ever told him to lay down. He couldn't do it. His heart ain't as black as all that."[29]

The highest offer for Shikat's services came out of Columbus, Ohio, from a promoter named Al Haft. Haft had been working in professional wrestling since around 1910, first as a wrestler and later by organizing cards around the Midwest. As a competitor, he was talented and well-trained enough to be hired as the first-ever wrestling coach at The Ohio State University in 1921. As a businessman, he would later become a pioneer in television by broadcasting his shows weekly on Cincinnati's Crosley Broadcasting Corporation.

Haft was at the center of a new partnership between Jack Curley's former partner Jack Pfefer, Strangler Lewis's former manager Billy Sandow, and a young Detroit-based promoter named Adam Weismuller, which was competing directly with Curley's group in several markets. Haft's philosophy of the wrestling business was simple: "Build men whom you can control and who are with you," he'd told Pfefer. "Whenever you put key men over whom you can't control, then they give you orders and that makes life miserable."[30] Taking ownership of Shikat's heavyweight championship would not only strike a direct hit against Curley and his partners, but it would also bolster the standing of Haft's group in the numerous states where athletic commissions recognized Shikat's new title claim.

Shikat accepted Haft's offer of $50,000, as well as enough bookings in the group's cities to keep him busy into the summer. Haft's group also began raiding Curley's employees, hiring away anyone they could. "Now is the time to hit as hard as possible," Haft wrote to Pfefer in April.[31] "Even if they die," Pfefer responded, "they will not win this battle with me."[32]

To block Shikat from going to work for their competition, Curley and his associates used the contract Shikat had signed with Paul Bowser as the basis for booking him into matches in Illinois, Pennsylvania, and Missouri—bookings they knew Shikat would never honor. It was a cunning countermove intended to provoke those states' commissions into suspending Shikat when he failed to appear. A suspension in any of those three states would lead, in turn, to reciprocal suspensions in many others. Shikat responded by telling reporters that in the two years since he'd signed the contract with Bowser, his affairs had been handled, instead, exclusively by Curley's New York office. The contract with Bowser, he said, was a sham. Nonetheless, the existence of the paperwork on file with athletic commissions around the country led to the outcome that Curley's group had hoped for. By the end of March, Shikat had been suspended from wrestling in almost thirty states.

In a race to keep Shikat from dropping his championship claim to another of Haft's wrestlers in one of the few states where he was still allowed to work, Curley's group filed formal charges against Shikat for breach of contract in April. A restraining order was issued on April 16, 1937, that prevented Shikat from wrestling anywhere at all. The resulting trial, formally named "Joe Alvarez vs. Richard Shikat and Al Haft," became national news. Professional wrestling, a sport long shrouded in secrecy, was going to open its books up in federal court. Some observers wondered whether it would survive the scrutiny.

FIGURE 22. Promotional poster for Ali Baba. Reproduced from the original held by the Department of Special Collections of the Hesburgh Libraries, the University of Notre Dame.

CHAPTER 21

The Game Is on the Level

ON THURSDAY, APRIL 23, 1936, Jack Curley sat in the witness box of a federal courthouse in Columbus, Ohio, for more than five hours in front of an overflowing room, answering hard questions about the integrity of his life's work. Yes, he was part of an arrangement with five other promoters to share profits and fend off competition, but no, that arrangement did not constitute a trust. "I'd like to get in a trust," Curley joked. "I've been in the promotion business forty years, and I'm still hustling for a living. A fellow could do better than that in a trust."[1] He denied, as well, instructing Dick Shikat to lose in his match with Danno O'Mahony. His most headline-grabbing statement, though, was one he'd made before. "I never even heard of a wrestling match being fixed," Curley testified. "The game is on the level."[2] Dan Parker followed the trial more closely than any other reporter. Curley's testimony left him befuddled. "It only goes to prove that a boss often doesn't know what is going on in his own organization," Parker wrote. "Or does it? Anyway, it must prove something."[3]

Curley's testimony didn't prove anything. In it, he directly contradicted most of the accusations laid out by Shikat's defense team, which only added to the surreal silliness of the trial. Perhaps it had all been one flat-out, well-rehearsed lie after another delivered by Curley to protect the sport he held so dear. It is also possible that Curley's testimony was the truth. Perhaps he really had never used his substantial influence to guide the outcome of a professional wrestling match. Or maybe his story was just true enough that he could offer it up under oath—true because after decades of experience with sports, entertainment, and politics, he still believed that no matter how hard you tried, you couldn't guarantee the outcome of even a high school Christmas pageant.

Immediately following Curley's testimony, Judge Mell Underwood dissolved the restraining order on Shikat, allowing him to return to wrestling. Shikat left the courthouse in Columbus that day and caught a late flight to Detroit, where promoter Adam Weismuller had scheduled him to appear the next evening. "What are we left with if Shikat is thrown tonight or suffers some injury?" complained the attorney for Joe Alvarez and Paul Bowser in a failed final attempt to keep the restraining order in place.[4]

Shikat's opponent in Detroit was a wrestler named Ali Baba. Baba was, in reality, Harry Ekizian, a former US naval officer born in the port city of Samsun in the Ottoman Empire in 1901. As a teenager, he had lost both his parents and two siblings during the Armenian Genocide. In 1932, after several years of naval service, he relocated to Los Angeles, where he worked in film and as an auto mechanic before turning to professional wrestling.[5] He tried a variety of gimmicks before settling on the character of Ali Baba. To become Ali Baba, Ekizian shaved his head and grew a horseshoe mustache that he twisted to fine points. He posed for photographs wearing a maroon fez and, once in the ring, wrestled barefoot. Some Detroit writers even took to calling him "The Terrible Turk," an invocation, whether they knew it or not, of Yusuf İsmail, who had unintentionally originated the character fifty years earlier and then drowned before he could return home and leave the wrestling business in America behind him.[6]

When Ali Baba climbed into the ring on April 24, 1936, to face Shikat in front of 8,000 spectators at Detroit's Olympia Hall, the cynics of the bunch had little doubt who would leave as champion. Shikat, they reasoned, would take any chance he could find to rid himself of his now burdensome championship. It was hardly a surprise to them, then, when Baba slammed Shikat to the mat after forty-six minutes and pinned him to become the new heavyweight champion. The more credulous of the crowd, though, were convinced they'd witnessed a Detroit miracle. "They can't fix Ali Baba," said one fan sitting ringside. "He doesn't understand the language."[7]

Shikat spent the night at Detroit's Receiving Hospital complaining of an injured pelvis. By Monday morning, he was back in Columbus to appear for trial, bruised, walking with crutches, and promising to give testimony that would turn professional wrestling inside out. "The testimony given so far by the plaintiff's witnesses stinks," his counsel said, "but a story that rings true will be told when we put Shikat on the stand."[8]

Shikat never got the chance to tell his story. Now worthless to Curley and his partners, they immediately moved to drop the charges against him. Shikat's exposé would ultimately be limited to a 3,000-word deposition that contained a minimum of fireworks, but that was all the more revealing in how it made plain just how casually and completely wrestlers and matches were manipulated.[9]

Freed of his troublesome championship and with the case against him wrapping up, Dick Shikat's worries should have been over. Instead, his problems were only beginning. His loss to Ali Baba in Detroit was declared invalid by the influential New York State Athletic Commission based on an almost parodic line of thinking: Since the Detroit match had been deemed an exhibition according to the Michigan commission, the New York commission, which only two years earlier had equated wrestling matches with acrobatic acts, could not recognize Ali Baba as the new champion.[10] For him to claim the championship in New York, they announced, he would need to beat Shikat in the state, under their rules. The decision forced Shikat to leave Columbus and to wrestle with Ali Baba again, this time for a nearly empty house at Madison Square Garden on May 5, 1936. It was Jack Pfefer's inaugural promotion at the Garden, a night he'd been dreaming of for years. He'd built bridges and burned them down, been crossed by his partners and crossed them in spades, all to get to this evening, and just 4,000 people bothered to show up.

Shikat lost in just less than fifty-four minutes, a formality of a match that was convincing enough for the New York Commission to recognize Ali Baba as the new champion.[11] Later that evening, back at his hotel, Shikat received the news that his wife of nine years, Erika, had been involved in a horrific single-car accident three miles east of Columbus earlier that day. She had been traveling to promoter Al Haft's home in Reynoldsburg along National Road when her car's engine caught fire. In a panic, she swerved and struck a curb, sending her car skidding and rolling for 150 feet. She suffered heavy burns on her face and body and was taken to Columbus's St. Francis Hospital in critical condition.[12]

Shikat returned to Columbus. A week later, on May 12, 1936, with his wife lying in critical condition just one mile away, he sat alone in a courtroom listening as the federal case against him was formally brought to an end. He left the courtroom immediately to return to the hospital.[13] Erika Shikat passed away two days later from her injuries. A grief-stricken Shikat took her remains to Dresden, Germany, to lay them to rest.

Ed Contos, the promoter responsible for organizing matches in Baltimore, Maryland, liked to think that working in the wrestling business had taught him something about how the public thinks. He had a story, for example, that he liked to use to demonstrate the incredulity of the modern wrestling fan. On June 25, 1936, Contos had traveled to Washington, D.C., to take in a night of matches at Griffith Stadium, the 27,000-seat baseball park that had hosted ceremonial first pitches from every president since William Taft. The first match that evening, the "curtain raiser," as it was known to promoters, was a throwaway match between two tough forty-something veterans named Mike Romano and Jack Donovan. After about thirteen minutes, Donovan threw Romano down with a headspin. With the fans shouting, "Give it to him," Donovan stepped over Romano and took hold of his wrist and head for what was likely to be the planned finish. Holding Romano in his arms, Donovan suddenly felt him go limp all at once. The referee stopped the match and declared Donovan the winner. Physicians from the audience rushed into the ring and tried to revive the unconscious Romano. A piece of dark fabric, possibly a ring robe, was laid across his torso while they waited for him to be carried from the ring.

Romano would be declared dead later that night. The initial cause was rumored to be a broken neck, but doctors later attributed his death to coronary occlusion. It was a long-standing condition for Romano that had worsened over time, a coroner's inquest later found. It remains unknown whether any athletic commission in any state where he'd recently performed had identified the issue during the standard pre-bout examinations or whether Romano had any idea that he had been risking his life every time he entered the ring.

When Ed Contos remembered the evening, he liked to stick with the rumor that Romano's heart had nothing to do with it—that he had died instantly after having his neck accidentally snapped. Whether he preferred that version for some reason or simply didn't believe the coroner's report can't be said. Still, what struck Contos as most remarkable from that evening was the audience's reaction. "Fans, being human, at least most of them, are always afraid they are not getting their money's worth," he said. "There lay Romano, a tough campaigner of countless ring battles, sprawled motionless on the canvas. He was dead! Yet the restless crowd took up the chant, 'Fake! Fake! Get up and wrestle, you bum!'"[14]

FIGURE 23. Jack Curley. Reproduced from the original held by the Department of Special Collections of the Hesburgh Libraries, the University of Notre Dame.

CHAPTER 22

Such a Muddle

JULY 7, 1937, kicked off what would turn into a string of searingly hot summer days across the Midwest and East Coast. More than 300 people would die from heat-related incidents before temperatures cooled. In Chicago, eleven people were injured when lightning struck beachgoers trying to beat the heat at Diversey Beach. Coney Island, the Rockaways, and Jones Beach reported their largest crowds in New York history.[1]

Jack Curley had turned sixty-one just three days earlier. The blond ringlets that had once been the inspiration for his adopted surname were now long gone, replaced by thin wisps of white hair that he brushed across his otherwise bald head. He was old enough to be thought of as a grand old man of American sport and had outlived many of his contemporaries, some of whose names would be remembered long after Curley's own would be forgotten. He'd been married to his wife Bessie for sixteen years, was still close to his two grown children from his previous marriage, and had an estate in Long Island, where he socialized with writers, athletes, and dignitaries. He and Bessie stumped for the New Deal whenever they could. In his free time, he talked religion with his friend, the rationalist philosopher M. M. Mangasarian.

He was living the life that he'd left San Francisco to chase down in 1893 as a stowaway on a Chicago-bound train. Reflecting on the improbability of it all, he concluded that his best days were still ahead of him. "I have not yet reached the slippered and pantalooned age, where a pipe, a glass, a warm chimney corner, and a few old friends are all that I desire," he'd written just a few years prior. "I am busier now than I ever have been before. My interests are broader, my friends and acquaintances more numerous, my goals more glittering."[2]

Curley had been angling to create a national alliance of like-minded businessmen for almost as long as he'd been involved in professional wrestling—one that would help people take the sport more seriously, organize it, and enforce some kind of structure. But after forty years of work, things were in as much disarray as ever. Between Ali Baba's April 1936 victory over Dick Shikat in Detroit and January 1937, six wrestlers in the United States had made claims—often overlapping—to the heavyweight championship. Serious sportswriters in the major cities who might have otherwise given wrestling a begrudging pass now openly derided it. "Such a muddle," Curley told them. "One champion more or less doesn't mean a thing in this business. . . . it's all a joke."[3]

Attendance at matches was down by one-third in most cities. Business in major hubs like Chicago and Philadelphia was off by as much as seventy-five percent. "New York is altogether dead," Chicago promoter Ed White wrote to Jim Londos in an attempt to coax him back from Greece, where he was living. "What the game needs is a New Deal. Wish you were here. It is the opportune time to do something constructive."[4]

Of almost as much concern to Curley as his anemic gates were his ever-realigning business relationships. After the Columbus trial, the partners with whom he sometimes worked and sometimes feuded made and broke agreements on what felt like a night-by-night basis. The main sources of conflict, as always, were who had stiffed whom on a debt, who was sending their wrestlers to which city, and what promoters were infringing on which other promoters' territory. How personally any of them took all of it or how much resentment they harbored toward each other is hard to say. In the business of professional wrestling, transgressions rarely led to permanent rifts. It was a world full of snakes and devils; longevity required tolerating the ones you knew, no matter how many times they crossed you.

By summer 1937, Curley had split with his longtime friend and associate Toots Mondt. Mondt had moved west to Los Angeles, where he managed a minor coup by brokering a deal to have Chicago Bears star and future College and Pro Football Hall of Fame inductee Bronko Nagurski recognized as a heavyweight champion. Nagurski was a popular and widely respected athlete, and while it was ridiculous to imagine that he could so easily defeat as many seasoned wrestlers as he had, his athletic pedigree lent a believability to his performances that spectators could go along with. "At last, we have a champion the world will go for," Mondt said. "I've been waiting for a man who can really catch the popular fancy. Nagurski is the man."[5] Such was the depressed state of wrestling, though, that convincing Nagurski to take the championship was said to have required a payment to him of $15,000 in cash, up front.[6] Long gone were the days of wrestlers paying promoters for the right to call themselves a champion.

Mondt was also rumored to be one of the primary unnamed sources of information for writer Marcus Griffin's book *Fall Guys: The Barnums of Bounce*, which had been published that May. Griffin had been a one-time press agent for Mondt in the early 1930s, and *Fall Guys* was a bracing tell-all. It gave inside details on the squabbling and petty arguments that defined the wrestling business in the 1930s. Far from trying to argue for wrestling's legitimacy, Griffin placed it somewhere between the theatre stage and a flea circus. "It's not the sport of kings," he wrote, "but the entertainment of the hoi polloi."[7] The book was published by Reilly & Lee (a major publishing house at the time), and Warner Brothers was said to be interested in turning it into a movie.[8] In any other sport, such attention would have been an embarrassment, but inside professional wrestling, Griffin's book was largely met with shrugs. Griffin guessed that 98% of wrestling fans were convinced that matches were above board.[9] He was grossly overestimating. By 1937, pro wrestling had been exposed, embarrassed, belittled, and mocked in every newspaper in the country. Still, there was reason to believe that the steady stream of ridicule only served to make some fans even more passionate.[10] People who continued to go to the matches did so for any number of reasons, but a desire to witness an evening of honest athletic competition was almost never one of them.

To help him fend off competition from Mondt and others, Curley had renewed his partnership with Boston's Paul Bowser and, improbably, with his former rival, Jack Pfefer. As Curley's plans for a fall and winter run of shows were being finalized with his new partners, he had begun involving his twenty-six-year-old son Jack Jr. more closely in his dealings. Everyone knew that the days of baseball stadiums full of breathless fans longing to catch a glimpse of Jim Londos or lines stretching for blocks to see Gus Sonnenberg flatten his opponent with a flying tackle were gone. Everything was running on fumes—yet not a single person involved in professional wrestling could be convinced that business would stay down for good.

With his exclusive lease on Madison Square Garden up, Curley relocated his weekly program of matches to the smaller, less expensive Hippodrome Theatre on Sixth Avenue. Along with the change in venue came the move of his office from its longtime location in the Times Building on Forty-second Street, overlooking Broadway, to a new location a mile away at Radio City. Curley's close friend, author and screenwriter Gene Fowler, mourned the move as a passing of some essential spirit from the Great White Way: "When wrestlers move from Broadway, and keeper Curley goes, the grand street is a sucker's beat with bums and picture shows. The curb where Canfield watched the throng; the walk where Brady stood is filled with tarts and apple carts; so I'll stay away for good."[11]

Curley's plan was for a slate of thirty shows to begin that fall, with occasional evenings in the grander Madison Square Garden for major matches. His last show there that March had drawn 7,000 people—a disappointment in any other year but in 1937 a reason for hope.[12] He'd survived more slumps than he cared to remember. His business had weathered a world war, a flu pandemic, and a global depression. The people would come back. They always came back for Jack Curley.

Curley had marveled to reporters more than once about his knack for dodging death. Though he was almost certainly exaggerating, he'd claimed to have tickets to travel on the doomed voyage of the ocean liner *Lusitania* in May of 1915, opting out of his trip only after last-minute objections from his then-wife.[13] He'd claimed, as well, to have been scheduled to travel on TWA Flight 6, which crashed on the evening of May 6, 1935, in a field near Atlanta, Missouri, killing New Mexico Senator Bronson Cutting and four others. An hour before leaving for the airport to catch the flight, he'd opted to travel by train instead. He'd just had a feeling, he said.[14] Call it a showman's premonition.

What Curley didn't talk much about were the health scares that had haunted his later years. He'd spent most of 1928 hospitalized with a mastoid infection and been hospitalized again in July 1934 for what was characterized as a major operation.[15] In June 1935, he'd been carried out of Fenway Park on a stretcher, an episode blamed on an "upside down stomach."[16] His weight, long a source of humor for writers, was always a concern, as well.

Curley typically started summer days with a 7:30 a.m. game of tennis with his wife, followed by breakfast. He would then drive his sixteen-cylinder Cadillac into the city to his office to spend the remainder of the day working.[17] It's very likely he followed close to that same routine on Monday, July 12, 1937. It was day six of the crushing national heatwave. By 2:30 that afternoon, the temperature in New York had risen to eighty-seven degrees, and the humidity had grown swampy and suffocating. Shortly before 3 p.m., a darkness fell. Broadway became so black that its office buildings lit up and its theatres illuminated their marquees. The darkness was followed by a thirty-minute thunderstorm that slashed through the city. Rain fell so fast and heavy that sewers became overwhelmed. Water flooded into the Park Avenue tunnel leading into Grand Central Station, snarling traffic on the tracks and marooning trains underground.[18]

Curley left the city and returned home to Great Neck that evening. Sometime around midnight, he began feeling ill and put himself to bed. At 12:45 a.m., he suffered a massive heart attack. His wife and daughter called a physician to the house who attempted to revive him, but they were too late.

News of Jack Curley's death reached newspapers later that day. It came as a shock to the sports community, and tributes poured in immediately. Yankees owner Jacob Ruppert called the promoter's death a great loss to sports. "Curley was honest and sincere," he said. "Sports could use more like him." The *New York Times* ran a long obituary, and writer Hype Igoe penned a heartfelt remembrance of him in the *New York American*. The *Daily News* featured a banner headline announcing his death on its rear-facing page. In Chicago, where Curley had spent his formative years and experienced some of his most lasting successes, he was remembered as "a far more romantic figure in the realm of exciting promotional adventures than the immortal P. T. Barnum."[19]

When Curley was laid to rest at a funeral chapel in Flushing on Wednesday, July 14, 1937, a crowd of more than 500 people attended, including politicians, sports stars, journalists, writers, and entertainers. The crowd was so large that police had to detour traffic away until the service was finished. Of Curley's on-and-off business partners, only Jack Pfefer, Paul Bowser, and Ray Fabiani were present at the service. Pfefer, shaken by the sudden loss, was bereft. He told several people in attendance how glad he was that he and Curley had resolved their differences before it was too late. He would soon fill his scrapbook for 1937 with seventeen pages of clipped and pasted articles on Curley's life. "Curley's last show not only turned them away but sent them home with a smile," wrote Dan Parker. "Death was reduced to a pleasant adventure on which he embarked with the optimism of a true showman."[20]

But the business of wrestling could stop for no single man—not even the one who'd all but built it. Before the memorial service was even finished, a fellow promoter approached Bowser and Pfefer and, with tears filling his eyes, made an offer to take Curley's place in their partnership.[21]

The situation left behind in the wake of Curley's death was hardly pleasant. Even if he was far from the omnipotent mastermind that he was often accused of being, he had acted as a centering force in an otherwise messy and cutthroat business. "He was, through thick and thin, the father confessor of the wrestling business," wrote one sportswriter.[22] He'd been at it longer than anyone, had known everyone, and had proven himself more than capable of soothing bruised egos and settling otherwise explosive disputes. Professional wrestling minus Jack Curley was rudderless.

His son, Jack Jr., made immediate plans to step into his father's role in New York wrestling, but unexpected competition from other promoters for Curley's wrestlers and clubs drove him out of business almost immediately. A splashy memorial show for Curley held at Madison Square Garden in September 1937 attracted fewer than 3,000 people. The sparsely attended night was a sad denouement. A final attempt to stage another wrestling show at the Garden was made six months later. It would be the last one held there for almost eleven years.[23]

"The game died along with Jack Curley," wrote columnist George Barton. "[Professional wrestling] isn't worth a plugged nickel in Gotham anymore."[24]

Everywhere you looked, business was slumping. By the end of the 1930s, promoters desperate for paying customers were willing to try anything. They filled rings with mud, fish, and feathers and molasses, and set wrestlers to work in them. The wrestlers themselves, always looking to excite the crowd, turned more and more to violence and gore. Where once blood capsules and dives through the ropes would suffice, they now beat each other with weapons and produced blood either by slicing their foreheads with razor blades or by smashing their knuckles into an opponent's eyebrow or temple, or directly behind their ear, a method they called "the hard way."[25]

"One hardly knows whether to blame the greed of the wrestling promoters . . . or the public for the exhibitions staged today in public places under the name of wrestling," wrote Paul Gallico. "The wrestling fan of today, turning his back upon fine art, demands brutality and realism and is getting it to the point where the wrestling show, to continue to pack them in, has had to overstep every limit of decency and good taste."[26]

In 1941, *Esquire*'s Curt Riess wrote a kind of obituary for professional wrestling. Earlier that year, aspiring promoters had attempted to revive wrestling in New York by staging something they called "honest wrestling." An astonished Riess pressed then-president of Madison Square Garden, Colonel John Reed Kilpatrick, on just why, after years of proof that it was simply impossible to make pro wrestling work without a healthy degree of theatrics and subterfuge, he was backing their bid. Kilpatrick, it turned out, was no fan of wrestling. His motivation—of which he made no secret—was purely mercenary. "He immediately produced his reason in the form of some very interesting and secret-looking books," wrote Riess. They were the ledgers for the years 1930 to 1933, and they told the tale of wrestling's golden years in dollars and cents.

Despite Kilpatrick's optimism, the revival of "honest wrestling" was stopped before it could even begin when it was revealed that one of the wrestlers scheduled for the main event had been offered a bribe to take a dive.[27] The whole affair rekindled memories of wrestling's heyday a decade earlier, when thousands would wait in line outside arenas around the country for a chance to see the grapplers. For Riess, it reignited the question of just what any of it had been about:

A few years ago, I went to a wrestling match in Los Angeles with the movie actor Peter Lorre, who was a wrestling addict. . . . [He] came for one single purpose. He wanted to see a fake bout. On this particular evening, the bout did not develop along the usual rapid lines. Mr. Lorre was disgusted. "Phooey," he said, and got up. "Sport!"

Mr. Lorre will be grieved to learn that he is nothing but the average wrestling patron. The average paying customer has always come not to see an honest wrestling bout but to see a fake bout and act wise about it. Jack Curley knew this very well. And the relations between him and his public were something like those between cat and mouse. The public came and paid and lamented that it was all phony. Curley never did anything to discredit this belief. . . .

He made money—and all the promoters made money—not because you could fool the people so easily but because you couldn't fool them. The wrestling public were suckers all right, but inverted suckers. There was only one thing that worried them: the awful possibility that a bout might be on the level. . . . Wrestling became the sport of the wise guys. The people who didn't give a damn what went on before their eyes, who only wanted to know what was going on behind the scenes. The people with the backstage urge.

Well, boys, it's all over now. A show can't run forever. Even a sport, a real sport, can only live so long. Wrestling as we knew it belonged to a certain era. It belonged so much to that era that moral indignation about it would be beside the point. Every era has the sport it deserves.[28]

FIGURE 24. Promotional flyer produced by Jack Pfefer and Toots Mondt. From the author's personal collection.

Epilogue

Paradigmatically Fake for Real

PROFESSIONAL WRESTLING, OF course, didn't die with Jack Curley. There were bad years and worse years for much of the 1940s, and the business was kept alive largely through the efforts of a groundbreaking group of women. None were more popular than Mildred Burke. Born Mildred Bliss on August 5, 1915, in Coffeyville, Kansas, she'd dreamed of becoming a wrestler since seeing her first professional match in her late teens. She met and later married Billy Wolfe, an abusive, philandering former wrestler, in the summer of 1934. Wolfe wooed Burke with his stories of life on the road, trained her, and put her to work performing in carnivals and small arenas where she was frequently matched against men. Just a bit over five feet in height and rarely weighing more than 140 pounds, Burke turned out to be a tenacious grappler and charismatic performer. She developed a signature look: crisp white tights paired with white boots, topped with a rhinestone-bejeweled ring robe. By 1944, she was performing in front of crowds of more than 10,000 people, and by 1946, she was said to be making $25,000 per year. If correct, that amount is enough to place her among the era's highest-paid athletes. As her fame grew, she began dressing in furs, full-length floral dresses, and diamonds layered on top of diamonds. "Women's wrestling wasn't going to be any freak show while I was champion," she would later write.[1]

Wolfe parlayed Burke's success into a business training and managing female wrestlers. In his prime years at the beginning of the 1950s, he was bringing in $250,000 a year. He was the unquestioned czar of women's wrestling, and treated the Columbus, Ohio, gym where he recruited new wrestlers as a combination training camp and brothel. Burke and Wolfe split in 1953, and a protracted legal battle between the two contributed to stymieing her career. She opened her own business training and booking female wrestlers, and later worked on two films about female wrestlers. She died on February 18, 1989, after suffering a stroke, at the age of seventy-three.

Pro wrestling's popularity took off following the end of World War II thanks primarily to its ubiquity on the new medium of television. Professional wrestling and television were a natural fit from the very first broadcast of matches in 1939.[2] Wrestling was cheap to produce, required no sets or scripts, and could often be shot with just a single stationary camera, unlike baseball and football.[3] Matches were easily understood at a glance, the lengths of individual bouts could be readily tailored to fit the strictures of a broadcast schedule, and wrestlers, unlike boxers, could perform weekly or even daily, if required. NBC added wrestling to its lineup in 1940, at a time when stations were only running for a handful of hours each day. By the late 1940s, some stations were airing wrestling as many as six nights per week.

No wrestler commanded attention during this era like Gorgeous George. Born George Wagner in Butte, Nebraska, in 1915, he'd been a struggling wrestler in the Pacific Northwest before deciding, at the encouragement of his wife, to marcel his dyed-blond hair, dress in flowing capes sewn by his mother-in-law, and affect an outrageous pomposity. Drawing on the theatrics Wilbur Finran had pioneered a decade earlier as Lord Lansdowne, George employed a valet who would spray the ring with perfume, and he treated the audience with a high-handed disdain.[4] He was an immediate sensation, exploding into living rooms across America in November of 1947. That year, there were approximately 16,500 television sets in America. A decade later, there were almost 50,000,000. Gorgeous George was responsible for moving more than his fair share. "I don't know if I was made for television, or television was made for me," he would famously quip.[5]

Whip smart with a titanic bravado, George would directly influence Muhammad Ali, Elvis Presley, James Brown, and Bob Dylan—to name some of his most famous fans. A prolific drinker, womanizer, and spender, he lived high and hard. In December 1963, he suffered a heart attack in the Hollywood flophouse where he had been reduced to living and died penniless on the day after Christmas. He was just forty-eight. At his memorial service four days later, ever the showman, he was laid to rest in an orchid-colored casket and dressed in his signature purple satin robe with a high collar of white ruffles.[6]

By then, for many people in sports and popular culture, the further they stayed away from pro wrestling, the better. To many, it was a flimsy, low-rent put-on; entertainment for mouth breathers and yokels who didn't know any better. A small contingent of admirers came to recognize in it some degree of artistry, though few could be convinced of Jack Curley's long-standing hope for it to be taken seriously as sport. The wrestlers themselves pressed on. They performed night after night, traveling countless miles between shows to entertain crowds that could range from a few hundred people in a high school gymnasium to thousands in the Atlanta Omni, or the Boston Garden, or the Louisiana Superdome. All the while, despite endless goading and insults, they never let on that it was all a very complicated and combustible bit of stagecraft. By the 1970s, wrestling, as critic Richard Meltzer lovingly wrote, had become "*uniquely* fake, *archetypally* fake, paradigmatically *fake for real* . . . the needle-threading, universe-belching master of its own persona."[7]

Wrestling promoters of the era, most of whom conducted their business in almost the exact same manner as their predecessors in the 1920s and 1930s, were notorious for their lack of interest in preserving the past. An investigation by the United States Department of Justice in the 1950s into anti-trust practices among promoters had only served to further convince them of what their forefathers had already known: the shorter and more obscure the paper trail, the less could be pinned on them.[8]

The business of professional wrestling had a way of treating its most significant innovators coldly. There were no Hall of Fame inductions, no unions, and no pensions. Shunned by the sports world and abandoned by the wrestling world, the men who invented professional wrestling were all but forgotten.

In early 1936, future heavyweight champion Lou Thesz was still just a young wrestler working in Minneapolis for the promoter Tony Stecher. Stecher had stayed active in wrestling and become a powerful figure following his run as manager for his beloved brother Joe during Joe's reign as champion in the 1920s. Joe Stecher, the one-time sports idol known as the Scissors King, had not fared as well. After losing his fortune during the Great Depression, Stecher had been forced to return to wrestling full time. Always known as a fierce competitor, his role in the 1930s had been to lose on demand to younger stars. After a suicide attempt sometime in that decade, he was committed to the St. Cloud Veteran's Hospital in St. Cloud, Minnesota, in 1934.

Hoping to cheer him up, Tony arranged for Thesz and several other young performers to wrestle with Joe in private at a Minneapolis gym. On the mats, Thesz remembered, Stecher became a different person: "Here was a man in his forties who had been in a mental hospital for several years and hadn't trained or wrestled a lick during that period, and he went out onto the mat with a bunch of hungry, well-conditioned athletes and ate every one of them alive."[9] It was a rare moment of pleasure for Stecher, who would remain institutionalized for the rest of his life. He died in 1974 at the age of eighty.

On the morning of June 3, 1933, William Muldoon passed away from the effects of prostate cancer at his farm in Purchase, New York. He was laid to rest on a high, grassy plot of land in Valhalla, New York. Obituaries listed his age as eighty-eight, but his true age was eighty-one.[10] He'd used different birth dates throughout his life in an attempt to appear older than he actually was. It made his claims of having served in the Civil War more plausible, and his boasts of being able to ward off the effects of aging with exercise all the more convincing. He could be a vain, moralizing fussbudget, but even at his worst, he commanded and received respect. Author Theodore Dreiser immortalized him as the domineering and petty, yet magnetic, Culhane, the Solid Man, in his 1919 book *Twelve Men*. "With no knowledge of or interest in the superior mental sciences or arts or philosophies, still [Culhane] seemed to suggest and even live them," Dreiser wrote.[11] Muldoon claimed to have never read Dreiser's book. "My neighbor told me not to," he told a reporter. "He said it might annoy me."[12]

Muldoon had served on the New York State Athletic Commission since its inception, and had presided with such gravity that some took to mockingly calling him "The Duke of Muldoon" when he was safely out of earshot.[13] And though at times his rulings could seem inconsistent or overreaching, he steered boxing, and to a lesser degree wrestling, through a perilous period in the 1920s during which the continued legality of both was not always guaranteed. His work, in many cases, served as a template for other cities and states as they struggled to issue their own regulations.

Dr. Ben Roller, the athlete-turned-physician-turned-athlete who was a star for Jack Curley for much of the 1910s and who elevated suffering in-ring injuries to an artform, died in New York on April 20, 1933, from pneumonia at the age of fifty-seven. He'd returned to medicine after retiring from the ring, married twice, and mostly tried to distance himself from the antics of the wrestling business.[14] Though most press notes of his passing made prominent mention of his wrestling career, he would no doubt have been pleased that the headline of his obituary in the *New York Times* referred to him only as a retired surgeon. Roller's one-time manager Ole Marsh, who'd battled with Roller and Jack Curley during the surreal Seattle fall of 1909, stayed active as a manager and promoter through the end of the 1930s. He died in 1952 at the age of eighty-four in Yamhill County, Oregon, and was buried in a plot on his family's farm.

"Farmer" Martin Burns, who along with Marsh had trained Frank Gotch and been a champion wrestler in his own right during the wild days of pro wrestling at the turn of the twentieth century, died in 1937 at the age of seventy-five. Wrestler Milo Steinborn had met Burns when the aged Farmer traveled to New York toward the end of his life. "The old geezer was still pretty spry," Steinborn remembered. "He asked me to try and strangle him, sticking his neck out and loosening his collar. I really didn't want to do it. He was an old man. But, when I tried to fake it, he said, 'Come on, Milo, give it a real try.' So I really squeezed. His eyes never bulged. He was one tough old man."[15]

Burns moved to his daughter's house in Council Bluffs, Iowa, after injuring his spine in a gym accident, a health fanatic to the very end. He'd long been left behind by the boom years of the 1930s, with its exaggerated theatrics and antics, but he never gave up the hope of discovering the next Frank Gotch. Cornered by a reporter during an evening of matches at the Council Bluffs Auditorium a handful of years before his death, a horrified Burns exclaimed, "Why, this isn't wrestling. There isn't a real wrestler living today who can't toss any of these actors any time he wants to."[16] He claimed to have wrestled more than 6,000 matches during his career and trained more than 1,600 students. Referencing President Herbert Hoover, Burns famously declared, "Only one man out of Cedar County, Iowa, ever made more money than I did, and he got to be President of the United States."[17]

Mort Henderson, who, with his black hood and elaborate efforts to avoid reporters as the Masked Marvel, had captivated audiences in the winter of 1915 at New York's Metropolitan Opera House, died in 1939 at the age of sixty. He'd begun a second life as a police officer, leaving his wrestling career far behind. Samuel Rachmann, the businessman responsible for the 1915 tournament, left wrestling immediately after the tournament was over. He began working in film distribution near the end of the 1910s and played a critical role in importing early German masterpieces to America, most notably Ernst Lubitch's *Madame DuBarry*. Rachmann returned to Germany in the 1920s and parlayed his success into a position with the country's famed UFA films. He lived fast and wild in post-war Berlin, indulging his twin loves of the arts and excess. He died of heart disease in 1930, deep in debt, at the estimated age of fifty-two.[18]

Wayne Munn, who unknowingly brought wrestling into a new age during the first few months of 1925 with his brief, manufactured run as heavyweight champion, died in January 1931 from kidney disease. He was only thirty-five. Munn abandoned his sports career at the end of the 1920s and started over in the oil business in Texas. Press reports of his death attributed the disease that took his life to injuries sustained in his earliest matches, an unlikely but not impossible claim. At his funeral service in San Antonio, he was called "a martyr to the game."[19]

Stanislaus Zbyszko, who had embarrassed Munn with the off-script thrashing that cost him his championship in March 1925, died at the age of eighty-eight on September 23, 1967, on his farm in St. Joseph, Missouri. Though he struggled financially after losing much of his savings during the Great Depression, Zbyszko stayed busy in his later years, promoting wrestling in Argentina and training aspiring performers. In 1933, he successfully sued the *New York American* for $25,000 in damages for comparing him to a gorilla. Zbyszko's lawyer, the prominent civil liberties attorney Arthur Garfield Hays, who had represented John Scopes and Sacco and Vanzetti, as well as participated in the Scottsboro Boys trial, cited Zbyszko's charm in the witness box as the reason for the generous settlement.[20] Zbyszko capped his career with a celebrated performance in director Jules Dassin's 1950 film noir classic *Night and the City*, as the aged, idealistic Greco-Roman wrestler Gregorious.[21] Zbyszko's younger brother, Wladek, who lived with him in Missouri, died less than one year after him on June 10, 1968, at the age of seventy-five.

George Hackenschmidt, the world-famous Russian Lion who dominated wrestling rings around the world in the first decade of the 1900s, retired after his Labor Day 1911 loss to Frank Gotch. After surviving a stint as a German prisoner of war during World War I, he married, settled in France, and finally relocated to England. He turned his attention

to philosophy, authoring a number of books on the subject before passing away on February 19, 1968, at the age of ninety. He was survived by
his wife Rachel, who donated his personal papers to the H.J. Lutcher
Stark Center for Physical Culture and Sports at the University of Texas
in Austin.

Reginald Siki, the first Black wrestler to gain national fame, spent his
life in constant motion. After leaving New York, he traveled the world
before finally settling in Germany in October 1937. He was a featured
performer everywhere he went, but had his life upended during World
War II.[22] He was taken into custody by German police in April of 1942
and imprisoned, along with several hundred other American civilians,
in Tittmoning Castle in south-eastern Bavaria. He was released in
March 1944 and returned to America, where, now in his mid-forties and
penniless, he would improbably manage to rebuild his wrestling career.
He became a regular performer, first in Massachusetts and finally in Los
Angeles, where he worked steadily in front of large audiences. He died of
a heart attack just four days shy of his forty-ninth birthday on Christmas
Eve 1948. The story that he had been born abroad, instead of in Kansas
City, proved so impenetrable that his death certificate listed his place of
birth as Africa.[23]

Lou Daro, the king of wrestling in California, saw his empire collapse
by the end of the 1930s. In 1935, an auto mechanic and World War I
veteran named William Focher was killed by police following an incident after one of Daro's shows, in which Focher had tried to collect from
Daro on an eight-year-old unpaid repair bill of just $37.44. Daro was
drubbed in the press for his role in involving the police in the dispute but
absolved of any responsibility for Focher's death. He went on to establish
a trust fund for Focher's widow and nine-year-old son later that year.[24] A
heart attack in 1936 left Daro bedridden for three months and clinging
to life. "I want to quit—I'm tired," he wrote a fellow promoter just four
weeks before falling ill. "The few years I have left I'm going to take it easy.
What's the use of worrying? What's the use of killing yourself? What's
it all about?"[25]

His problems did not end there. On April 19, 1939, a special commission of the California State Assembly chaired by Assemblyman Chester
Gannon opened public hearings into the conduct and oversight of professional wrestling and boxing in the state. A retired wrestler named
Richard Thompson testified to low payouts, shabby working conditions,
and lax oversight of wrestlers' health and safety by commissioners.

"Your ability doesn't mean anything," he said. "You have got to take orders or get out." Daro himself avoided testifying, claiming illness. In his place, his younger brother and business partner Jack stood for a withering series of questions about the tactics the brothers employed to undermine their competitors, including donations to gubernatorial candidates, judges, sheriffs, and district attorneys, as well as alleged kickbacks to state oversight officers and athletic commission members. Uncovered, also, were steady payouts totaling almost $30,000 per year to sportswriters, allegedly in return for favorable coverage, though Jack Daro preferred to label them as being for the "building of good will."[26]

Pressed on the integrity of wrestling matches, San Francisco matchmaker and former wrestler Joe Malcewicz refuted claims that wrestlers rehearsed their matches, and denied ever dictating the outcome of a match he was promoting. He admitted that the wrestlers may decide between themselves to put on a show for fans, but in the end, he said, "the best man wins":

Assemblyman Tenney: Well now, I don't know a whole lot about wrestling, but you have had lots of experience. I have heard wrestlers say that if they put on a show—that is, went in on an actual contest and wrestled, without all of the fireworks and showmanship, that nobody would come to see those matches. Do you believe that's true?

Joe Malcewicz: Well, they come.

Assemblyman Tenney: Well, they have the fireworks and all of the theatricals. But I say if they just went in and wrestled.

Joe Malcewicz: Well now, I will give you an illustration. If I was wrestling with you, I would have a hell of a hippodrome, but my outcome would be just the same—I would beat you.

Assemblyman Tenney: If you wrestled with me—

Joe Malcewicz (interrupting): But I would have a hell of a lot of fun doing it. But I would beat you.

Assemblyman Poulson: You would hippodrome it.

Joe Malcewicz: But if you were pretty tough and strong and were giving me hell, there would be no fooling.

Gannon's hoped-for reforms would never materialize, though as many as twenty newspapermen would lose their positions following the hearing.[27] The fallout from the investigation helped to depress already declining attendance numbers in the state. Daro's lease on the Olympic Auditorium expired in 1941, formally ending his reign in the city. He died in Los Angeles on July 11, 1956, after a long illness.[28]

Danno O'Mahony, whose loss to Dick Shikat in 1936 set off the lawsuit that turned professional wrestling on its head, stayed active on and off into the late 1940s. He opened a successful restaurant in Santa Monica, California, which he named "The Irish Whip," and served in the United States Army in World War II. On the evening of November 2, 1950, while on a trip home to Ballydehob, he crashed into a stalled truck parked on a dark stretch of road, breaking both his legs and several ribs. He died the next day at the age of thirty-eight and was buried with a hero's funeral. Dick Shikat wrestled on and off into the 1950s. He died on December 3, 1968, at the age of seventy-one.

Paul Bowser, the powerful Boston-based promoter who discovered O'Mahony and engineered his rise to fame, died on July 17, 1960, at the age of seventy-four. He never stopped promoting wrestling but devoted much of his attention in his later years to his love of harness racing. Though Jack Curley is often cited as the most influential promoter in wrestling, Bowser deserves at least as much credit for the boom years of the late 1920s and 1930s. Few of Bowser's contributions during that era were as transformational as his discovery of Gus Sonnenberg, the fiery but tormented former college football star and one-time heavyweight champion.

Sonnenberg lived a stormy, non-stop life after his initial success in the late 1920s. He married actress Judith Allen in 1931, but the pair divorced two years later. He remarried in 1934 but again divorced within only a few years. "Each loved me because I was a wrestler, but each promptly insisted that I become a bond salesman," he later said. "When I asked if they would be content to share about $50 a week which this would mean, instead of my wrestler's income, they got mad and didn't love me anymore."[29] He stayed active as a wrestler through the 1930s, though nagging injuries and a worrisome drinking problem dogged him later in the decade.[30] Driving home from a match in July 1932, he was involved in a head-on automobile accident in which a police officer was killed. Sonnenberg was charged with manslaughter and driving under the influence of alcohol but was acquitted in March 1933 after a headline-grabbing trial.

He was back in a Massachusetts courthouse the next month, suing the *Boston Herald* for $1,000,000 in damages resulting from the newspaper's 1929 articles that referred to his matches as a "racket." Sonnenberg claimed that besides hurting his reputation and drawing power, the articles caused him severe mental anguish. "I didn't feel like putting my head out of the window," he told the jury.[31] After only twelve hours of deliberation, they declared themselves unable to reach a unanimous decision. [32]

He joined the Navy in 1942 as a physical instructor but fell ill the next year with a mysterious illness that was later diagnosed as leukemia. He was hospitalized for the last eight months of his life, and died on September 12, 1944, at the age of forty-six. "I get sick and disgusted with [wrestling]," Sonnenberg had once said at the height of his fame. "I have hated myself and everybody else connected with the sport many a time. But after all, I make a lot of money, and I'd be a fool not to make it while I can. Wrestlers don't last very long, you know, and when they're through being famous, they're still just wrestlers, and there isn't any place for them in the scheme of things."[33]

Of all his in-ring contemporaries, Jim Londos fared the best. Though his pace slowed considerably as he aged, he would still occasionally wrestle well into the 1950s. Londos carved out for himself a level of autonomy unlike any wrestler since. A proud and unyielding presence in the ring, in his private life he was said to be humble and friendly. He dedicated his retirement to charitable work, his avocado and citrus farm in Escondido, California, and his wife and three daughters. He died of a heart attack on August 19, 1975, at the age of eighty-one.

Billy Sandow stayed active in wrestling into the 1950s as well, wielding varying amounts of influence, though never as much as when he was the aggressive, visionary manager for "Strangler" Ed Lewis. Even into his early eighties, Sandow never stopped agitating for new opportunities in the business. "Wish you would call on me some time," he wrote to a fellow promoter in 1966. "I have a great idea for something sensational."[34] He retired to Portland, Oregon, and longed to have a book written about his life. He would invite reporters over to his house to look through his boxes of newspaper clippings, journals, and other memorabilia, but his long-hoped-for book never materialized. He died on September 15, 1972, at the age of eighty-eight.[35]

Strangler Lewis wrestled his final match in Honolulu, Hawaii, on January 25, 1948, at the age of fifty-seven. Two months later, he failed

California's physical examination for wrestlers and had his license revoked, effectively ending his career.[36] Struggling for money and with his health declining, earning an income was hardly optional for the aging Strangler. But even more than the money, Lewis loved and missed performing. "I'm still a bit of an egoist," he told a reporter. "I like to have people liking me, cheering for me. Even a few boos aren't too hard to take."[37]

Lewis found work late in the 1950s as a publicity man for wrestler Lou Thesz, who had risen to considerable fame during wrestling's second golden age. Wrestlers of that era found gaining respect from sportswriters to be nearly impossible. "I couldn't walk into a newsroom and tell the sports editor, 'I'm a great wrestler, and I'll be appearing here Tuesday night,'" Thesz later wrote. "Ed could do it, though, because he had unbelievable charm in addition to a great reputation."[38] Lewis retired for good in the early 1960s. Legally blind after decades spent battling trachoma, he turned to preaching, claiming that God would heal him. "This is just another test to prove the allness, the omnipotence of God," said a then-seventy-five-year-old Lewis. "I'm going through a beautiful experience."[39] A series of strokes left him confined to a veterans' hospital in Muskogee, Oklahoma, where he died on August 7, 1966, at the age of seventy-six. One of his only visitors during that time was Jack Pfefer, an undoubtedly welcome face from Lewis's heyday as the ruler of the wrestling ring.

After Jack Curley's death in 1937, Pfefer had redoubled his efforts to establish a foothold on the East Coast. With his irresistible quotes and a personality he cultivated to be as cartoonish as even the most outrageous of his wrestlers, he inspired reams of media coverage. Jack Miley wrote about him for *Collier's*, A.J. Liebling for the *New Yorker*, and Joseph Mitchell for the *World-Telegram*. "A honest man can sell a fake diamond if he says it is a fake diamond," he told Liebling. "Only if he says it is a real diamond ain't he honest. These loafers don't like that I say wrestling is all chicanery—hokum, in other words."[40] In 1940, *Life* called Pfefer the most important wrestling promoter in the country, just after quoting him as saying, "Mine profession, eet's a phoney."[41]

Pfefer ruled over his domain from his thee-room office suite on the tenth floor of the Times Building in Manhattan, which he decorated in a firecracker red and gold color scheme. ("I'd hate to be in this joint when it goes off!" one of his wrestlers joked.)[42] He covered its walls with framed photographs of the wrestlers he'd worked with and known. The photographs of those he felt had betrayed him hung under a sign labeled "Dead Wrestlers." "Among them were photographs of several living wrestlers," deadpanned Mitchell. "It is a way Mr. Pfefer has of getting even."[43] His wrestling shows, he argued to Liebling, should be considered artistic successes even when they weren't commercial ones. "The trouble, according to him," Liebling wrote of Pfefer, "is that the moneyed clientele has ceased to believe in wrestling as a sport and has not yet learned to appreciate it as a pure art form."[44] "I don't tell people my wrestling shows are on the level," Pfefer told another reporter. "I guarantee them they're not."[45]

Pfefer did all he could to bring audiences along to his vision. He pushed a massive, 600-pound phenom named Martin Levy ("That's short for Leviathan," remarked a *Paramount News* commentator covering a Levy training match), who wrestling fans knew better as "The Blimp."[46] "Some night he'll drop dead in a ring," Pfefer joked. "God forbid!"[47] He managed as well a Gorilla Man, The Mysterious Mystery, and a wrestler he dubbed King Kong. "A wrestler has to be an exceedingly grotesque person to win Mr. Pfefer's respect," wrote Joseph Mitchell. "So long as citizens will pay to see wrestlers moan and grunt and burp and slap the mat in agony, he is willing to take their dollar bills."[48]

Pfefer actively promoted matches through the end of 1967, outlasting almost every one of his competitors from thirty years prior. Though his stature faded over the years, he remained a ferocious businessman. "I have proven in all the long years that I can take care of myself and hope to do so as long as I will be able to fight," he told a fellow promoter in 1952.[49] Shaped by his years spent in the whirlwind of the New York wrestling wars of the 1930s, he never stopped seeing the business as infested with "rats," "schemers," and "double-crossers." Pfefer, as one writer put it, "lived for revenge. He never forgave the bigwigs, and he never trusted the high echelon of pro wrestling ever again."[50] He died in a Norwell, Massachusetts nursing home on September 13, 1974, at the age of seventy-nine. In 1977, what he had deemed his "museum collection" was donated to the University of Notre Dame by Eddie Einhorn, the future owner of the Chicago White Sox, who had acquired it in 1974. The collection, a total of almost five tons of photos, letters, telegrams, scrapbooks, posters, and other memorabilia Pfefer lovingly preserved over the course of his career, now represents the best available window into wrestling's colorful and contentious history.

Pfefer's on-again off-again friend and partner Joseph "Toots" Mondt worked in wrestling into the late 1960s. He is as responsible for the shape of modern professional wrestling as anyone. As he aged, the once-dangerous grappler's movements took on what one reporter described as a "slow grace, like an aging Sherman tank."[51] He helped to manage the careers of some of the most famous performers of the 1950s, 1960s, and 1970s, including Antonino Rocca and Bruno Sammartino. In August 1957, Mondt partnered with New York promoter Vincent J. McMahon to form Capitol Wrestling. McMahon's father, Jess, had been a one-time boxing promoter at Madison Square Garden, and had worked with Jack Curley in the early 1930s to stage wrestling on Long Island.

Mondt and McMahon established the World Wide Wrestling Federation (WWWF) in 1963. Using the vast network of connections Mondt had cultivated over his 40-year career, McMahon turned their business into a powerful force in the Northeast. "People want as much action as they can get," said Mondt, "and we give it to them."[52] Mondt formally retired in 1969 and moved to St. Louis, Missouri, with his long-time wife Alda. He died of pneumonia on June 11, 1976, at the age of eighty-two. In the years following Mondt's death, the WWWF would only continue to grow. In 1982, it was sold to McMahon's son, Vincent K. McMahon, who reshaped it first into the World Wrestling Federation (WWF) and later into the global juggernaut now known as World Wrestling Entertainment (WWE).

Jack Curley shepherded professional wrestling into the twentieth century and was responsible for establishing it as an enduring style of entertainment. The template he helped to build has proven remarkably durable. By the end of the 1920s, the matches he was putting on were different only by a matter of degrees from the professional wrestling matches of today. When he passed away, critics had fully expected pro wrestling to go the way of flea circuses, dance marathons, cakewalks, nonstop indoor bike races, and the other oddball entertainments Curley had championed at one time or another. Curley probably never had a doubt that wrestling would continue without him, though he would have been amazed, horrified, and amused by what it has become.

In 1965, Charley Rose, an eccentric former boxer and matchmaker who had once shared an office with Curley and had gotten to know him well, penned a remembrance for his long-dead friend for *Ring* magazine.

"Jack was the strangest character in the history of sports promotion," Rose wrote. "He knew art. He was a connoisseur in antique furniture. He knew everybody from the White House to the old Garden in New York." Rose reminisced about their time together in a world now long-buried, of seat-of-your-pants shows conceived of in saloons and financed by gamblers and mobsters and of events that promised to be thrilling, even if they couldn't always be guaranteed to be honest.

Curley, he wrote, "was one of the most remarkable promoters wrestling yet has seen, father of the mat game as we know it now." Rose knew that everything had moved on without them, that his generation of wise guys had long ago been relegated to deep, deep storage. Still, Rose had seen them all and known them all. This obituary for Jack Curley, written almost thirty years after his death, was Rose's tiny way of trying to keep the memory of his friend alive while he still could. It was the remembrance Jack would have wanted. "My most interesting years," Rose wrote, "were spent in association with Curley. Never a dull day, never a dull hour."[53]

Acknowledgments

WHAT WE KNOW about the history of professional wrestling has been collected, published, analyzed, and argued over by a tiny, remarkable group of amateur historians over just about the last fifty years. It was one of the great pleasures of my life to get to interact with most of them during my almost ten years of work on this book. They were, without fail, generous with their knowledge and time, eager to talk, and some of the kindest and funniest people I ever expect to get to meet. There is no doubt that without their help, this book would not exist. Most have written excellent books of their own, which you can find in the bibliography and which, when taken together, give a much more complete history of pro wrestling than can be told in a book like mine.

Steve Yohe opened his home and his entire archive to me without hesitation. He was always available to answer thorny questions, check my interpretation of events, engage in long, rambling conversations about things that happened a century ago, and ultimately point me in the right direction, no matter what I asked. Mark Hewitt and Tim Hornbaker both went above and beyond by reading drafts of my work, and by sending me crucial documents; in particular, Strangler Lewis's unpublished biography, Max Jacobs's unpublished articles, and the court files from the 1936 Columbus trial. The amazing Greg Oliver and Steve Johnson of *SLAM! Wrestling* provided me with an incredible amount of information on Jim Londos and others and helped me connect to fellow historians.

Also remarkably helpful were Scott Beekman and the late Don Luce, who were crucial in chronicling the life of William Muldoon as well as helping me understand the roots of wrestling in the United States. Susan Grant of Hawaii kindly shared her remarkable research into the murky life and times of Ole Marsh and the Mabray Gang. Scott Teal at Crowbar Press has published a number of indispensable books on wrestling history and was helpful anytime I needed a hand. Koji Miyamoto, Phil Lions and Jon Lister helped me research the lives of Yusuf İsmail, George Hackenschmidt, and others; Tom Burke and Eddy Portnoy helped me with my research on Jack Pfefer.

Many special thanks, too, to Jason Micallef, who helped me land on the idea of basing the book around the life of Jack Curley. Without him, I'm not sure this would have ever gotten off the ground. Julie Fogh helped and supported me from day one. Lindsay Shane Oliver was my remarkable editor, and her tireless guidance, enthusiasm, and encouragement helped me overcome my many bouts with self-doubt and bad writing. Suzanne Rindell gave me endless encouragement early in the process and was incredibly generous with her time and contacts. Ray Tennenbaum and Irv Muchnick contributed invaluable feedback of their own, along the way.

Lifelong thanks, as well, to Mike Edison, for many things, but for the subtitle, in particular; Keith Eliot Greenberg; Jeff Leen; Bob Bryla, Michael Murphy, and Johnny Griffin for their assistance with photographs and other artifacts; Eve Brandel, Mark Brailsford, and the family of Reginald Siki; Jon Strickland; Jan-Christopher Horak at the UCLA Film & Television Archive for his help on the life of Samuel Rachmann; Richard Baumann and Bill Sandow, Billy Sandow's grandsons, who opened up Billy's collected papers to me; Chris Swisher; Charlie Thesz; Amy Reading, who shared her research on the Mabray Gang without a second thought; Court Bauer; Neal Pease; Richard White; Mike Chapman; and Olga Bogatova.

For their generous assistance sorting out issues related to boxing, thank you to Arly Allen; Peter Benson; Gerald Gems; Steven Riess; Mike DeLisa at the Cyber Boxing Zone; and Tracy Callis, Dan Cuoco, and everyone at the International Boxing Research Organization.

A huge thanks to all of the remarkable librarians and archivists who bent over backwards and never seemed to lose patience with my requests to help track down obscure documents and dig through endless boxes of paper. Their dedication to their work was a constant source of inspiration. In particular, there were Natasha Lyandres, George Rugg, Gregory Bond, Sara Weber and all of the staff at the University of Notre Dame's Hesburgh Library, home to the remarkable Jack Pfefer collection;

Vanessa Nastro at the Port Washington Public Library, who helped suss out just what went on between Jack Curley and Huey Long at Sands Point; Maris Mägi at the Estonian Sports and Olympic Museum, who helped me track down George Hackenschmidt's unpublished memoir; Cindy Slater at the H.J. Lutcher Stark Center for Physical Culture and Sports in Austin; Gwyneth G. Hanrey at the Dayton History Center, who helped me research the death of Erika Shikat; everyone at the New York State Archives for their help with the records of the State Athletic Commission; Christy Orquera at the Great Neck Library; Leila Mattson at the Great Neck Historical Society; Sarah LeRoy at the National Archives at Kansas City, who did unbelievable work locating the court files for the Mabray Gang; the staff of the San Francisco, Columbus, New York, and Boston Public libraries; and Daniel Levy at the University of Washington. Thanks, too, to everyone at the University of Missouri for their belief in this project, especially Andrew Davidson, Mary Conley, and Adam Criblez.

And endless blessings upon all the friends and family who supported and encouraged me along the way: Jay Walsh, Tom Beaujour, Tim and Elizabeth Bracy, Rebecca Coseboom, Michael Rivo, Jack Cheevers, Ryan Walsh, Cory Brown, Julie Werblez, Carmen Chacon, and my family—Dennis Fogh, Marilyn Mcadoo, Tim Fogh, Darlene Flynn, and Steve, Chris, Erin, Terry, Bryan, Sam, Hannah, Abby, Paige, Carole, John, and my wonderful wife, Shannon.

Notes

Prologue
The Kingfish Takes a Powder

1. Judith Goldstein, *Inventing Great Neck* (New Brunswick: Rutgers University Press, 2006), 3.

2. Goldstein, *Inventing*, 30.

3. Richard D. White, email message to author, April 18, 2019.

4. "Huey Long Socked at L.I. Club Party, And, O, His Story," *Daily News* (New York, NY), August 29, 1933; "Huey Long Victim of Asparagus," *The Times* (Munster, IN), August 31, 1933.

5. Thomas Harry Williams, *Huey Long* (New York: Vintage Books, 1981), 648–50.

6. "Merger on O'Mahoney," *Time*, August 12, 1935.

7. "Socker is Sought," *Washington Post*, August 30, 1933.

8. Pat Robinson "Huey Not Hard Boiled; Just Softly," *Times* (Munster, IN), August 31, 1933; "Nation-Wide Drive Led Against Long," *New York Times*, September 1, 1933; Jack Curley, "Jack Curley, Well Known Sportsman, Offers His Story of How He Acted as Nurse to Huey Long After Incident at Sands Point Club," *New York Enquirer*, September 3, 1933.

9. "Huey Long Is Said to Have Been Punched," *Sacramento Bee*, August 28, 1933; "Long Amid Bedlam Denounces Foes," *New York Times*, August 30, 1933.

10. "Who Hit Huey Long, and Why? Attack on Senator Mystifies," *Brooklyn Times Union*, August 29, 1933; "Long Amid Bedlam."

11. Williams, *Huey Long*, 654; "Long Amid Bedlam"; Richard D. White, *Kingfish: The Reign of Huey P. Long* (United Kingdom: Random House Publishing Group, 2009), 186.

12. "Nation-Wide Drive."

13. White, *Kingfish*, 186.

14. "Huey Long Booed in His Home State," *New York Times*, October 17, 1933.

15. White, *Kingfish*, 267.

16. Jack Curley to Huey Long, September 9, 1933, The History Center, Port Washington Public Library, Port Washington, New York.

17. Nat Fleischer, "Forty Years in Sports," *The Ring*, July 1934.

18. "Sporting Squibs," *Lincoln Star*, May 4, 1918; Jack Curley, "Jack Curley, Dabbler in Everything, Tries Hand at Managing Enrico Caruso," *Des Moines Register*, March 5, 1936.

19. Joe Williams, "By Joe Williams," *Knoxville News-Sentinel*, November 1, 1929.

20. Jack Curley with Frank Graham, "Memoirs of a Promoter," *The Ring*, May 1930, 7.

21. "Merger on O'Mahoney." According to the Theodore Roosevelt Center at Dickinson State University, Roosevelt did not wish for any honorary pallbearers. His casket may have, instead, been carried by porters. Curley may have been telling the truth regarding his presence at the president's funeral, but it is impossible to know for sure.

22. Curt Riess, "Honesty Is the Worst Policy," *Esquire*, December 1, 1941.

23. John Rickards Betts, *America's Sporting Heritage: 1850–1950* (Reading: Addison-Wesley Publishing Company, 1974), 169; "At Random in Sportdom," *Asbury Park Press*, June 17, 1915.

24. Charles Cochran, *Secrets of a Showman* (London: William Heinemann, Ltd., 1925), 114.

25. Jack Miley, "Circus Men, Scribe Fears, Putting Rasslin' Near Brink," *Detroit Free Press*, April 27, 1936.

26. Alva Johnston, "Cauliflowers and Pachyderms," *New Yorker*, July 28, 1934, 20.

27. Neil Harris, *Humbug: The Art of P.T. Barnum* (Boston: Little, Brown, and Company, 1973), 216.

Chapter 1
The Glamour of the Streets and the Life That Seethed About Them

1. Curley, "Memoirs," May 1930, 6; Information on San Francisco's wharf comes from the San Francisco Maritime Museum.

2. "Jack Curley, World's Biggest Promoter, Got Start in Life as a Newsboy in St. Louis," *Quad City Times*, April 4, 1920; "Jack Curley Dies Suddenly in Home," *Brooklyn Daily Eagle*, July 12, 1937; Lewis Francis Byington, *The History of San Francisco* (Chicago: S.J. Clarke Publishing Company, 1931), 350.

3. "Gloria In Excelsis, The Centennial Fourth in San Francisco," *San Francisco Chronicle*, July 6, 1876; Alan Ziajka, *Lighting the City, Changing the World* (San Francisco: University of San Francisco, 2014), 8–10.

4. Johnston, "Cauliflowers," 24; Jack Miley, "A Tribute to Curley," *Daily News* (New York, NY), July 13, 1937.

5. The *Langley San Francisco Directory* for the years 1888–1894 lists Henri Schuhl (spelled Henry in 1888) as conductor for the Geary Street Railroad. He lived at 1411 ½ Buchanan Street in 1888 and then at 1433 O'Farrell Street. This is almost certainly Curley's father, and these years would seem to conform to Curley's story of having arrived back in the city as a teenager. The same name does not appear in any preceding directory for the city. This could add evidence to the idea that Curley was not actually born in San Francisco, but it's also possible that the family did not have a fixed address when Curley was born.

6. Curley, "Memoirs," May 1930, 6.

7. Curley, "Memoirs," May 1930, 6.

8. Roger Kahn, *A Flame of Pure Fire* (New York: Harper Collins, 2012), 4; "Dempsey Knocked Out," *Boston Daily Globe*, August 28, 1889.

9. Joseph S. Page, email message to author, October 22, 2018; Curley, "Memoirs," May 1930, 6.

10. Curley, "Memoirs," August 1930, 35; Curley, "Memoirs," May 1930, 6.

11. Fleischer, "Forty Years." The fights Curley is referencing are the James Corbett and Bob Fitzsimmons heavyweight championship fight in Carson City, Nevada, on March 17, 1897, and the Bob Fitzsimmons and Peter Maher fight for the heavyweight championship on February 21, 1896, in Langtry, Texas.

12. Jack Curley, "How I Broke Into the Game," *News*, November 16, 1928. Curley is likely exaggerating here. According to an August 15, 1893, report in the Muncie *Evening Press*, a fire was set in the arena's ticket office by a group of "interlopers" denied entrance to the fight. According to that report and others, the fire was extinguished before setting off a panic and the fight ended with Greggains being knocked out in the fifteenth round.

13. Jack Curley, "Memoirs," May 1930, 6.

14. John Lardner, "The Pay Off," *Boston Globe*, July 13, 1937.

15. Tex O'Rourke, "Jack Curley Returns to Boxing," *The Ring*, December 1927.

16. "Sullivan and Ryan Meet," *New York Times*, January 20, 1885.

17. Lorena Hickok, "Tennis Promoter Likes Show Business," *Reno Gazette Journal*, February 18, 1931.

18. Gene Smith and Jayne Barry Smith, *The Police Gazette* (New York: Simon and Schuster, 1972), 104–7.

19. Ty Cobb, "Inside Stuff," *Nevada State Journal*, May 28, 1944.

20. Curley, "Memoirs," May 1930, 8.

21. "Jack of All Trades, But Master of Mat, That's Versatile Curley," *Daily News* (New York, NY), January 4, 1931.

22. Jack Curley, "Getting the Gate," *Liberty*, March 26, 1932.

23. Betts, *America's Sporting*, 121, 162; David G. Schwartz, *Roll The Bones* (Sheridan: Gotham Books, 2006), 338–40.

24. Richard C. Lindberg, *Gangland Chicago* (Lanham: Rowman & Littlefield, 2016), 36.

25. Curley, "Getting the Gate"; Curley, "Memoirs," October 1930, 34.

26. Curley, "Memoirs," October 1930, 34.

27. Curley, "Memoirs," October 1930, 34–35.

28. Curley, "Memoirs," October 1930, 47.

29. "Graft Hunters Get Five Heads; Craig A Victim," *Chicago Tribune*, December 15, 1903.

30. "Dies Riding In Street Car," *Chicago Tribune*, September 17, 1905.

31. Jack Curley, "Bullfight Promotion Stunt Shortest of Curley's Career," *Star Tribune* (Minneapolis, MN), March 4, 1936. Curley's claims of it being the first bullfight in America are plainly false. "I did know whether bullfights had been held in this country before that, but I had never heard of any," Curley later wrote, "and besides, someone else prepared the posters." The prospect of the bullfight did raise concerns

across Montana, culminating in a wire from the state's governor to the sheriff of Silver Bow County threatening an intervention from the state militia if Curley's event was allowed to proceed. "There was talk of Sodom and Gomorrah, frightful iniquities, cruelty to animals and, above all, desecration of the Sabbath," Curley later wrote. A defiant Curley began the day with a parade, the head matador riding in an open barouche with a troupe of bull fighters and mounted picadors following behind. Reports out of Butte, though, do not seem to indicate that his stadium was destroyed. He may be conflating his bullfight with one that had occurred in St. Louis the prior month. At that event, a pine arena was set aflame by a crowd enraged by the cancelation of a planned bullfight. For more information, see "Bullfight Stopped, But Crowd Is Mad And Wrecks Place," *Butte Miner*, June 6, 1904; "Governor Gets Bullfight Appeal," *The Butte Miner*, August 13, 1904; and Curley, "Memoirs," November 1930, 21.

32. Johnston, "Cauliflowers," 24.

33. Jack Curley, "42 Years on the Sports Trail," *Pittsburgh Sun Telegraph*, March 2, 1936. This story, too, is likely an exaggeration on Curley's part. Kellerman, for her part, makes no mention of Curley in *My Story*, her unpublished memoir. Angela Woollacott, author of *Race and the Modern Exotic: Three Australian Women on Global Display*, which includes a chapter on Kellerman, confirmed in an email exchange on April 28, 2019, that there's a possibility that Curley made an adjustment to the suit that influenced Kellerman's final design but that he can't be given the main credit.

34. Tom Anderson, "Jack Curley, the Promoter," *Nashville Banner*, January 21, 1931.

35. A.J. Liebling, "From Sarah Bernhardt to Yukon Erik," *New Yorker*, November 13, 1954, 132–49.

36. Johnston, "Cauliflowers," 21.

Chapter 2
A Fake Verisimilitude

1. Scott Beekman, *Ringside: A History of Professional Wrestling in America* (Westport: Praeger Publishers, 2006), 1.

2. Charles Wilson, *The Magnificent Scufflers: Revealing the Great Days When America Wrestled the World* (Brattleboro, VT: The Stephen Greene Press, 1959), 26–54.

3. John C. Meyers, *Wrestling: From Antiquity to Date* (St. Louis: Von Hoffman Press, 1931), 68; Beekman, *Ringside*, 19–21.

4. "The Gladiators," *San Francisco Chronicle*, November 15, 1874.

5. "The Gladiators"; "A Put-up Job: The Great Wrestling Match Between Miller and Bauer," *San Francisco Chronicle*; May 29, 1875; Scott Beekman, email message to author, September 2, 2019.

6. Byington, *History*, 171.

7. Schwartz, *Roll*, 218, 236–37.

8. "A Put-up Job," *San Francisco Chronicle*.

9. "A Put-up Job," *San Francisco Chronicle*; "Roman Wrestling: How the Recent Matches Have Been Arranged—The Swindle Exposed," *San Francisco Chronicle*, June 1, 1875.

10. "Municipal Police Athletic Club," *New York Times*, April 8, 1877; "Miscellaneous City News—The Police Athletic Club," *New York Times*, March 24, 1887; "Policemen as Pugilists: A Club Fight in the Street," *New York Times*, March 23, 1878.

11. Scott Beekman, email messages to author, September 2–3, 2019.

12. "Harry Hill is Dead," *New York Times*, August 28, 1896; "A Successful Benefit," *National Police Gazette*, May 12, 1894; Luc Sante, *Low Life* (New York: Farrar, Straus, and Giroux, 1991), 109–10. Hill's club, as historian Luc Sante wrote, epitomized the ascendancy of vice in America from the gutter to the status of institution. Hill's shows of force to manage his crowd, as Sante writes, were often staged.

13. "The Wrestling Match," *Brooklyn Times Union*, March 21, 1877.

14. Scott Teal and J Michael Kenyon, *Wrestling in the Garden: The Battle for New York* (Gallatin: Crowbar Press, 2017), 14–15.

15. Teal and Kenyon, *Wrestling,* 12, 14; "Wrestling," *Brooklyn Daily Eagle*, October 27, 1879.

16. "Muldoon Defeats Bauer," *New York Times*, January 20, 1880; "Muldoon Defeats Bauer," *National Police Gazette*, January 31, 1880. Bauer was a tough, dangerous character later in his life. After returning to California, he set himself up as a saloon owner and pimp. Operating out of Los Angeles's red light district in an area called "Hell's Half Acre," he controlled a stretch of Alameda Street that came to be known as "Little Paree." He was a landlord to hundreds of women who rented rooms for two dollars a day. Inside, they serviced as many as thirty men a day, catering to the lowest-paying customers in the city. It was brutal and dehumanizing work that Bauer exploited for all he could. In 1896, the *Los Angeles Herald* estimated that he was clearing a minimum of $30,000 in profits, and likely much more. When Bauer died in 1901, the *Los Angeles Times* took the unusual step of celebrating over his grave. Bauer, the paper wrote, "lived off the earnings of fallen women, and even to that class he was cruel to a surprising degree. The adage which enjoins saying only good of those who are dead cannot apply to him, and among those who felt his cruelty the news that he is no more will be received with a feeling of satisfaction." See "A Grinding and Sinful Monopoly," *Los Angeles Herald*, March 3, 1896; "'King of Little Paree' Pays Wages of Sin," *Los Angeles Times*, December 31, 1901; and "'King' Unmourned," *Los Angeles Times*, January 3, 1902, for more information.

17. "Muldoon–Rigal," *Daily Alta*, June 5, 1883. Muldoon's technique of using advance men to promote his shows was similar to a method used in traveling medicine shows in which show employees would arrive days ahead of the show to seek out townspeople who could vouch for the supposed cures.

18. Betts, *America's Sporting,* 61; Beekman, *Ringside,* 16.

19. Smith and Smith, *The Police Gazette,* 13–19; Elliot J. Gorn and Warren Goldstein, *A Brief History of American Sports* (Urbana: University of Illinois Press, 1993), 117. Fox grew wealthy enough to commission the building of a seven-story, $250,000 structure in 1883 near the corner of Pearl and Dover Streets in Manhattan.

20. Steven Johnson and Greg Oliver, *The Pro Wrestling Hall of Fame: The Storytellers* (Toronto: ECW Press, 2019), 21.

21. Graham Noble, "The Life and Death of The Terrible Turk," *Eurozine*, May 23, 2003; Phil Lions email message to author, September 24, 2022.

22. William A. Brady, *Showman* (New York: E.P. Dutton & Company, 1937), 210, 211, 215–16.

23. A. J. Liebling, "The Opera House Slugger," *New Yorker*, October 30, 1937.

24. "Yusuf Fouled Roeber," *New York Times*, March 27, 1898.

25. "Wrestlers Have a Fight," *New York Times*, May 1, 1898.

26. Liebling, "Opera."

27. Brady, *Showman*, 221.

28. Liebling, "Opera."

29. "The Strangler's Match," *The Enquirer* (Cincinnati), February 17, 1886.

30. Mark Hewitt, *Catch Wrestling: A Wild and Wooly Look at the Early Days of Pro Wrestling in America* (Boulder, CO: Paladin Press, 2005), 8.

31. Robert K. DeArment, *Bat Masterson: The Man and the Legend* (Norman: University of Oklahoma Press, 1979), 361, 367.

32. Hewitt, *Catch*, 1.

33. Edward Hitchcock and Richard Nelligan, *Wrestling, Catch-as-Catch-Can Style* (New York: American Sports Publishing Company, 1898), 3.

34. Gorn and Goldstein, *Brief History*, 17–18.

35. L. A. Jennings, "'Rough-And-Tumble': The Deeply Southern Tradition of Nose-Biting, Testicle-Ripping, and Eye-Gouging," Vice.com, September 22, 2016; Interview with Mark Hewitt, January 12, 2022; Beekman, *Ringside*, 37.

36. Westbrook Pegler, "Westbrook Pegler Says," *Washington Post*, January 15, 1931.

37. "Evan Lewis a Winner," *Buffalo Evening News*, June 21, 1898.

38. Pegler, "Westbrook Says."

39. Graham Noble, "Life and Death"; Johnson and Oliver, *Storytellers*, 24.

40. Lou Thesz and Kit Bauman, *Hooker* (Gallatin, TN: Crowbar Press, 2011), 30–32.

41. Harley Race and Gerry Tritz, *King of the Ring* (New York: Sports Publishing, 2004), 5; Joe Nickell, *Secrets of the Sideshows* (Lexington, KY: University of Kentucky Press, 2005), 62–63.

42. Ed Lewis, unpublished manuscript; Hjalmar Lundin, *On the Mat and Off: Memoirs of a Wrestler* (New York: Albert Bonnier Publishing House, 1937), 67. In a February 4, 1924, article from the *Kansas City Times* ("Playing A 'Safe' Game"), Ed Lewis was described as "looking like a veritable Job, afflicted with boils."

43. Thesz and Bauman, *Hooker*, 48.

44. Hewitt, *Catch*, 5.

45. Interview with Charlie Thesz, May 21, 2019.

46. Scott Teal, *Wrestling Archive Project: Classic 20ᵗʰ Century Mat Memories; Volume 1* (Gallatin: Crowbar Press, 2015), 194–95.

47. Pat Laprade and Dan Murphy, *Sisterhood of the Squared Circle* (Toronto: ECW Press, 2017), 15–22.

48. "Karpe's Comments," *Buffalo News*, August 17, 1923; Jan Todd, "The Mystery of Minerva," *Iron Game History*, vol. 1, no. 2, 14–17.

49. Todd, "The Mystery." Minerva retired from the stage in 1910 and became a successful real estate investor in New York and New Jersey. She died on September 1, 1923, from cancer.

50. Thesz and Bauman, *Hooker*, 32. Gus Schoenlein often wrestled under the name Americus, and was well known not only in Maryland but in many other states where he appeared.

51. Liebling, "From Sarah Bernhardt," 132–49.

52. Lewis, unpublished manuscript.

53. Lewis, unpublished manuscript. In his column in the August 1, 1937, *New York Daily Mirror*, sportswriter Dan Parker wrote, "Whenever you see a picture of a wrestler in a hospital bed staring at you from the sports pages, you can bet that in 99 cases out of 100 the faker is so bursting with health he's a menace to himself. The hospital cot finish is now generally adopted to make an inferior wrestler's 'victory' over one of his betters look kosher."

54. Will Connolly, "A Mat Traitor or Rasslin Killjoy," *San Francisco Chronicle*, February 4, 1936.

55. Thesz and Bauman, *Hooker*, 48.

56. Robert Edgren, "Pardello Said To Be Pioneer of Modern Time Wrestling Game," *Dayton Daily News*, October 4, 1931; Greg Oliver and Steven Johnson, *Pro Wrestling Hall of Fame: The Heels* (Toronto: ECW Press, 2010), 9.

57. Grantland Rice, "Rasslin' Gets A Toe Hold," *Collier's*, March 14, 1931.

58. Interview with Bill Apter, August 26, 2018. The word "kayfabe" is frequently used to refer to this practice. As a writer for several magazines dedicated to professional wrestling, Bill Apter had more access to the inside world of wrestling than perhaps any other non-wrestler or promoter. When I asked him how we would describe kayfabe, he answered, "'Keeping the family secret' is what [kayfabe] really meant. Magicians kayfabe the way they do their tricks. They don't break the unwritten code and let the public in on how the business of trickery operates. It was the same back when kayfabe was the unwritten law in pro wrestling."

59. Thesz and Bauman, *Hooker*, 33–34.

Chapter 3
Americans Believe Him Next to Invincible

1. Nat Fleischer, "Gotch Made U.S. Mat Mad," *Ring Wrestling*, September 1963.

2. Jack Curley, "Wrestling's Dark Horse," undated clipping.

3. Mike Chapman, email message to author, August 6, 2021. There is some debate over what year Gotch was born, and dates fluctuate between 1876 and 1878. The date listed on Frank Gotch's mausoleum is April 27, 1877, which is the date used here.

4. Mike Chapman, *The Life and Legacy of Frank Gotch: King of the Catch-as-Catch-Can Wrestlers* (Boulder, CO: Paladin Press, 2008), 3.

5. Tim Hornbaker, "Frank Gotch Wrestling History," *Legacy of Wrestling*, September 23, 2022. http://www.legacyofwrestling.com/Gotch.html.

6. Chapman, *Life*, 6.

7. Curley, "Wrestling's Dark Horse."

8. Martin Burns, *The Life Work of "Farmer" Burns* (Omaha: A.J. Kuhlman, 1911), 106.

9. Burns, *Life Work*, 49.

10. Lundin, *On the Mat*, 49.

11. Burns, *Life Work*, 89.

12. Burns, *Life Work*, 28.

13. Amy Reading, *The Mark Inside: A Perfect Swindle, a Cunning Revenge, and a Small History of the Big Con* (New York: Alfred A. Knopf, 2012), 13.

14. In his life, Marsh would refer to himself by a number of different names. His birth name was Joe Carroll Marsh, but he would work as Joe Marsh, Joe Carroll, and J. C. Marsh, as well as under other names. Later in his life, he used Ole Marsh, which is what is used throughout this book for consistency.

15. Alva Johnston, *The Legendary Mizners* (New York: Farrar, Straus & Young, 1953), 78.

16. "Frank Gotch Made $40,000 From Alaska Mat Campaign," *Milwaukee Free Press*, April 8, 1917.

17. Milton MacKaye, "On the Hoof," *Saturday Evening Post*, December 14, 1935.

18. Steve Yohe, "A Review of the Nine Frank Gotch/Tom Jenkins Matches," Wrestling Classics. http://wrestlingclassics.com/.ubb/ultimatebb.php?ubb=get_topic;f=10;t=0 02261;p=1. Gotch and Jenkins's first match, technically speaking, was held sometime in October 1900 in Humboldt, Iowa. It was a private match, and not related to the series they wrestled later that decade.

19. "Murmurs About the Big Match," *Cleveland Plain Dealer*, February 5, 1905. For one example of many, see: Cotton Calvert "Turk Is Babe Before Gotch," *Joliet Evening Herald-News*, April 15, 1909. It describes a 1909 Gotch match promoted by Jack Curley that Calvert called "one of the merriest fakes ever pulled over the eyes of the American public." However, Gotch, he continued, "I know to be above suspicion."

20. "Gotch–Jenkins Bout Not a Fake," *Minneapolis Tribune*, March 26, 1905. For more information, see also, "Jenkins Pins Gotch in Wrestling Match," *New York Times*, March 16, 1905.

21. George Hackenschmidt, *The Way to Live: Health & Physical Fitness* (London: Health & Strength Limited, 1908), 107.

22. "How Gotch Won a Title Without a Fall," *Buffalo Enquirer*, April 6, 1908.

23. Cochran, *Secrets*, 110; Hackenschmidt, *The Way*, 144; Graeme Kent, *A Pictorial History of Wrestling* (London: Spring Books, 1968), 146–55.

24. Cochran, *Secrets*, 112.

25. Robert Edgren, "Roosevelt's Grip Makes 'Hack's' Eyes Get Briny," *Evening World* (New York), March 23, 1908.

26. "Hackenschmidt, the Russian Lion, Who is Matched to Wrestle Frank Gotch, Has Never Been Defeated" *Washington Post*, February 23, 1908.

27. "Champion Wrestler Quits, Exhausted," *New York Times*, April 4, 1908. Sadly, no footage of the match has survived.

28. George Hackenschmidt, *The Russian Lion* (unpublished manuscript in possession of author) 241.

29. Hackenschmidt, *Russian*, 242.

30. "Champion Wrestler Quits."

31. "Hackenschmidt Concedes Frank Gotch Best Man in the World," *Salt Lake Herald Tribune*, April 5, 1908.

32. "Hackenschmidt Concedes."

33. George Siler, "Gotch Wins World's Wrestling Championship by Making 'Russian Lion' Quit," *Chicago Tribune*, April 4, 1908; Tim Hornbaker, "Frank Gotch."

34. "Grapplers Ready for Big Contest," *New York Times*, September 3, 1911. Tracing the history of wrestling's championship claims is a convoluted and all but hopeless task. During the 1800s, champions had tended to be localized to countries, states, or towns, or to specific styles of wrestling. Athletes could and did declare themselves the champion of virtually anywhere. William Muldoon once even declared himself the champion of the universe. Hackenschmidt's 1905 claim to be world champion is generally accepted by historians as the beginning of an incredibly twisted line of champions in the catch-as-catch-can style, which was emerging as the most popular style of wrestling by the 1900s.

35. "Gotch Flops Pole in Easy Victory," *Chicago Tribune*, June 2, 1910.

Chapter 4
I Never Miked an Honest Man

1. Curley, "Memoirs," December 1930, 43.

2. Tim Hornbaker, "The Master of Medicine and Gimmicks: Dr. B.F. Roller," Legacy of Wrestling, September 23, 2022, http://www.legacyofwrestling.com/RollerBio.html; "Died in Doctor's Office," *Philadelphia Inquirer*, May 18, 1903; untitled clipping, *Pennsylvania Gazette*, May 15, 1933; University of Pennsylvania, email message to author, March 2, 2020.

3. Fred Beell and Jack Carkeek are two essential figures in wrestling history. Beell was a German-born wrestler who had trained under Evan Lewis. He is one of the only wrestlers ever to gain a clean win over Frank Gotch. Beell's victory over Gotch came in New Orleans on December 1, 1906, in a match that was almost certainly rigged. Wrestler Ed Lewis, in his memoir, called it a "betting coup" for Gotch, and it's long been suggested that Gotch took advantage of his "can't lose" reputation to pull a swerve on overconfident gamblers. If the match, indeed, was a fake, the wrestlers' work in the ring was sophisticated enough that newspaper writers and the fans didn't openly suspect it. Jack Carkeek was a Zelig-like figure born in Rockland, Michigan. He was a well-trained and respected wrestler, as well as a silver-tongued entertainer. He'd traveled the country with William Muldoon, been a star in England, where he was billed as the "King of Wrestlers," and was one of the most feared grapplers on multiple continents for much of the late nineteenth century.

4. "131,500 is Fortune Netted by Bunco Gang in Seattle," *Seattle Star*, August 23, 1906; "Bunco Men Leave Between Night and Early Morning," *Seattle Star*, August 24, 1906.

5. "Must Stop All Wrestling Fakes," *Vancouver Daily World*, October 20, 1906.

6. Curley, "Memoirs," January 1931, 34.

7. Curley, "Memoirs," January 1931, 34.

8. Susan Grant, email message to author, July 28, 2019; Curley, "Memoirs," January 1931, 35; "How the Fake Wrestling Or 'Big Stores' Game Is Worked," *Seattle Daily Times*, October 8, 1909. How honest Curley and Marsh were being in their initial protestations is impossible to establish. Curley would write later that Marsh

had insisted on being cut in on proceeds from the Exposition, a demand Curley claimed to have laughed at. There is no evidence Curley had links to the kinds of organized swindles Marsh was later connected with, but there is a preponderance of circumstantial evidence that would at least place him, Frank Gotch, Farmer Burns, and others in the orbit of those eventually arrested. Evidence also exists that would suggest Marsh and Curley were at least familiar with each other prior to Curley arriving in Seattle, including an inscribed photograph from Curley that Marsh kept in his possession until his death.

9. Advertisement for Roller–Warner Match, *Seattle Star*, September 22, 1909. Like many barnstormers, Bert Warner used multiple names during his career. In Seattle, he was known as Bert Shores.

10. "Warner Shows Up Dr. Roller's Game," *Seattle Star*, September 25, 1909; "Rowdy Scenes at Wrestling Match," *Victoria Daily Times*, September 25, 1909.

11. "Warner Shows."

12. Curley, "Memoirs," January 1931, 35.

13. "Warner Shows"; "Rowdy"; "Roller Caught With the Goods," *Butte Daily Post*, October 2, 1909.

14. "Dr. Roller Arrested," *Seattle Star*, October 4, 1909.

15. Curley, "Memoirs," January 1931, 41. Charges against Ben Roller were dropped when Kenneth C. Beaton, managing editor of the *Star*, learned of Marsh's arrest.

16. "Joe Carroll, Alias Ole Marsh, Arrested," *Seattle Daily Times*, October 8, 1909.

17. David W. Maurer, *The Big Con: The Story of the Confidence Men* (New York: Anchor Press, 1999), 22–26.

18. Maurer, *Big Con*, 22–26.

19. "Carkeek Under Arrest," Sioux City Journal, August 27, 1910.

20. United States v. J.C. Mabray, et al., District Court of the United States, District of Nebraska, Omaha Division, January 15, 1910.

21. Maurer, *Big Con*, 103–4.

22. "Traveled 3,000 Miles to Be Swindled," *Atlanta Constitution*, March 18, 1910.

23. Raymond A. Smith, Jr, "John C.Mabray: A Con Artist in the Corn Belt," *The Palimpsest* 64, no. 4 (July–August 1983): 123–39.

24. Joe Marsh to Jack Pfefer, September 15, 1939, Jack Pfefer Wrestling Collection, Hesburgh Libraries, University of Notre Dame.

25. James J. Hawkins, *Mabray and the Mikes* (Little Rock, AR: Democrat Print and Lithographing, 1910), 107.

Chapter 5
When a Mayor Leaves Office He's an Ex-Mayor, Isn't He?

1. Geoffrey C. Ward, *Unforgivable Blackness: The Rise and Fall of Jack Johnson* (New York: Vintage Books, 2006), 23–25. Johnson would later write that many battle royals were "framed up," with a group of boxers agreeing in advance to work together so one would be guaranteed to win, and then split the victor's purse between them. During the Springfield battle royal, Johnson had to fight off one such group, knocking all four men out. When one had tried to get back on his feet and continue fighting, Johnson had told him, "If you get up, I will kill you."

2. Ward, *Unforgivable*, 27-29; Curley, "Memoirs," July 1930, 18–19, 49.

3. Curley, "Getting the Gate."

4. Jack London, "It Was Not 'Too Much Johnson' But 'All Johnson' For Tommy Burns Did Not Have a Look-In to Win Fight," *Philadelphia Inquirer*, December 27, 1908.

5. "Jeffries Will Meet Johnson," *Los Angeles Times*, March 1, 1909.

6. Randy Roberts, *Papa Jack: Jack Johnson and the Era of White Hopes* (New York: The Free Press, 1983), 85.

7. Ward, *Unforgivable*, 168–69.

8. Rex Beach, "Rex Beach Sizes Up the Fighters," *The Boston Globe*, July 2, 1910.

9. James Jeffries with Eddy Orcutt, "Inside Those Ropes," *Saturday Evening Post*, August 17, 1935.

10. Johnston, "Cauliflowers," 20.

11. Curley, "Memoirs," February 1931, 45.

12. Ward, *Unforgivable*, 217.

13. Charles Samuels, *The Magnificent Rube: The Life and Gaudy Times of Tex Rickard* (New York: McGraw-Hill, 1957), 175.

14. Hugh S. Fullerton, *Two Fisted Jeff* (Chicago: Consolidated Book Publishers, 1929), 292.

15. Curley, "Memoirs," February 1931, 45.

16. Curley, "Memoirs," March 1931, 36.

17. Curley, "Memoirs," March 1931, 37.

18. Curley, "Memoirs," March 1931, 36. It's now assumed that Curley had planned to bring Gama to America to wrestle Frank Gotch, as several references to Gotch were planted in newspaper articles leading up to the match. If that was the plan, a tour of America never materialized. Gama returned to India at the end of the year and would live and perform there for over 40 more years.

19. Curley, "Memoirs," March 1931, 37.

20. It was somewhere around the time of this trip to Europe that Roller began claiming injuries with a hilarious frequency. He repeatedly injured his shoulders and knees, broke his ribs over and over, and was unusually susceptible to being knocked unconscious.

21. Cochran, *Secrets*, 117.

22. Neal Please, "Mighty Son of Poland: Stanislaus Zbyszko, Polish Americans, and Sport in the Twentieth Century," *Polish American Studies*, Vol. 74, No. 1, (Spring 2017): 7–26.

23. Johnston, "Cauliflowers," 23; Curley, "Memoirs," April 1931, 42.

Chapter 6
The Sodden Earth Never Closed Over a Deader One in the World

1. Curley, "Memoirs," May 1931, 45.

2. "Bars Wrestling Promoters," *New York Times*, February 7, 1913; Hugh S. Fullerton, "The Gotch–Hackenschmidt Fake That Failed," *Reno Gazette Journal*, November 18, 1914.

3. "'Never Again' Says Public of Fiasco," *Tacoma Times*, September 5, 1911.

4. H. E. K., "Big Mat Go Like Ajax vs. Ulysses," *Chicago Tribune*, September 3, 1911.

5. "Bout to Settle an Old Grudge," *Scranton Truth*, August 15, 1911.

6. John Kieran, "Sports of the Times," *New York Times*, April 14, 1938. An alternate version of what happened was presented by a wrestler named Ad Santel (Adolph Ernst), and advanced in wrestler Lou Thesz's biography *Hooker*. Santel, Thesz claimed, said that he was responsible for injuring Hackenschmidt's knee, and that he was paid $5,000 by Frank Gotch to do so. Santel was a dangerous wrestler and capable of inflicting injury. It is not impossible that his claim is true, but the consensus among the researchers consulted is that it is not. Additionally, Curley stuck to the story of Roller accidentally injuring Hackenschmidt's knee throughout his life. In this case, given that there is no other evidence to contradict his story, we'll give Curley the benefit of the doubt.

7. Curley, "Memoirs," June 1931, 44.

8. Curley, "Memoirs," June 1931, 44.

9. Hackenschmidt, *Russian*, 297.

10. Hackenschmidt, *Russian*, 296, 298.

11. "Human Tide Surges on Wrestling Arena," *Los Angeles Times*, September 4, 1911.

12. Curley, "Memoirs," June 1931, 44; H. E. K., "Gotch Downs Hack in 2 Quick Falls with All Bets Off," *Chicago Tribune*, September 5, 1911.

13. Jack Curley, "Curley Recounts Gotch–Hackenschmidt Feud," *Minneapolis Star Tribune*, March 1, 1936; Pegler, "Westbrook Pegler Says"; Curley, "Memoirs," June 1931, 44.

14. "Gotch Champion Wrestler of World," *New York Times*, September 5, 1911; Hackenschmidt, *Russian*, 299.

15. "Gotch Defeats Hackenschmidt Without Ever Extending Himself," *Los Angeles Herald*, September 5, 1911; Marcus Griffin, *The Annotated Fall Guys: The Barnums of Bounce*, annotated by Steve Yohe and Scott Teal (Gallatin: Crowbar Press, 2019), 114.

16. "Lion Easy Prey," *Baltimore Sun*, September 5, 1911; "Should Return Money Bet," *Norfolk Weekly News-Journal*, September 15, 1911.

17. Arthur Daley, "Sports of the Times," *New York Times*, February 13, 1949.

18. Lloyd Kenyon Jones and E. W. Clark, "Champion Frank Gotch Conquers Hackenschmidt in Less Than 20 Minutes of Actual Wrestling," *Chicago Inter Ocean*, September 5th, 1911; Fullerton, "The Gotch-Hackenschmidt Fake."

19. Griffin, *Annotated Fall Guys*, 114–15.

20. Curley, "Memoirs," June 1931.

21. Jones and Clark, "Champion Frank Gotch."

22. "Humboldt Goes Mad," *Sioux City Journal*, September 5, 1911; "Tribune Branch Offices Crowded," *Chicago Tribune*, September 5, 1911.

23. Kieran, "Sports of the Times"; "Gotch Defeats Hackenschmidt."

24. Hackenschmidt, *Russian*, 300.

25. H. E. K., "Gotch Downs."

26. Curley, "Memoirs," June 1931, 16.

27. "'Never Again.'"

28. Luke Stadel, "Wrestling and Cinema, 1892–1911," *Early Popular Visual Culture*, 2013, Vol. 11, No. 4, 342–64. Gotch and Hackenschmidt's match would be the last-known wrestling match committed to film for almost a decade. All copies of it, as well as any other film of Frank Gotch wrestling, have been lost.

29. "Police Fight Gaming," *Chicago Inter Ocean*, September 5, 1911.

30. Curley, "Memoirs," June 1931, 16.

31. "Wife Divorces Jack Curley," *Chicago Tribune*, September 16, 1911; "Jack Curley's Wife Secures a Divorce," *Buffalo Commercial*, September 18, 1911; "Wrestling Promoter Is Sued by His Wife," *Hutchinson Gazette*, September 15, 1911.

Chapter 7
The Greatest Promotional Odyssey of Modern Times

1. Arly Allen, *Jess Willard: Heavyweight Champion of the World (1915–1919)* (Jefferson, NC: McFarland & Company, 2017), 11. Floto's boss at the *Post*, Harry Tammen, was so taken with Floto's name that he appropriated it for the circus he had purchased as an investment, rechristening it as the Sells–Floto Circus. It operated under that name until being acquired by Ringling Brothers in 1921.

2. Curley, "Memoirs," July 1932, 26.

3. John Lardner, *White Hopes and Other Tigers* (New York: J. B. Lippincott Company, 1947), 20, 27, 41.

4. Roberts, *Papa Jack,* 126; Ward, *Unforgivable,* 258.

5. Johnston, "Cauliflowers," 20.

6. Roberts, *Papa Jack,* 131.

7. Curley, "Memoirs," July 1931, 43. Curley had initially hoped to hold the fight in Madison Square Garden but had been rebuked. Other Black fighters were appearing in New York, and the denial seemed to stem from a personal grudge against Johnson held by the state's boxing commissioner. "I guess that's discrimination for you," Johnson had said in response. "As an American citizen, why have I not the same right to box in New York as anyone else?"

8. Ward, *Unforgivable,* 280.

9. "Jack Curley to Wed," Morning Examiner (Bartlesville), May 23, 1912.

10. Curley, "Memoirs," July 1931, 43.

11. "Called Fido, Husband Fights," *Chicago Tribune*, June 1, 1912.

12. "Check for $31,100 Is Handed Johnson at Noon," *San Francisco Call*, July 5, 1912.

13. Abe Pollock, "Johnson Outclasses Fireman from Start," *San Francisco Call*, July 5, 1912.

14. Graham, "Memoirs," July 1931, 43.

15. Ward, *Unforgivable,* 284.

16. Ward, *Unforgivable,* 293–94; Charles J. Johnson, "The Short, Sad Story of Cafe de Champion—Jack Johnson's Mixed-Race Nightclub on Chicago's South Side," *Chicago Tribune*, May 25, 2018.

17. Ward, *Unforgivable,* 346.

18. John D. McCallum, *The World Heavyweight Boxing Championship: A History* (Radnor: Chilton Book Company, 1974), 76.

19. Curley, "Memoirs," August 1931, 34–35. Harry Frazee had been the financial backer behind the Jim Jeffries tour of 1910 and is best known by sports fans as the man who purchased the Boston Red Sox in 1916. Frazee famously sold Babe Ruth's contract to the New York Yankees in 1919. This began what Red Sox fans refer to as the "Curse of the Bambino," a drought of World Series wins that ran from 1918 to 2004. Curley told the story of the genesis of the Johnson fight on at least two occasions: once to *New York American* writer Frank Graham for a series in *Ring* magazine and a different version to Graham that was referenced in John D. McCallum's book *The World Heavyweight Boxing Championship*. The details are slightly different in each version, including variations in the order in which Johnson and Willard were signed for the bout. The version from *Ring* magazine is used here, as it is the version used in other books about Johnson and because it has the most in-depth telling of the story.

20. Samuels, *Magnificent Rube,* 179.

21. Johnston, "Cauliflowers," 20.

22. Curley, "Memoirs," August 1931, 34.

23. An excellent, if perhaps not wholly reliable, chronicle of Johnson's time in Russia can be found in the article "Jack and The Game," by Finis Farr in the June 22, 1959, issue of *Sports Illustrated*. Johnson, his new wife, and nephew were hurried out of Russia under what Johnson called the five-and-ten-law. "That means five minutes to pack and ten minutes to get out of town," he wrote. Johnson claimed to have connections with the Russian royal family through the promoter of his stage show that he was working with at the time. When Johnson was forced to exit Russia quickly, he not only had to leave fast but had to do it with what was apparently a nasty hangover. The night before, he claimed, he'd tried to go drink for drink with Rasputin and come out on the losing end.

24. "Syndicate Backs Willard," *New York Times,* September 14, 1914; Curley, "Memoirs," August 1931, 45–46; Johnston, "Cauliflowers," 20.

25. "Villa Sanctions Boxing," *New York Times,* January 1, 1915.

26. Grantland Rice, "The Sportlight," *Kansas City Star,* April 1, 1915.

27. Allen, *Jess Willard,* 14. *The Heart Punch* was directed by Stuart Paton, who is perhaps most famous for filming the 1916 version of *20,000 Leagues Under the Sea*. Paton is credited with writing, producing, and directing *The Heart Punch,* though Curley would later credit himself with conceiving the idea for the film and directing it.

28. Johnston, "Cauliflowers," 22.

29. Curley, "Memoirs," September 1931, 39.

30. "Willard Wins Heavyweight Title from Jack Johnson," *Lancaster Examiner,* April 7, 1915; "Jack Johnson vs. Jess Willard," BoxRec, September 23, 2022, http://boxrec .com/media/index.php/Jack_Johnson_vs._Jess_Willard.

31. "'Have My Wife Get Out of Here,' Said Johnson After 24th Round," *Washington Post,* April 6, 1915.

32. Damon Runyon, "Johnson Laid Low by Fist of Kansas in Twenty-Sixth," *San Francisco Examiner*, April 6, 1915.

33. Ward, *Unforgivable*, 380.

34. "32,000 At Fight; Receipts $110,000," *New York Times*, April 7, 1915.

35. "Promoters Of Big Fight at Havana Are Under Arrest," *Des Moines Tribune*, April 7, 1915; "Jack Curley in Court," *Victoria Daily Times*, April 7, 1915.

36. Ed W. Smith, "Cat Family Has Little on Curley for Lives," *Salt Lake Telegram*, October 1, 1918. Curley would claim that the amount was $1,500.

37. "Curley Leaves Debts Behind," *New York Times*, April 8, 1915; "Willard Given Rousing Welcome When His Boat Is Docked at Key West," *Los Angeles Herald*, April 8, 1915.

38. Curley, "Memoirs," October 1931, 36.

39. Ward, *Unforgivable*, 382.

40. Curley, "Memoirs," October 1931, 36.

41. "Golden Smile Ruined," *Washington Post*, April 12, 1915.

42. "Jack Curley and Others Get Cold Deal," *The Evening News* (Wilkes-Barre, PA), July 20, 1915.

43. Dan Streible, "A History of the Boxing Film, 1894–1915," *Film History* 3, no. 3 (1989): 235–57; "Won't Allow Fight Films Shown in the United States," *Dayton Daily News*, April 7, 1915.

44. Marcus Griffin, *Wise Guy: James J. Johnston: A Rhapsody in Fistics* (New York: Vanguard Press, 1933), 120–27. Hearing that Weber was willing to pay $50,000 to the person who could find a way to bring the films into the United States, boxing promoter James J. Johnston, who'd famously said he'd succeeded by "the sweat of my imagination," went as far as projecting the film from a camera located on one side of the Canadian border and capturing the images on negative film running on another machine located just twelve inches away on US soil. The transfer worked as planned, but a judge ordered the film destroyed, ruling that a metal chain running between the two machines and keeping them in sync violated the law. "Court decisions like that almost make a guy decide to give up thinking for a living," Johnston later said.

45. Westbrook Pegler, "Johnson Admits, In Book, Willard Bout Was Framed," *Washington Post*, August 12, 1927.

46. Ward, *Unforgivable*, 385–86. The film was distributed around the world but was unseen in America. Copies of the film were considered lost until the early 1960s.

47. Jack Johnson, *In the Ring and Out* (Detroit: Gale Research Company, 1975), 201; "Johnson Asks $50,000 for Losing to Willard," *Washington Post*, July 23, 1915.

48. Ward, *Unforgivable*, 370–71. Any appeals to Bryan clearly did not sway him. Prior to the fight, Bryan sent word to officials in Havana to refuse Johnson a passport.

49. "Jack Curley Dies; Sports Promoter," *New York Times*, July 12, 1937.

50. Ward, *Unforgivable*, 369.

Chapter 8
Call Me Desdichado

1. Lorraine Glennon, *The 20ᵗʰ Century: An Illustrated History of Our Lives and Times* (North Dighton: JG Press, 2000), 56; John Koegel, *Music in German Immigrant*

Theatre, New York City, 1840–1940 (Rochester: University of Rochester Press, 2009), 341–45.

2. "Wrestling In Favor Again," *New York Times*, October 31, 1915; "Champions of Mat in New Tourney," *New York Times*, November 7, 1915.

3. Lewis, unpublished manuscript.

4. "Wrestling Is Booming Here," *Herald News* (Passaic, NJ), November 23, 1915; Advertisement for "Second International Wrestling Tournament," *Evening World* (New York), November 27, 1915; Lewis, unpublished manuscript.

5. Lewis, unpublished manuscript. According to Ed Lewis, "Athletes were pretty much rated on their 'color' and their box office. The way each vied with the other for applause and acclaim, was as deft a battle of bow-purloining, scene-embezzling, and other felonies of the theatre as ever besmeared a stage."

6. "Tofalos Makes a Hit," *The Brooklyn Daily Eagle*, December 8, 1915; John J. Fleeson, "Wrestlers Go Through Their Parts in Double Quick Time," *Brooklyn Times Union*, January 12, 1916; "Wrestlers Growl Till Curtain Drops," *New York Times*, December 2, 1915; John J. Fleeson, "Wrestling Once More Popular," *Brooklyn Times Union*, December 20, 1915.

7. "'Scissors' Hold is Only One Used by Stecher in Subduing His Mat Rivals," *St. Louis Post-Dispatch*, December 12, 1915.

8. "Wrestlers Get Scrappy," *Brooklyn Daily Eagle*, December 4, 1915.

9. "'Masked Marvel' Wonder in More Ways Than One," *Washington Post*, January 9, 1916. For more information on the Masked Marvel, see "Masked Wrestler Wins," *New York Times*, December 10, 1915; "No Doubting the Fact That Masked Marvel is Henderson," *Brooklyn Daily Eagle*, December 27, 1915; "At a Woman's Whim He Stoops and Conquers," *San Francisco Chronicle*, January 23, 1916.

10. "Interest In Wrestling Tournament," *Courier-News* (Bridgewater, NJ), January 5, 1916.

11. Zoe Beckley, "'Kill Him,' Women at Wrestling Match Cry Out to Black-Masked Hero Who Thrills All New York," *Washington Post*, December 21, 1915.

12. Samuel Rachmann v. Mort Henderson, Superior Court of New York County, February 10, 1916.

13. Johnson and Oliver, *Storytellers*, 25–30.

14. "Woman's Whim."

15. "No Doubting the Fact That Masked Marvel is Henderson," *Brooklyn Daily Eagle*, December 27, 1915.

16. Samuel Rachmann v. Mort Henderson, Superior Court of New York County, February 10, 1916.

17. "Man in the Mask to Meet Stecher," *New York Times*, January 26, 1916.

18. "Stecher Throws Masked Marvel," *New York Times*, January 28, 1916.

Chapter 9
The People Booed; They Thought Frank Was Faking

1. Yohe, *Ed "Strangler" Lewis: Facts Within a Myth* (Vancleave: Ramble House, 2015), 8.

2. "World Champion Wrestler and Contestant Who Meet for Title in Evansville Tonight," *Evansville Press*, October 20, 1915.

3. "World Champion Wrestler," *Evansville Press*, October 20, 1915.

4. "Gotham Gets Info on One J. Stecher," *Omaha Daily Bee*, December 12, 1915.

5. "Nebraska Lad Is Wrestling Champ," *Omaha Daily Bee*, July 7, 1915.

6. "Nebraska Lad."

7. "Minister Gives Wrestling Match a Boost," *Butte Miner*, February 1, 1916.

8. "Nebraska Lad.;" "Joe Stecher Wins the Championship," *Fremont Tribune*, July 6, 1915; "Cutler Credits Stecher's Skill," *Omaha Daily Bee*, July 7, 1915.

9. "Gotch Comes Out of Retirement to Wrestle Ad Santel," *Austin American*, February 10, 1916.

10. "Frank Gotch Is Very Ill," *Star-Gazette* (Elmira, NY), May 4, 1916.

11. Yohe, *Facts Within*, 7, 9.

12. Lewis, unpublished manuscript, 19.

13. Yohe, *Facts Within*, 7.

14. Ralph Friedman, "Billy Sandow, The Jason of Wrestling," *The Sunday Oregonian*, February 12, 1967.

15. Lewis, unpublished manuscript.

16. Lewis, unpublished manuscript, 63. Lewis is referring to Benjamin Bosse, mayor of Evansville from 1914 to 1922.

17. Attendance figures for the match vary from 10,000 to 20,000 people, with 18,000 being the most commonly cited number.

18. Nat Fleischer, "Non-stoop Mat Bout," *The Ring*, July 1934.

19. Lynn Mucken, "Lewis' Manager Recalls July 4th Match," *Oregonian*, July 6, 1969.

20. "Will Probably Wrestle Again," *Wood County Reporter* (Grand Rapids, WI), July 13, 1916.

21. Stu Pospisil, "In 1916, Wrestlers Had a Stranglehold on the City," *Omaha World Herald*, July 4, 2016. Lewis would maintain for years that the match had been legitimate. His dodging and stalling, he claimed, were part of a deliberate strategy designed to wear Stecher down. And though the match would damage his reputation in some parts of the country, Billy Sandow claimed afterward that Lewis's asking price for matches rose higher than ever as a result of his being able to stay in the ring for such a long period of time with Stecher.

22. "Gotch Snaps Leg in an Exhibition Bout at Kenosha," *Chicago Tribune*, July 19, 1916.

23. George Strickler, "Referee Tells His Version of Debated Fall," *Chicago Tribune*, April 9, 1933.

24. "Gotch Snaps Leg."

25. "Stecher Good at Wrestling Early," *Daily Oklahoman*, July 2, 1916.

26. "No Rice for Joe," *Fremont Tri-Weekly Tribune*, December 12, 1916.

27. Lundin, *On the Mat*, 126–35.

28. "Caddock is Given Decision in Match with Joe Stecher," *Des Moines Register*, April 10, 1917; "Referee Sherman Presents His Case," *Des Moines Register*, April 15, 1917.

29. "What the Principals Say About the Result," *Omaha Daily News*, April 10, 1917; Charley Sherman, "Stecher, His Manager, and Sherman Make Statements," *Des Moines Register*, April 11, 1917.

30. Thesz and Bauman, *Hooker*, 58. Rumors have long persisted that the actual cause of Gotch's death was syphilis.

31. "Famous Wrestler Dies at His Home at Humboldt, IA., Sunday," *Quad City Times*, December 17, 1917.

32. "Frank Gotch Only Shadow of Former Wrestling Champ," *Winnipeg Tribune*, June 7, 1917.

33. "Special Trains to Funeral of Gotch," *Des Moines Tribune*, December 19, 1917.

34. "Fortunes in Pugilism," *Times Dispatch* (Richmond, VA), November 3, 1918.

Chapter 10
The Knockers and Scandalmongers Will Be Chased to the Woods

1. Marie B. Swanton v. John Curley, 273 N.Y. 325, 7 N.E.2d 250 (N.Y. 1937).

2. Charley Rose, "Jack Curley in Class by Himself as Promoter," *Ring Wrestling*, February 1965.

3. "Chairman Wenck is on the Grill of Cross-Examination for Four Hours at Albany," *New York Times*, January 31, 1917.

4. "Boxer is Killed in Ring," *New York Times*, January 31, 1917.

5. "Whitman Wants New Boxing Law," *New York Times*, February 1, 1917; "Legislature Passes Slater Bill, Killing Boxing In New York," *New York Times*, May 11, 1917.

6. "Promoter Jack Curley Makes Boxing Defense," *Star Gazette* (Elmira, New York), February 6, 1917; "Legislature Passes Slater."

7. "Willard Is Through," *The Province* (Vancouver, British Columbia), July 10, 1917.

8. Jack Curley, "Temperament Woe of Promoters," *Pittsburgh Sun Telegraph*, March 4, 1936. On a gate of $21,000, Curley paid Fulton and Dempsey $12,500 each, resulting in a $16,000 loss to Curley and his partners.

9. Damon Runyon, "Dempsey Knocks Out Fulton in 23 Seconds," *San Francisco Examiner*, July 28, 1918; Joe Vila, "Took Fulton While to Confess," *Philadelphia Inquirer*, February 4, 1919.

10. Brian Cronin, "Did Boxer Jack Dempsey Use Loaded Gloves When He Won His First Heavyweight Title?" LA Times, August 31, 2011. https://www.latimes.com/archives/blogs/sports-now/story/2011-08-31/did-boxer-jack-dempsey-use-loaded-gloves-when-he-won-his-first-heavyweight-title.

11. Damon Runyon, "By Damon Runyon," *Miami Tribune*, November 21, 1924.

12. Smith, "Cat Family." One sideline Curley explored during this time was a tour with the Italian tenor Enrico Caruso. In the summer of 1917, Curley managed a run of twelve Caruso shows in cities from New York to Denver. Rumors circulated, too, that Curley was at the center of an arrangement to bring a professional hockey team to New York to be a part of the National Hockey Association, although a deal never materialized. In 1926, Tex Rickard would succeed in establishing an NHL team, the New York Rangers. For more information, see "Montreal Critics Have New Scheme," *The Province* (Vancouver, British Columbia), January 11, 1916; "New York May Have Big Time Hockey," *Ottawa Citizen*, February 17, 1923; "Sporting Squibs"; Jack Curley, "Caruso Gay Figure, Valentino Vain Type," *Pittsburgh Sun-Telegraph*, March 5, 1936.

13. Lewis, unpublished manuscript.

14. Cy Sherman, "Caddock Wins in Dazzling Style," *Lincoln Star*, February 10, 1918.

15. "Stecher Eludes Zbyszko's Grasp," *New York Times*, March 2, 1918; "Pole Butts Lewis and Loses Match," *New York Times*, March 19, 1918; "Zbyszko Disqualified for Fouling Lewis," *Atlanta Constitution*, March 20, 1918. Wladek Zbyszko's nationality was a nagging problem throughout the time of America's involvement in World War I. In May 1918, Zbyszko was arrested by federal officials and held for several days over immigration issues. Doubt over his citizenship was depressing attendance at his matches outside of New York. To settle the issue, a lawsuit (certainly a ruse) was filed by Curley's business partner, Louis Meyer, alleging that Zbyszko had struck him after an argument in which Meyer called him a German. "I am one-hundred percent American," Zbyszko testified. The case was dismissed after Meyer was unable to show any injury from the struggle, but the story, with Zbyszko's words to the judge intact, made papers nationally. For more information, see "He Spanked Promoter Meyer," *New York Herald*, October 10, 1918.

16. Teal and Kenyon, *Wrestling*, 33–39; Yohe, *Facts Within*, 33–36.

17. Yohe, *Facts Within*, 32; "Zbyszko Is Victor in Bout with Lewis," *New York Times*, December 23, 1917.

18. Harry B. Smith, "Listen to the Wrestlers and their Debates," *San Francisco Chronicle*, June 1, 1917. Curley submitted a typed letter to reporters, promising not only to stake his entire fortune on the match but that he was "willing to be stopped at the ferry from ever again entering San Francisco unless the match proves to be on the dead level."

19. Yohe, *Facts Within*, 20, 25; Mucken, "Lewis' Manager Recalls." After Ed Lewis's five-hour match with Joe Stecher on July 16, 1916, Sandow planted a story with reporters that Lewis went out dancing after the match while Stecher spent the night in the hospital. Later in life, Sandow would claim Stecher suffered permanent brain damage from an Ed Lewis headlock. "He's still in a hospital in Minnesota and they won't allow newspaper men to interview him," he said, elliptically referring to Stecher's hospitalization for mental illness.

20. "Caddock and Stecher May Set New Wrestling Gate Record," *Buffalo Commercial*, January 15, 1920.

21. Igoe, "Joe Stecher Beats Earl Caddock For Wrestling Championship," *Des Moines Tribune*, January 31, 1920; "Stecher Defeats Caddock in Lively Tussle for World's Wrestling Title," *New York Times*, January 31, 1920; Yohe, *Facts Within*, 42. The surviving footage of the match can be seen at https://www.youtube.com/watch?v=18wMsQs LMGI.

22. "Week's Gross at Garden, $2,500," *Variety*, February 13, 1920.

Chapter 11
Much That Is Undesirable and Unfair Has Crept into the Sport

1. Swanton v. Curley. It's possible that Bessie was his fourth wife, as Curley's first wife had claimed he was married once before their marriage. Curley's personal life was complicated at best and ugly at times. Besides accusations of having abused his

first wife, his second wife, Marie, sued him for child support in 1935. She initially sued for $20,000 and was awarded somewhere between $6,000 to $7,500, the smaller amount due largely to the statute of limitations on her suit. Under the terms of the original divorce, Curley was allowed to provide for the children whatever amount he deemed necessary based on his past generosity in caring for them. But Curley's idea of generosity after the marriage was over, her lawyer said, was "not to pay one red cent." According to Marie, Curley talked her out of requiring him to pay a fixed amount. "That was because he was afraid I would put him in Ludlow Street Jail if he fell behind in his payments," she testified. "Those were the exact words he said to me." Asked why she agreed to the arrangement, she stated, "He was very glib. He has a very glib tongue and is a good talker. He talked me into a lot of things."

2. "Governor Miller Signs the Simpson Bill Regulating State Boxing and Wrestling," *New York Times*, May 15, 1921.

3. Charles F. Mathison, "Wrestling Rules Require Changes," *New York Herald*, November 8, 1921.

4. New York State Athletic Commission Minutes, 1921, 110. Available at: https://digitalcollections.archives.nysed.gov/index.php/Detail/collections/2940.

5. Curley, "Memoirs," January 1932, 42.

6. Curley, "Memoirs," February 1932, 23.

7. Donald L. Miller, *Supreme City: How Jazz Age Manhattan Gave Birth to Modern America* (New York: Simon & Schuster, 2014), 400–1.

8. "Tex Rickard Gets Madison Sq. Garden," *New York Times*, July 13, 1920; Teal and Kenyon, *Wrestling*, 40.

9. Interview with Geoff Pesek, May 30, 2020. In Ravenna, where he lived for almost all of his life, John Pesek was something of a living tall tale. Locals claimed, certainly falsely, that he'd murdered three men. Others claimed that he was so strong that he could swing a log chain over his head. Pesek himself claimed that he'd retired from wrestling as a millionaire, and—again certainly false—that he had been standing next to Babyface Nelson when the gangster was gunned down by FBI agents in 1934. One of his favorite publicity gimmicks, which he continued performing late into his life, was to let an automobile drive over his stomach.

10. Max Jacobs, *Milo and the Halitosis Kid*, 70.

11. Hewitt, *Catch*, 153.

12. Mark Hewitt, "The Saga of the Trust Buster—The Life and Times of Marin Plestina," article in possession of the author.

13. "The Wrestling Game," *Des Moines Register*, June 26, 1918; "Championship Wrestling Matches Don't Look Good," *El Paso Herald*, February 27, 1918.

14. "Marsh In Huge Expose of Mat 'Trust,'" *Collyer's Eye*, February 8, 1919.

15. "Noted Wrestling Manager Is Visiting in Vancouver," *The Vancouver Sun*, December 5, 1918. Strangler Lewis, in his unpublished manuscript, scoffed at the notion that Curley was some kind of all-powerful mastermind of the wrestling business. "This, of course, was not only a psychological and physical impossibility, it is also a mathematical absurdity," Lewis wrote. "While it is conceivable and possible that Curley might have been an arranger of schedules, the cost of this overhead, the intricacy of the detail, temperaments, and conditions as they were at the time . . .

made any control for any duration of time impossible. There was little reason for a combine. If a man was a good card, he could find a place."

16. Dr. B. F. Roller, "What's Wrong with Wrestling—and How to Right It," *Physical Culture*, March 1919, 49–50, 78–80, 82–84. *Physical Culture* was owned by an eccentric magazine magnate named Bernarr MacFadden. He'd begun the magazine in 1899 and used it to promote his views on fitness and diet. His own best press agent, he'd changed his name from Bernard to Bernarr, he said, because it sounded more like a lion's roar. By the end of 1920, *Physical Culture*'s readership had grown to half a million readers. MacFadden spun that success into a series of magazines, the most famous being *True Story* and *True Detective*. By the end of the 1920s, his fortune was said to be close to $30,000,000. For more information on the life of Bernard MacFadden, see Gerard Jones's excellent *Men of Tomorrow: Geeks, Gangsters, and the Birth of the Comic Book* and Ben Yagoda, "The True Story of Bernard MacFadden," *American Heritage*, December 1981.

17. "Jack Curley's Attitude," *Des Moines Tribune*, April 29, 1919.

18. Teal and Kenyon, *Wrestling*, 38. Cartoonist Thornton Fisher satirized this in his cartoon titled "Wrestling has 'Come Back'" in February 2, 1920's *Evening World*.

19. "What About Plestina?" *Des Moines Register*, July 7, 1918.

20. The William J. Burns International Detective Agency to W. I. Biddle, September 23, 1921, Collection of Mark Hewitt.

21. Burns Agency to Biddle, September 23, 1921.

22. "Workings Of Marin Plestina and J.C. Marsh Are Exposed," *The Gazette*, October 24, 1921; Lewis, unpublished manuscript.

23. "Hooks and Slides," *Star-Gazette* (Elmira, NY), March 20, 1928.

24. Hardy K. Downing, "Downing's Fight Dope," *Salt Lake Telegram*, November 27, 1921; "Hooks and Slides."

25. Vincent Treanor, "Bout Had All the Earmarks of A 'Frame Up in Advance," *Evening World*, November 15, 1921.

26. Plestina was reported to have suffered a corneal abrasion to his right eye and a less serious injury to his left, which he had treated at the Manhattan Eye and Ear Hospital. "The injury indicated that the patient had either been struck or scratched," Plestina's doctor told the *New York Times*. "Such an injury, although painful, is found invariably not to be serious." Treanor, "Bout"; "Plestina Wins on Foul from Pesek," *New York Times*, November 15, 1921; "John Pesek Fouls Marin Plestina," *Sacramento Union*, November 15, 1921; "Pesek Barred from Wrestling Here After Foul Performance," *New York Tribune*, November 15, 1921.

27. Treanor, "Bout"; "Need Pesek Worry Regarding the Trust?" *Brooklyn Daily Eagle*, November 23, 1921.

28. Charles F. Mathison, "Pesek Denounced by Own Manager," *New York Herald*, November 17, 1921.

29. Louis DeCasanova, "Pesek Says He Worked Under Orders from Lichenstein," *Brooklyn Daily Eagle*, November 23, 1921.

30. Treanor, "Bout;" DeCasanova, "Pesek Says."

31. W. C. Vreeland, "Forced Out of New York, Wrestlers of the Trust Seek 'Green Grass;' in West," *Brooklyn Eagle*, May 14, 1922.

32. "At The End of The Rope," *Kansas City Star*, December 4, 1921; "Rickard's Fight with Wrestling 'Trust' Develops," *Decatur Herald*, November 22, 1921.

33. "No More Licenses, Boxing Ultimatum," *New York Times*, December 30, 1921.

34. Charles F. Mathison, "Honest Wrestling or None in Garden," *New York Herald*, November 16, 1921.

35. "Zbyszko Retains Wrestling Title," *New York Times*, November 29, 1921. Muldoon also used the occasion to introduce another new rule. Instead of being required to force each other's shoulders to the mat, under his "flying falls" rule, a fall would be called as soon as a wrestler's shoulders touched the mat, even if it was just for a moment. Though they were standard in Greco-Roman and early Lancashire-style wrestling, flying falls had been discarded in the transition to catch-as-catch-can. Muldoon believed they would speed matches up and confound attempts at fixing matches, as any wrestler who unexpectedly lost their footing was at risk for an unplanned loss. In the Lewis-Zbyszko match, Lewis was declared the loser after he inadvertently let both of his shoulders touch the mat as he was squirming out of a neck and crotch hold.

36. W. C. Vreeland, "Muldoon Says Gamblers Tried to Fix Big Bout," *Brooklyn Daily Eagle*, December 12, 1921.

37. "Rickard In Tombs; 8 Jurors Selected," *New York Times*, March 21, 1922; "Jurors Speedily Free Tex Rickard," *Boston Daily Globe*, March 29, 1922.

38. "Son Of Former President Appears as Character Witness for Tex Rickard," *Fort Worth Star-Telegram*, March 25, 1922; "State Rests Case Against Rickard," *New York Times*, March 24, 1922; "Rickard Not Guilty; Verdict 12:19 a.m.; Jury Out 91 Minutes," *New York Times*, March 29, 1922.

39. "Dempsey–Lewis Mixed Match Is More Bunk," *Brooklyn Daily Eagle*, December 3, 1922; Frank Menke, "Sport-O-Graphs," *Press and Sun Bulletin* (Birmingham, AL), March 16, 1922; Frank Menke "Native Hicks of New York Out-Hick the Hickiest Hicks of Hicksville," *Record-Journal* (Meriden, CT), January 22, 1923.

Chapter 12
The Crowd Seemed Bent on Inflicting Bodily Harm

1. Menke, "Sport-o-graphs"; Yohe, *Facts Within*, 47–58.

2. Yohe, *Facts Within*, 247–57.

3. Lewis, unpublished manuscript. 4

4. Tim Hornbaker, "Tom Packs Wrestling Biography," *Legacy of Wrestling*, September 23, 2022. http://www.legacyofwrestling.com/Packs.html. Packs was born Anthanasios Pakiotis on August 15, 1894, in Poulithra, Arcadia, Greece. He was brought into wrestling by Jim Londos, and the pair would work together to great success over the coming years.

5. Little definitive information is known about the early life of Cora Livingston. She is thought to have been born between 1886 and 1893 in Buffalo, New York, and to have been raised by nuns following the death of her parents. She is considered to be the finest of the early female wrestlers and the first to be truly schooled in grappling, with some sources claiming she was trained by the legendary Dan McLeod. Her first known match was in March 1906, and by the end of that month she was

being billed as a world champion. She married Paul Bowser in 1913, and Bowser featured her as a star attraction at his shows in Boston. She reigned as the undisputed champion of women's wrestling for much of the 1910s and '20s, retiring from the ring in 1935. In retirement, she was a noted horse trainer at the couple's estate in Lexington, Fair Oaks Farm. She and Bowser remained married until Livingston's death on April 22, 1957. For more information, see *Sisterhood of the Squared Circle* by Pat LaPrade and Dan Murphy and *She's a Knockout!: A History of Women in Fighting Sports* by L.A. Jennings.

6. "Chief McShane Bans Wrestling Bouts at Local Auditorium," *Sacramento Star*, December 22, 1922; Cecilia Rasmussen, "In L.A., He Was King of the Ring," *Los Angeles Times*, June 3, 1996; "Pick Lou Daro For Manager," *Los Angeles Times*, February 4, 1925; Yohe, *Facts Within*, 71–73; Max Jacobs, *The Role of the Promoter in Professional Wrestling*, 30. As a strongman, Daro bent dimes, broke chains, and tore decks of trading cards in half. As a wrestler, he appeared at the 1915 Manhattan Opera House tournament promoted by Samuel Rachmann. To generate publicity for that event, he laid down at 47th and Broadway with plans to allow a car to drive over his chest. A quick-acting patrolman intervened, instead, and arrested him for disorderly conduct.

7. Ray Tennenbaum, "Sleeperhold, Part 1," September 23, 2022, http://www.ray-field.com/content/article/sleeper-hold-part-1; Tim Hornbaker, *National Wrestling Alliance: The Untold Story of the Monopoly That Strangled Pro Wrestling* (Toronto: ECW Press, 2007), 95.

8. Hornbaker, *National Wrestling Alliance*, 94–97.

9. Bob Broeg, "Joe (Toots) Mondt: 'Policeman in Tights,'" *St. Louis Dispatch*, February 1, 1976.

10. Hornbaker, *National Wrestling Alliance*, 94–96.

11. Frank O. Klein, "Tricks of Mat 'Trust' Shown in Letters of Mondt," *Collyer's Eye*, October 27, 1923.

12. "Probe Mat Game in Illinois," *Muncie Evening Press*, June 7, 1927.

13. Jimmy Wheeler, *The Italian Temper: The Story of How Alphonse "Babe" Bisignano Turned Out All Right* (Eat Sleep Wrestle, 2020), 31; Thesz and Bauman, *Hooker*, 77–79; Joe Jares, *Whatever Happened to Gorgeous George?* (Gallatin, TN: Crowbar Press, 2015), 88.

14. Thesz and Bauman, *Hooker*, 63–64.

15. Sante, *Low Life*, 85.

16. Ben Singer, email message to author, March 7, 2022.

17. Dana Stevens, *Camera Man: Buster Keaton, The Dawn of Cinema, and the Invention of the Twentieth Century* (New York: Atria Books, 2022), 64; Eileen Bowser, *The History of the American Cinema: The Transformation of Cinema; 1907–1915* (Berkeley: University of California Press, 1990), 2.

18. Ben Singer, *Melodrama and Modernity: Early Sensational Cinema and Its Contexts* (New York: Columbia University Press, 2001), 149–220; Richard Koszarksi, *History of the American Cinema: An Evening's Entertainment, 1915–1928* (Berkeley: University of California Press, 1990), 181.

19. Interview with Mark Hewitt, March 3, 2022.

20. Brady, *Showman*, 209. It wouldn't be until the 1950s that philosopher Roland Barthes would explore the connection between theatre and wrestling in detail with his essay "The World of Wrestling." It's from that essay that his endlessly quoted observation that, "There is no more of a problem of truth in wrestling than in the theatre," is taken. Wrestling promoter Ed Contos, who oversaw wrestling in Baltimore, Maryland, would put it more bluntly during an interview in 1954 when he said, "Blood and thunder are what the fans want. There must be a villain and hero. If you don't give it to them, by golly they will manufacture them! You can't buck the public taste and stay in the wrestling business." Whether Contos had read Barthes, sadly, can never be known.

21. "Ernie Dusek vs. Sandor Szabo" (wrestling match)," 71st Regiment Armory program, November 27, 1933. Jack Pfefer Wrestling Collection, Hesburgh Libraries, University of Notre Dame.

22. Lewis, unpublished manuscript.

23. Interview with Kevin Sullivan.

24. Jacobs, *Milo*, 49–50.

25. Yohe, *Facts Within*, 70–71.

26. Lewis, unpublished manuscript.

27. W.C. Vreeland, "Curley Hasn't Any Interest in Wrestling Venture Save As Agent, Says Zimmermann," *Brooklyn Daily Eagle*, January 21, 1923; "Sports Brevities," *San Bernardino Daily Sun*, November 15, 1922.

28. Chester L. Smith, "The Village Smithy," *The Pittsburgh Press*, April 25, 1936. That Curley had never heard of Valentino before agreeing to manage his tour is a highly dubious claim. Though he spent most of his career promoting sports, he did occasionally work as a tour manager for traveling shows. Besides Valentino, he had worked with the British suffragette Emmeline Pankhurst, likely as part of her appearance at Madison Square Garden in October 1913, dancer Vernon Castle, opera star Enrico Caruso, and the Vatican Boys Choir, who he managed on their 1919 tour of America. The tour visited fifty-six cities and was said to have been the first time since its formation in the fourth century that the choir left Rome. The choir was made up of seventy-two members ranging in age from eight to seventy and must have been a nightmare to manage, with eighteen of the members initially prevented from leaving Ellis Island because of immigration issues, and many complaining of indigestion during the tour due to the steady diet of hotel food. The shows were all well attended, but the overhead must have been immense, and it was a bust financially.

29. Emily Leider, *Dark Lover: The Life and Death of Rudolph Valentino* (New York: Farrar, Straus, and Giroux, 2003), 237–38, 244–63.

30. Royal W. Jimerson, "Valentino Prize Medley Belittles Mob Scenes, Old Roman Holidays, *Minneapolis Star*, May 24, 1923.

31. Smith, "Village Smithy."

32. Hugh Fullerton, "Smith Election May Land Big Go in Gotham Ring," *Chicago Tribune*, November 8, 1922.

33. Al Copland, "Commish Eager to Know Where Curley Stands," *Daily News* (New York, NY), February 4, 1923; "Wrestling Show Off After Muldoon Acts," *Brooklyn Daily Eagle*, March 26, 1923; Vreeland, "Curley Hasn't Any"; Tim Hornbaker,

Capitol Revolution: The Rise of the McMahon Wrestling Empire (Toronto: ECW Press, 2015), 15–16.

34. Thomas S. Rice, "Will License Committee Stand for Boxers Barred by Rulings of Muldoon," *Brooklyn Daily Eagle*, April 11, 1923.

35. "Rickard is Denied Wrestling Permit," *New York Times*, December 29, 1923; Henry L. Farrell, "Tex Rickard Denied License to Stage Wrestling Bouts in Famous Garden," *Salt Lake Telegram*, December 30, 1923; Hornbaker, *Capitol Revolution*, 15–16.

Chapter 13
With a Touch of Bronchitis

1. Stecher had been publicly agitating for a match against Lewis for months, but Sandow had only thrown up a series of barriers and demands in response. On February 11, 1924, Stecher wrestled Toots Mondt in Kansas City, a match he needed to win before Sandow would grant him a match with Lewis. In the second fall, Mondt punched Stecher with a closed fist and was disqualified. Mondt's punch has been taken by historians as Sandow's method of sending a message to Stecher that any deals the group had were off.

2. Frank O. Klein, "Stecher Attacks Sandow," *Collyer's Eye*, March 1, 1924.

3. Yohe, *Facts Within*, 73–74.

4. Yohe, *Facts Within*, 73–74.

5. "Munn Still Is Too Big," *Kansas City Times*, December 12, 1924.

6. "Munn The New Champion," *The Kansas City Times*, January 9, 1925.

7. "Wild Scenes in The Hall," *Kansas City Star*, January 9, 1925.

8. "Wild Scenes," *Kansas City Star*, January 9, 1925; "Sport: Lewis vs. Munn," *Time*, January 19, 1925.

9. "Lewis' Career Probably Ended," *Morning Post* (Camden, NJ), January 10, 1925.

10. "Munn The New."

11. Eliot Asinof, *Eight Men Out* (New York: Henry Holt & Company, 1987), 112–14.

12. Yohe, *Facts Within*, 76; "'Big' Munn Not Here for Match," *Lincoln Journal Star*, January 22, 1925.

13. "Facts Show 'Strangler' Lewis Did Not Lose Title to Munn," *Denver Post*, December 2, 1925; "Munn Seeks Injunction Against Lewis and His Manager," *Joplin Globe*, January 24, 1925; "Lewis' Defeat Cost Him Trip Abroad and Nearly $200,000," *The Tennessean*, January 11, 1925.

14. "'Big' Munn Hands Zbyszko Trimming," *Wisconsin State Journal*, February 12, 1925.

15. Lewis, unpublished manuscript.

16. Please, "Mighty Son," 7–26.

17. "Zbyszko's Shape Peculiar," *Los Angeles Times*, July 5, 1924; Untitled article, *San Francisco Chronicle*, July 29, 1924.

18. Art Carlson, "Past 50th Milestone, Age Seems No Barrier to Stanislaus Zbyszko," *Miami News Herald*, April 27, 1925; "50-Year-Old Mat Expert Regains World's Crown," *Philadelphia Public Ledger*, undated clipping.

19. Sharon Cummins, "Old Orchard Beach Brothers Had Brains and Brawn," Sea Coast, August 20, 2009. https://www.seacoastonline.com/story/news/local/york -star/2009/08/20/old-orchard-beach-brothers-had/51703279007/.

20. "Joe Stecher Denies 'Fake' Confession," Journal Times (Racine, WI), February 19, 1925.

21. Paul Gallico, "Omaha Claims Joe Stecher Confessed," Daily News (New York, NY), February 20, 1925.

22. Henry Farrell, "Charges Trust Now Organized," Muncie Evening Press, February 19, 1925.

23. "Curt Comment," The Wichita Eagle, February 1, 1925.

24. Asinof, Eight Men Out, 29. Author F. Scott Fitzgerald, who lived close to Jack Curley in Great Neck and was close to many of the same people, had met Rothstein at least once. In Fitzgerald's 1925 book The Great Gatsby, he turned Rothstein into Meyer Wolfsheim, the man who fixed the World Series simply because he thought he could. The novel's Nick Carraway, upon meeting Wolfsheim, is staggered by the idea; "It never occurred to me that one man could start to play with the faith of fifty million people—with the single-mindedness of a burglar blowing a safe."

25. Johnston, "Cauliflowers," 20–21.

26. "'Big' Munn Set to Defend Title," Philadelphia Public Ledger, April 15, 1925.

27. "Sport: Big Munn," Time, April 27, 1925.

28. "Pole Scores Two Straight Falls Over Wayne Munn," Pittsburgh Post-Gazette, April 16, 1925. The likely substitute would have been John Pesek.

29. Gordon Mackay, "Cries of 'Double Cross,'" Philadelphia Inquirer, April 17, 1925.

30. Perry Lewis, "Zbyszko Will Probably Defend Title in Match with Joe Stecher Here," Philadelphia Inquirer, April 18, 1925.

31. "Munn Says He'll Get Title Back," Winnipeg Tribune, April 17, 1925.

32. "I'll Regain Championship Asserts Wayne 'Big' Munn," Philadelphia Inquirer, April 17, 1925.

33. "Munn Failed to Heed Wife; Lost Wrestling Title," Miami News, April 17, 1925.

34. "Condition Of Munn Is Little Improved," Evening Star (Washington, DC), April 17, 1925.

35. "Zbyszko Wins Mat Crown from Munn," Evening Star, April 16, 1925.

36. "Munn Able to Quit Sick Bed for Trip Home," Chicago Tribune, April 19, 1925.

37. "Giant Wrestling Champ on Edge for Title Tilt," Philadelphia Inquirer, April 15, 1925.

38. "Zbyszko and Lewis May Wrestle Again," Des Moines Tribune, April 20, 1925; Yohe, Facts Within, 79; "Mecom Starts Probe of Lewis' Title Claims," Shreveport Journal, September 20, 1927; "United States District Attorney Finds Lewis Has Best Claim to Title," Shreveport Times, October 2, 1927. In 1927, United States District Attorney Phillip Mecom investigated Lewis over complaints that he'd committed mail fraud by advertising himself as the heavyweight champion in newspapers, which were delivered via the mail. The question of Lewis's claim was tied to his loss to Munn, and his persistence in claiming a championship despite it. Mecom investigated the records of both Lewis and Joe Stecher to attempt to determine who held the

legitimate claim to declaring themselves champion. He concluded that Lewis's claims amounted to "puffing," a claim that might be exaggerated but which was impossible to prove false.

39. Mackay, "Cries of 'Double'"; "Wayne Munn Under Knife," *Wichita Falls Record News*, April 29, 1925; John Wray, "Wray's Column," *St. Louis Post-Dispatch*, April 20, 1925. It was reported that on April 29, 1925, two weeks after his match with Zbyszko, Munn had his tonsils removed in a Kansas City hospital. In a statement to reporters responding to Munn's claims of illness, Zbyszko said, "If Munn was sick, he had no business in the ring. But if he tries to belittle my victory with such an alibi, all I can say is let him get well, good and well and then call on me any afternoon and we shall go to Bothner's gymnasium and I shall throw him on his back, free of charge. This goes any time Munn gets well enough to feel he wants further proof that he cannot wrestle."

40. "'Big Munn' Blames Illness for Loss of Wrestling Crown," *Pittsburgh Daily Post*, April 17, 1925.

41. Westbrook Pegler, "Has Wrestling Ethics or Is It Just Business? Hear Curley," *Chicago Tribune*, January 12, 1931.

42. Lewis, "Zbyszko Will Probably."

43. "Stanislaus Zbyszko Loses to Stecher," *Philadelphia Inquirer*, May 31, 1925. Like Wayne Munn after he defeated Ed Lewis in January 1925, Zbyszko had filed suit against Lewis and Sandow, hoping to keep them from advertising Lewis's Decoration Day match as a championship bout. Zbyszko's action was something altogether different from Munn's, though. It was heard just days before Lewis's match in Michigan City. Had Zbyszko prevailed it would have sunk that match. The suit wasn't successful. Judge Hugo Friend, who had presided over the acquittal of eight Chicago White Sox players accused of conspiring to throw the 1919 World Series four years earlier, ruled that championships should not be won and lost in courtrooms. "If the court were to attempt to decide who is champion in this case, every athlete who deemed himself aggrieved in an athletic context would be rushing into court for relief."

44. "Wayne Munn Is Under Wing of Ed W. White," *Chicago Tribune*, September 13, 1925. Munn's success as a fighter during his first brief attempt at a boxing career was limited, at best. "Munn made his debut in the prize ring as a pro and was heralded as a coming rival to the Wild Bull of the Pampas (Luis Angel Firpo)," recounted Jack Curley. "After Munn's terrific swings had resulted in his being knocked out by an experienced opponent, he was christened 'The Wild Bull of the Canvas' by a wit."

45. "Andre Anderson Slain Because He Refused to 'Throw' Bout with 'Big' Munn," *Caspar Star-Tribune*, April 23, 1926.

46. "Fight 'Fixers' Dole Death to Munn's Conqueror," *Lincoln Star*, April 23, 1926.

47. Tim Hornbaker, "The Mob Kills Chicago's Heavyweight 'Hope," Legacy of Wrestling, September 23, 2022, http://www.legacyofwrestling.com/AndersonArticle .html.

48. Rose Keefe, *The Man Who Got Away*, 207; "Leo Mongoven, Survivor of the Prohibition Wars," *New York Times*, January 20, 1980. A little more than a year after his arrest, Mongoven was said to be one of the main targets of Al Capone's 1929 St. Valentine's Day Massacre, though he was ultimately not among the seven men

gunned down that morning. Improbably, he was able to leave organized crime, retire to a farm in Lee County, raise six children, and live quietly until his death in 1980. The killing of Andre Anderson was almost certainly one of the inspirations for Ernest Hemingway's 1927 short story "The Killers," in particular the doomed boxer, Ole Anderson.

Chapter 14
The Man Who Revolutionized Wrestling

1. Daley, "Sports of the Times."

2. Untitled article, *Boston Herald*, June 29, 1928.

3. Westbrook Pegler, "Why Wrestle? Mat Champion Solves Riddle," *Chicago Tribune*, May 22, 1930; Jan Isabelle Fortune, "'Dynamite' Gus on the Morning After," *Dallas Morning News*, May 25, 1930.

4. Dink Carroll, "Playing the Field," *The Gazette* (Montreal), September 15, 1944.

5. Damon Runyon, "Damon Runyon Says," *Nevada State Journal*, May 6, 1930.

6. Westbrook Pegler, "Sonnenberg Says He's Through Scrubbing Floors for a Living," *Nashville Banner*, May 25, 1930.

7. W. W. Heffelfinger, *That Was Football* (New York: Barnes, 1954), 118.

8. Tim Hornbaker, "Gus Sonnenberg Biography," Legacy of Wrestling, September 23, 2022, http://www.legacyofwrestling.com/GusSonnenbergBio.html.

9. David F. Egan, "Wrestling King is Victor in Boston," *Boston Globe*, March 15, 1928.

10. Surviving footage of the match is available at https://www.youtube.com/watch ?v=oiFV0aYgzNA.

11. Fortune, "'Dynamite' Gus".

12. David F. Egan, "Sonnenberg Pitches from Ring at Arena," *Boston Globe*, June 30, 1928.

13. Burt Whitman, "Wrestler Badly Hurt at Arena," *Boston Herald*, June 30, 1928. The stories of what really happened with Sonnenberg's hospital stay are varied. He was attended to by multiple doctors in the dressing room. He was then taken to a private hospital, despite the fact that the city's General Hospital was just minutes away. Gus was dressed and on his way to Providence the next day, against his doctor's advice, but was reported to have collapsed after trying to leave the hospital. How believable this story is is open to debate. He spent the weekend in the hospital.

14. David F. Egan, "Lewis Is Favorite, Expect 20,000 Crowd," *Boston Globe*, January 4, 1929; David F. Egan, "Mat Title Won by Sonnenberg," *Boston Globe*, January 5, 1929.

15. "Ask Sonnenberg About $100,000 Paid to Lewis," *Boston Herald*, April 6, 1933. Bowser later swore that Lewis promising to lose the championship was never part of the deal. This defies belief but when pressed on the matter under oath in 1932, Bowser never relented. In the same trial, Sonnenberg was asked, "Isn't it true that part of this agreement that you and Mr. Bowser entered into was that you were to get the championship?" Sonnenberg shot back, "That's an awful lie for you to say."

16. Pegler, "Sonnenberg Says." Author Jack Kerouac saw Sonnenberg perform in Lowell, Massachusetts, at the tiny Crescent Rink sometime in the early 1930s,

and would later recount the match in his piece, "In the Ring," available in the *Good Blonde & Others* anthology. Kerouac's father ran a boxing and wrestling club in Lowell and would occasionally promote matches in town. The arena was filled, Kerouac remembered, "in the incredible cigar smoke which always made me wonder how those guys could breathe let alone wrestle."

17. "Three State Commissions Bar Sonnenberg for Set-ups," *Boston Herald*, June 12, 1929.

18. "Sonnenberg Day On Stand," *Boston Herald*, April 5, 1933.

19. Charles Morton, *It Has Its Charms* (Philadelphia: Lippincott, 1966), 124–26. This practice wasn't restricted to wrestling, alone. In an attempt to bolster his reputation as "The Manassa Mauler" during a string of bouts in 1918, boxer Jack Dempsey was accused of having his sparring partners, as well as one of his good friends, fight against him under assumed names. For more information, see Bruce Evensen's *When Dempsey Fought Tunney*.

20. "Wrestling For Titles Great Flim Flam Game," *Boston Herald*, June 11, 1929.

21. "Mat Promoter Exposes Racket," *Boston Herald*, June 14, 1929.

22. "Wrestling For Titles."

23. Morton, *Charms*, 126.

24. "Sonnenberg Day."

25. "Sonnenberg Sees Promoter Today," *Boston Globe*, June 13, 1929; "Lewis' Manager Here Pressing for Match With 'Sonny,'" June 14, 1929.

26. "Judge To Give Charge Today in Sonnenberg Libel Case," *Boston Herald*, April 12, 1933.

27. "Sonnenberg To Defend His Title Against Lewis July 9," *Boston Herald*, June 15, 1929.

28. "Defence Opens in Libel Case," *Boston Herald*, April 11, 1933.

29. "Sonnenberg Got $172,997 From Bowser In 4 Years," *Boston Herald*, April 7, 1933.

30. David F. Egan, "Sonny Retains Wrestling Crown," *Boston Globe*, July 10, 1929; "Gus Sonnenberg Retains His World Wrestling Mantle in Three-Fall Match at Fenway," *Boston Herald*, July 10, 1929.

31. "Sonnenberg Got $172,997."

32. "Gus Sonnenberg Retains."

33. Pegler, "Why Wrestle?"

34. Andy Lytle, "Sport Rays," *Vancouver Sun*, December 12, 1931; Westbrook Pegler, "Nobody's Business," *Chicago Tribune*, June 6, 1930.

35. Interview with William Sandow, October 26, 2019; "Lewis Grappled Two Years Minus Good Eyesight," *Birmingham News*, February 16, 1927.

36. Lewis, unpublished manuscript.

37. Jacobs, *Milo*, 170.

38. "Sentenced For Attack on Gus," *Charlotte News*, November 13, 1929; "Gus Sonnenberg Gets Dose of Own Medicine and Suffers Injuries," *Selma Times-Journal*, October 23, 1929; Pegler, "Nobody's Business." This is one of the most confusing and truly kaleidoscopic incidents of this era. In 1934, Ladjimi sued Jim Londos for $30,800. The suit claimed that Londos had agreed to pay him $600 per week to suss

out future opponents. The suit never progressed, and little money appears to have ever changed hands between the two. Nonetheless, it helped fuel rumors that Londos had paid Ladjimi to attack Sonnenberg.

39. "The Sonnenberg Wrestling Racket," Boston Better Business Bureau, November 19, 1929; "Sonnenberg Spends Most of Day on Witness Stand," *Boston Herald*, April 5, 1933; Fortune, "'Dynamite' Gus."

40. William Braucher, "Grid Stars Bring New Life to Mat Racket," *The Capital Times* (Madison, WI), May 25, 1931.

41. Morris Markey, "Catch as Catch Can," *New Yorker*, April 18, 1931.

42. Curley Grieve, "Sports Parade," *San Francisco Examiner*, June 9, 1932.

43. "Sonnenberg Got $172,997."

44. "Sonnenberg Got $172,997."

45. Gene Kowske, "Gus Sonnenberg Defends 'Grunt and Groan' Game, *Tampa Times*, October 26, 1929.

Chapter 15
I Know Where They Grow

1. Alva Johnston, "Rule by Commission," *New Yorker*, July 28, 1928.

2. "Jim Browning vs. Ray Steele," (wrestling match), Madison Square Garden program, January 8, 1934, Jack Pfefer Wrestling Collection, Hesburgh Libraries, University of Notre Dame.

3. Johnston, "Cauliflowers," 24.

4. Mark Kelly, "It's Old, Old Trick," *Ogden Standard Examiner*, June 30, 1929.

5. "Infusion Of New Blood Made Wrestling What It Is Today," *Brooklyn Times Union*, April 5, 1930.

6. Swanton v. Curley.

7. "Six-Day Race Lost More Than $10,000," *New York Times*, January 22, 1929; "Bike Riders Start Suit to Get Purse," *Yonkers Statesman*, January 25, 1929.

8. "Tex Rickard Dies; Held Leading Place in World of Sport," *New York Times*, January 7, 1929. The man who remade sports in the 1920s was only fifty-eight when he died. A public viewing of his body was held at Madison Square Garden three days after his death and described by Paul Gallico in his book *Farewell to Sport*. The west end of the arena was transformed into an altar of flowers set amid ferns and palm trees, a pair of which almost met over Rickard's solid bronze coffin. Thousands attended, though the final crowd was far short of the overflow numbers that organizers anticipated. Gallico watched the scene from the arena's otherwise empty upper shelf sitting alongside several Garden staff. "Boy, I bet they've got him lashed down so he can't spin," one man joked. "Would he be revolving in that box if he saw this mob all coming in here off the cuff!"

9. "H.H. Frazee Dies Suddenly at 48," *New York Times*, June 5, 1929.

10. "Otto Floto Dies in Denver at 66," *New York Times*, August 5, 1929.

11. Swanton v. Curley; Rose, "Curley in Class."

12. Williams, "By Joe."

13. Williams, "By Joe."

14. Eddy Portnoy, email message to author, July 8, 2020; "Death of Jack Pfefer Verified, Nobody Else Like Him!" *Ring Wrestling*, undated clipping.

15. Jacobs, *Milo*, 158.

16. From the best available records, Pfefer knew Billy Sandow during his time in Chicago. It's possible that he met Toots Mondt via Sandow, and Mondt provided a connection to Jack Curley. According to a photograph contained in Notre Dame's Jack Pfefer Collection, Pfefer's first show in New York was held in 1925. Pfefer inscribed the photo as follows: "The first show promoted in New York by Jack Pfefer in the old famous Pioneer Club in 1925."

17. Jack Miley, "Jake's Juggernauts," *Collier's*, October 22, 1938; Eddy Portnoy, *Bad Rabbi: And Other Strange but True Stories from the Yiddish Press* (Stanford, CA: Stanford University Press, 2018), 185.

18. Jares, *Whatever Happened*, 87.

19. Joseph Mitchell, *My Ears Are Bent* (New York: Vintage Books, 2008), 105.

20. A.J. Liebling, "A Reporter at Large—Pull His Whiskers!" *New Yorker*, July 8, 1939, 57–65.

21. "Around the World with Master Showman Jack Pfefer," undated wrestling program from Tennessee, Jack Pfefer Wrestling Collection, Hesburgh Libraries, University of Notre Dame.

22. "I'll Meet You At—," *New York World-Telegram*, undated clipping.

23. "Mat Promoter at Three New York Clubs Admits His Wrestling a Fake," *New York Enquirer*, November 6, 1938.

24. Mitchell, *My Ears*, 105.

25. Liebling, "A Reporter."

26. Johnson and Oliver, *Storytellers*, 42; Griffin, *Annotated Fall Guys*, 102.

27. "Seeks Matman from Far East," *Star Press* (Muncie, IN), July 3, 1932.

28. Liebling, "A Reporter," 57–65; "Angels' International Row Ends in $250 Fine," *Los Angeles Times*, October 5, 1945; Jacobs, *Milo*, 199; Jares, *Whatever Happened*, 86.

29. Tennenbaum, "Sleeperhold, Part 1."

30. Interview with George Rugg, June 6, 2019; "Jack Pfefer Wrestling Collection," University of Notre Dame, October 15, 2022, https://archivesspace.library.nd.edu/repositories/3/resources/1548.

31. "American Fighters, Not Foreigners, Have Best Claim to Crown," *Brooklyn Eagle*, December 19, 1926. In the early 1920s, a story existed in New York in which Curley had one of his staff meet each new wrestler at the docks, where they were presented with an expensive fur-lined coat. "It wasn't cat's fur, either," wrote reporter W.C. Vreeland. The coat was intended to make them look prosperous and intimidating. Once the wrestler had been sufficiently photographed wearing the coat, Curley would put it back into storage, only ever breaking it out again when he had a new foreign wrestler to promote.

32. Paul Gallico, "His Manager Named Him," *Daily News* (New York, NY), March 15, 1931.

33. Francis E. Stan, "Wrestling Has Its 'Ivory' Hunter," *Sunday Star* (Washington, DC), March 27, 1932.

34. Frank Menke, "Sport-o-Graph," *Great Falls Tribune*, January 29, 1926.

35. "A Perfect Physical Specimen of Aframerican Manhood," *Pittsburgh Courier*, September 25, 1926; Robert L. Jones "Reginald Siki—the Abyssinian Panther," *Boxing and Wrestling News*, May 1931.

36. Menke, "Sport-o-Graph;" "Poulios Offers New Wrestlers on Coming Card," *Hartford Courant*, May 7, 1932; Jamie Greer, "The Pioneers: Viro Small—The First African American Wrestler," lastwordonsports.com, February 1, 2018, https://lastword onsports.com/prowrestling/2018/02/01/viro-small-first-african-american-wrestler/. His ring name of Siki was undoubtedly a reference to the Senegalese-born boxer Battling Siki, who was popular at the time. One story has it that American soldiers who had seen Battling Siki fight in Europe gave the name to Reginald after seeing him box, though it is likelier that Berry either adopted the name himself or was given it by a promoter.

37. "Color Bars Him," *Winnipeg Tribune*, October 27, 1923; "Lewis Wary of Siki as Foe for Mat Bout," *Chicago Tribune*, December 2, 1923. It's worth noting that while professional wrestling in the twentieth century was integrated long before other professional sports like baseball, football, and basketball, it wouldn't be until 1992 that a Black wrestler, Ron Simmons, would win a nationally recognized heavyweight championship.

38. "Selects Race Athletes for New Biblical Production," *Pittsburgh Courier*, August 21, 1926; "Reginald Siki in Films," *Pittsburgh Courier*, December 25, 1926.

39. Jeremy Schaap, *Cinderella Man* (New York: Houghton Mifflin, 2005), 49.

40. "Shikat Pressed to Defeat Calza," *Brooklyn Times Union*, March 11, 1930.

41. Edward J. Neill, "'Exhibition' Or 'Show' Must Be Term for Events," *Star Tribune* (Minneapolis, MN), April 9, 1930. In an article in the *Dayton Daily News* from June 27, 1973, a wrestler named "Tiger" Joe Marsh gave this curious statement: "It was Damon Runyon's idea in New York in 1933 to make wrestling matches exhibitions. Then every state started to do it. Of course, you don't wrestle as hard in an exhibition, but there was no put on." While older wrestlers are famous for overstating their successes, misremembering dates, and conflating events, calling out Runyon as having a hand in guiding the athletic commission's decision is noteworthy, and is not an impossible scenario to imagine, given his influence in the city at the time.

42. Noel Busch, "'Wrestling Cat' Escapes the Bag," *Daily News* (New York, NY), April 9, 1930.

43. Ed Hughes, "Latest 'Commish' Edict Against 'Wrasslin' Is Classic of Comicality," *Brooklyn Daily Eagle*, April 9, 1930.

Chapter 16
The Golden Goose

1. Roscoe McGowen, "22,000 See Londos Retain Wrestling Title by Throwing McMillen in Garden," *New York Times*, January 27, 1931; Joel Sayre, "The Pullman Theseus," *New Yorker*, March 5, 1932.

2. McGowen, "22,000 See"; Noel Busch, "Jim Londos Takes 20:47 To Down Foe," *Daily News* (New York, NY), December 30, 1930.

3. Teal and Kenyon, *Wrestling,* 58–59; Sayre, "Pullman Theseus." Attendance numbers at wrestling shows during this era were notoriously inflated. Where there were discrepancies in reported numbers, the lower number was deferred to.

4. Steven Johnson and Greg Oliver, *The Pro Wrestling Hall of Fame: Heroes & Icons* (Toronto: ECW Press, 2012), 1–3.

5. Wilfrid Smith, "Mr. Alger, How Did You Miss Londos' Story," *Chicago Tribune,* August 12, 1934.

6. Sayre, "Pullman Theseus."

7. Sayre, "Pullman Theseus."

8. W. J. McGoogan, "10,567 Fans Paid $19,774 to See Match; Londos Received About $6700 and Steele $4000," *St. Louis Post-Dispatch,* February 21, 1931; Jesse A. Linthicum, "5,000 See Londos Throw Daviscourt to Retain Wrestling Championship," *Baltimore Sun,* March 4, 1931; Perry Lewis, "Arena Jammed, Thousands Turned Away as Londos Successfully Defends Title," *Philadelphia Inquirer,* March 7, 1931.

9. Damon Runyon, "Lenglen, Nurmi, Cobb Excelled in Grace Field," *Lancaster New Era,* December 12, 1931.

10. Sayre, "Pullman Theseus."

11. Thomas Hauser, *The Boxing Scene* (Philadelphia: Temple University Press, 2009), 122.

12. Bob Husted, "The Referee," *Dayton Herald,* January 8, 1932. This is noted in many descriptions of Londos, but Ohio promoter Al Haft's quote in this article is particularly compelling: "The fans who pay to see Londos know that he's going to win, but they turn out just the same. Why? Simply because Londos is a colorful performer on the mat. . . . He gets in and out of tight jams. The crowd likes that. Finally, Londos wins as everybody knew he would, but the fans go home satisfied. The next time Londos wrestles they will again be on hand." Haft was also known later in life to show footage of Londos in the ring to young wrestlers to educate them on the proper way to work.

13. Liebling, "From Sarah Bernhardt."

14. Interview with Steve Yohe, May 11, 2018.

15. Heywood Broun, "Sport for Art's Sake," *Vanity Fair,* September 1921, 69.

16. "Unemployment Statistics during the Great Depression," *U-S-History.com,* October 15, 2022, https://www.u-s-history.com/pages/h1528.html.

17. Tommy Armour, "I Make an Athletic God," *Vanity Fair,* December 1934.

18. Smith, "Mr. Alger, How."

19. Markey, "Catch as Catch."

20. Westbrook Pegler, "Fighters Seem to Need Groans of Mat Business," *Chicago Tribune,* June 1, 1931; Westbrook Pegler, "Are Wrestlers People?" *Esquire,* January 1, 1934.

21. Herman Hickman, "Rasslin' Was My Act," *Saturday Evening Post,* February 6, 1954.

22. Paul Gallico, "Beware! General," *Daily News* (New York, NY), October 26, 1934.

23. Ted Carroll, "Jack Pfefer, Master of Ballyhoo," *Wrestling*, August 1969; Hickman, "Rasslin' Was My Act."

24. Paul Gallico, "Form of Public Suicide," *Daily News* (New York, NY), January 27, 1932.

25. Interview with Kevin Sullivan.

26. Grieve, "Sports Parade."

27. Pegler, "Are Wrestlers People?"

28. Pegler, "Fighters Seem."

Chapter 17
If I Were to Tell You the Real Inside about Wrestling, I Probably Would Spend the Night in the Tombs Instead of at Home

1. Markey, "Catch as Catch."

2. "'Miss 'Tarzan,' 'Terrible Tessy Terry' To Battle for Women's Boxing Title," *Brooklyn Times Union*, November 17, 1932.

3. "Slinky Marathoners Start Doing Their Dance Tomorrow," *Brooklyn Daily Eagle*, February 10, 1932; "Sport Static," *Sioux City Journal*, March 13, 1932; Carol Martin, *Dance Marathons: Performing American Culture in the 1920s and 1930s* (Jackson, MS: University Press of Mississippi, 1994), 31–32. Curley's marathon in Brooklyn dragged out for more than three months and attracted legal problems along the way. A warrant for Curley's arrest was issued for what a grand jury called "unhealthful and degrading" work conditions for the dancers. Like pro wrestling matches, dance marathons were complicated mixtures of carefully managed stagecraft and true feats of skill and endurance. Successful marathons relied on staged dramatics to punctuate the often grinding monotony. Dancers took meals, had their hair done, received medical care, and slept all in full view of the audience and all with their feet shuffling along to the music to avoid elimination. That Curley seized on them as a business opportunity is hardly surprising.

4. Henry McLemore, "Big Bill Tilden Turning Back on Amateur Tennis," *Columbus Telegram* (Columbus, NE), December 31, 1930.

5. Westbrook Pegler, "Tilden Talks on His New Duties to Sports Public," *Chicago Tribune*, February 17, 1931.

6. Dixon Stewart, "Jack Curley Attempts to Sign French Stars for Pro Tennis Troupe," *Courier-News* (Plainfield, NJ), March 14, 1932.

7. Hank Casserly, "Hank Casserly Says," *Capital Times*, May 18, 1931.

8. Teal and Kenyon, *Wrestling*, 69.

9. Johnson and Oliver, *Heroes & Icons*, 4; Arthur J. Daley, "30,000 See Londos Retain Mat Crown," *New York Times*, June 30, 1931. Professional wrestling was insanely popular during the summer of 1931. Between June 29 and July 30, 75,000 people attended just three different wrestling shows: Jim Londos-Ray Steele at Yankee Stadium on June 29 (30,000 people), Henri Deglane-Ed Don George at Braves Field on July 14 (25,000 people), and Henri Deglane-Gus Sonnenberg, also at Braves Field, on July 30 (20,000 people). This isn't even to mention the weekly cards happening in Brooklyn, Los Angeles, St. Louis, and other cities that were drawing upwards of 10,000 people each.

10. Interview with Steve Johnson, December 26, 2017; Griffin, *Annotated Fall Guys*, 82.

11. Interview with Steve Johnson, December 26, 2017.

12. Ray Fabiani to Jack Pfefer, February 4, 1942, Jack Pfefer Wrestling Collection, Hesburgh Libraries, University of Notre Dame.

13. Liebling, "A Reporter."

14. Damon Kerby, "Eighteen Cities in Wrestling Circuit Controlled by Tom Packs," St. Louis Dispatch, January 7, 1931.

15. Milton MacKaye, "On the Hoof," *Saturday Evening Post*, December 14, 1935.

16. Hickman, "Rasslin' Was My Act." Herman Hickman, a one-time wrestler, professional football player, and later college football coach, detailed the life of a work-a-day wrestler in the 1930s in a piece he wrote for the *Saturday Evening Post* in 1954 called "Rasslin' Was My Act." One of his more colorful claims was that booking offices communicated with wrestlers working the circuit via Postal Telegraph Company and Western Union, two competing operators of national telegraph networks. Instructions for the evening's matches were sent out via one service, he wrote, and confirmations were sent back on the other. The messages were coded, with wrestlers referred to by nicknames such as Cannonball, Glendale, or Subway. Wrestlers were free to improvise their matches as they went along, as long as they adhered to the prescribed endings and completed them in the prescribed times. This is a wonderful anecdote and worth repeating but thus far no researcher has been able to verify it. If such telegrams were sent, no copies have survived.

17. "Grunts and Growls, Slams and Bangs, Blood and Thunder—Here They Come," *Pittsburgh Press*, March 15, 1931.

18. "Wrestling Muscle of Sandow Hustle Threatens Tussle," *Daily News* (New York, NY), February 3, 1931; "Cliques Clash," *Hartford Courant*, May 14, 1931; David Lidman, "Bowser Mat Group to Invade City; First Show on Saturday," *Richmond Times-Dispatch*, April 19, 1931.

19. Paul Gallico, *Farewell to Sport* (Lincoln: University of Nebraska Press, 2008), 313.

20. *Flesh*, directed by John Ford (1932; Beverly Hills, CA: Metro-Goldwyn-Mayer Corporation).

21. B. R. Crisler, "Mr. Pendleton and a Party of Five," New York Times, April 11, 1937.

22. Yohe, *Facts Within*, 124–25; "Lewis and Sandow Parting Company After 20 Years," *Commercial Appeal* (Memphis), January 23, 1932; Frank Menke, "Menke Sees Londos Beating Lewis in Groaning Where Strangler Once Threw Jim," *Tampa Tribune*, February 15, 1932; George Barton, "More Blood on The Wrestling Moon," *Star Tribune* (Minneapolis), May 25, 1932.

23. Griffin, *Annotated Fall Guys*, 120; Thesz and Bauman, *Hooker*, 73.

24. Al Warden "Along Sport Paths with Al Warden," *Ogden Standard-Examiner*, December 3, 1931.

25. "Lewis and Sandow Part," *Kansas City Star*, December 22, 1931; "Billy Sandow on Trail of That Title Again," *St. Louis Star and Times*, October 4, 1932. Of his split

with Ed Lewis, Billy Sandow said, "I told Ed I thought he had reached his end. He disagreed with me. This difference of opinion caused our split."

26. Yohe, *Facts Within*, 124.

27. Griffin, *Annotated Fall Guys*, 119.

28. "As You Like It," *The Standard Union*, May 22, 1930; Hornbaker, *Capitol Revolution*, 31.

29. "War Threatens Wrestling Trust," *Nashville Banner*, April 7, 1932.

30. Teal and Kenyon, *Wrestling*, 68.

31. Hornbaker, *Capitol Revolution*, 58–64.

32. George A. Barton, "Between You and Me," *Star Tribune*, April 17, 1932.

33. "New York Body Bans Jim Londos," *Detroit Free* Press, October 1, 1932.

34. Yohe, *Facts Within*, 123; "New Wrestling Association Says Londos is Champ," *The Times* (Shreveport, LA), September 17, 1930.

35. Hornbaker, *Capitol Revolution*, 61.

Chapter 18
Flipflops and Acrobatics and All That Fake Stuff

1. Tom Doerer, "Rassle Racket Outgrows Vet," *Evening Star*, December 12, 1932. Wikipedia and other sources list Ed Lewis's birth year as 1891, but Lewis's biographer, Steve Yohe, contends based on his extensive research that Lewis was born in 1890.

2. Yohe, *Facts Within*, 127–28; Teal and Kenyon, *Wrestling*, 70; Paul Gallico, "Tale of a Shooting Match," *Daily News* (New York, NY), October 12, 1932.

3. Thesz and Bauman, *Hooker*, 49.

4. Teal and Kenyon, *Wrestling*, 72; Yohe, *Facts Within*, 129–30; Perry Lewis, "Steele's Elbow Wallop Brings Warning, Then Banishment," *Philadelphia Inquirer*, December 6, 1932.

5. Jimmy Powers, "The Punching Punchinellos," *Daily News* (New York, NY), December 7, 1932; Henry McLemore, "Lewis Wins Over Steele on 'Foul' As His Mates Riot," *St. Louis Star and Times*, December 6, 1932; James P. Dawson, "Lewis Keeps Title: Is Victor on Foul," *New York Times*, December 6, 1932.

6. Albert W. Keane, "Connecticut Sportsdom Pays Tribute to Boxing Commissioner Tom Donohue," *Hartford Courant*, May 10, 1930; Albert W. Keane, "Calling 'Em Right," *Hartford Courant*, September 21, 1932.

7. "Everything 'All Set' to Give Irishman Mat Championship," *St. Louis Globe-Democrat*, April 11, 1933.

8. "'Bunch of Lies,' Says Promoter Answering $25,000 Bribe Story," *St. Louis Globe-Democrat*, April 13, 1933; "Pat O'Shocker Tells Story of Attempt to Bribe Him to Double Cross Londos," *St. Louis Post-Dispatch*, April 11, 1933; Keane, "Calling 'Em Right"; Griffin, *Annotated Fall Guys*, 127.

9. Mike Sielski, "Star in the Shadows," *Philadelphia Inquirer*, February 11, 2019; William Ritt, "Wrestling Pictures of Savoldi Tell Story of His Success in Grid Games," *Moline Daily Dispatch*, February 11, 1931.

10. Griffin, *Annotated Fall Guys*, 132. As historians Steve Yohe and Scott Teal point out in their reissued version of the book *Fall Guys: The Barnums of Bounce*, following

the Savoldi-Londos match, the Illinois Athletic Commission established a rule requiring referees to count out loud when determining a pinfall. This likely led to other Commissions adopting the same rule. In time, referees would take to slapping the mat three times as they counted a fall.

11. George Strickler, "On the Square or Not? 6,800 Fans Wonder," *Chicago Tribune*, April 8, 1933.

12. Edward J. Neil, "Joe Savoldi's Win Over Londos Tickles Bowser-Curley Faction," *Macon Telegraph*, April 16, 1933; Frank Reil, "No Wonder Savoldi Prefers to Wrestle," *Brooklyn Daily Eagle*, April 25, 1933.

13. George Strickler, "Referee Defends Action in Awarding Fall to Savoldi," *Chicago Tribune*, April 9, 1933.

14. "Kill-or-Cure Treatment for Mat Game Is Plan of Promoter Here," *St. Louis Star and Times*, April 12, 1933.

15. "Savoldi Leaves Ring, Decision Goes to Slagel," *Daily News* (New York, NY), June 27, 1933.

16. Dan Parker, "The Geometry Class Convenes," *Daily Mirror* (New York, NY), June 29, 1933. That the match was held at Staten Island's Coast Guard Pier, at an arena located on federal government property, made it the ideal location. The arena was outside the jurisdiction of the state athletic association, assuring that Slagel would not face repercussions in the state for his actions.

17. Sid Keener, "Sid Keener's Column," *St. Louis Star and Times*, April 12, 1933.

18. Edward J. Neil, "On the Sidelines," *Altoona Tribune*, March 1, 1933.

19. Tim Hornbaker, "The Unknown Heavyweight Champion of the World—The Turnover Scissors King—Jim Browning," Legacy of Wrestling, September 23, 2022, http://www.legacyofwrestling.com/Browning.html.

20. Jim Jennings, "Jim Browning Tosses Sonnenberg In 1:10:21," *Daily Mirror* (New York, NY), November 21, 1933.

21. Griffin, *Annotated Fall Guys*, 131.

22. Paul Bowser to Jack Pfefer, May 15, 1933, Jack Pfefer Wrestling Collection, Hesburgh Libraries, University of Notre Dame.

23. Griffin, *Annotated Fall Guys*, 135.

24. Ted Carroll, "Jack Pfefer, Master of Ballyhoo," *Wrestling*.

25. Mitchell, *My Ears*, 107.

26. Jack Pfefer, "'Double Crossed,' Says Pfefer, By Mat Trust," *Daily Mirror* (New York, NY), December 30, 1933.

27. Pfefer, "'Double Crossed;'" Dan Parker, "An Iron Major with A Heart of Gold," *Daily Mirror*, August 31, 1933.

28. Griffin, *Annotated Fall Guys*, 134; "Pfefer Splits with Curley," *The Front Page*, August 30, 1933.

29. "Jim Londos vs. Paul Boesch" (wrestling match), New York Coliseum advertisement, November 25, 1933, Jack Pfefer Wrestling Collection, Hesburgh Libraries, University of Notre Dame.

30. Paul Gallico, "Break it off: Nocturne in Wrestling," *Vanity Fair*, April 1934.

31. "Jim Browning vs. Ray Steele" (wrestling match), Madison Square Garden program, January 8, 1934, Jack Pfefer Wrestling Collection, Hesburgh Libraries, University of Notre Dame.

32. Jesse A. Linthicum, "Ring and Rasslin' Racket," *Baltimore Sun*, December 13, 1933.

33. Damon Kerby, "Sonnenberg and Steele to meet here; wrestling a happy family," *St. Louis Dispatch*, December 28, 1933.

34. Riess, "Honesty Is."

35. Milton MacKaye, "On the Hoof," *Saturday Evening Post*, December 14, 1935; Teal and Kenyon, *Wrestling*, 80. Jack Curley, for his part, maintained that he'd never had an aged wrestler whom he'd employed approach him begging for money after their career was over.

36. New York State Athletic Commission Minutes, August 17, 1933. Available at https://digitalcollections.archives.nysed.gov/index.php/Detail/objects/74138.

37. Joe Alvarez v. Richard Shikat and Al Haft, U.S. District Court, Southern District of Ohio, Eastern Division, No. 1180, April 27, 1936; Billy Fogarty, "Wrestling Groups Have Secretly Merged," *New York Enquirer*, December 3, 1933.

38. Fogarty, "Wrestling Groups"; Griffin, *Annotated Fall Guys*, 137; Jack Pfefer, "Pfefer Reveals More Details of Wrestling 'Mess,'" *Collyer's Eye & Baseball World*, January 13, 1934; "Minneapolis to See Much Better Shows as Result of Exchange," *Minneapolis Star*, December 27, 1933.

39. Alvarez v. Shikat and Haft.

40. Paul Gallico, "All's Quiet on the Rassling Front," *Los Angeles Times*, January 18, 1934.

41. "Jim Londos vs. Everette Marshall" (wrestling match), Philadelphia Convention Hall program with inscription by Jack Pfefer, December 15, 1933, Jack Pfefer Wrestling Collection, Hesburgh Libraries, University of Notre Dame.

42. "Dead! Londos Says 'No,'" *New York Daily Mirror*, December 20, 1934.

43. Griffin, *Annotated Fall Guys*, 135.

44. Mitchell, *My Ears*, 106.

Chapter 19
Teaching Atheism to Babies

1. "Dan Parker Dies, Sportswriter, 73," *New York Times*, May 21, 1967.

2. Hickman, "Rasslin' Was My Act."

3. "Dan Parker Dies."

4. Dan Parker, "Burp! Wrestling Is Exposed by Pfefer," *Daily Mirror* (New York, NY), December 28, 1933.

5. Dan Parker, "Pfail to Pfind Pfefer's Pflute," *Daily Mirror* (New York, NY), June 29, 1934.

6. Jack Pfefer, "'Double Crossed,' Says Pfefer, By Mat Trust," *Daily Mirror* (New York, NY), December 30, 1933.

7. Jack Curley, "Just Sour Grapes to M. Curley," *Daily Mirror* (New York, NY), December 29, 1933; Jack Curley, "Pfefer's Story Pack of Lies Claims Curley," *Daily Mirror* (New York, NY), December 31, 1933.

8. Untitled Article, *Daily Mirror* (New York, NY), January 3, 1934.

9. Edward Zeltner, "Miller Absent as Mat Probe Is Launched," *Daily Mirror* (New York, NY), undated clipping.

10. Marshall Hunt, "Solons Begin Investigation of Wrestling," *Daily News* (New York, NY), January 3, 1934.

11. Zeltner, "Miller Absent." The split between Miller and Pfefer was not permanent, and the pair would be in communication again by 1935, by which time Miller had moved to Florida and was attempting to establish himself in wrestling there. "[Miller] turned out to be just the heel you found him out to be in N.Y.," wrote Jim Downing, a Florida-based businessman with whom Miller was competing, in a letter to Pfefer dated June 28, 1935. By all indications, Miller's actions in 1933 very much caught Pfefer by surprise but were not considered unforgivable to Pfefer, who was famous for his ability to hold grudges.

12. "Testimony of Packs Heard in Mat Probe," *Daily Mirror* (New York, NY), January 9, 1934; Dan Parker, "Pfefer's Mat Expo Flivvers at Hearing," *Daily Mirror* (New York, NY), undated. Packs' quote was presented in an exaggerated accent in the original article. It has been edited here, but the original meaning has been maintained. Whatever testimony was taken that day, sadly, was not retained in the commission's records.

13. "Wrestling Probe Destined to be Bloomer," *Minneapolis Star*, January 9, 1934. Pfefer's quote was presented in an exaggerated accent in the original article. It has been edited here but the original meaning has been maintained.

14. "Rasslin's on the Level! Yep, State Solons Say So," *Daily News* (New York, NY), January 25, 1934.

15. "Mat Decision Creates Riot," *San Pedro News Pilot*, January 25, 1934; Claude Newman, "Seats Torn Up as Crowd Runs Wild at Match," *Hollywood Citizen News*, January 25, 1934.

16. Henry L. Farrell, "Hooks and Slides," *Selma Times-Journal*, January 29, 1934.

17. Doc Holst, "The Delicate Art of Mayhem," *Detroit Free Press*, August 25, 1940.

18. "Wrestling Peer, Monocle and All, Picturesque Character Whether or Off Padded Canvas," *Battle Creek Enquirer*, July 23, 1933.

19. "Finnegan Is Match Winner," *Lexington Herald*, July 29, 1937; "Wilbur 'Lord Lansdowne' Finran, 54, Pioneer Character Wrestler Succumbs," *Springfield Daily News*, November 30, 1959; Oliver and Johnson, *Storytellers*, 144.

20. Scott Teal, *Raising Cain: From Jimmy Ault to Kid McCoy* (Gallatin: Crowbar Press, 2020), 116, 166.

21. Johnson and Oliver, *Storytellers*, 55–60; "Julius Woronick," *Meriden Journal*, July 23, 1968.

22. "Dean Crushes Zaharias as 11,500 Cheer," *Los Angeles Times*, August 16, 1934. There is always the possibility, even the likelihood, that the 7,000 turned-away number is an exaggeration, but it underscores just how quickly Dean caught on with fans.

23. Johnson and Oliver, *Heroes & Icons*, 182–85.

24. Frank Leavitt to Jack Pfefer, March 11, 1937, Jack Pfefer Wrestling Collection, Hesburgh Libraries, University of Notre Dame; Jon Wertheim, "The Classified Case of the Pro Wrestler Who Helped Beat the Nazis," Sports Illustrated, May 30, 2022. https:// www.si.com/wrestling/2022/05/30/man-mountain-dean-wrestling-hitler-daily -cover; "'Man Mountain' Dean Dies at Work in Yard," *Chattanooga Daily Times*, May 30, 1953.

25. Frank Leavitt to Jack Pfefer, October 3, 1938, Jack Pfefer Wrestling Collection, Hesburgh Libraries, University of Notre Dame.

26. Fleischer, "Forty Years."

27. "Sportographs," *Star Tribune* (Minneapolis, MN), June 21, 1934.

28. Wray, "Wray's Column," September 20, 1934.

29. Yohe, *Facts Within*, 140–41.

30. "Sportographs," *Star Tribune* (Minneapolis, MN), January 24, 1934.

31. Fogarty, "Wrestling Groups."

32. Wilfrid Smith, "Londos Pins Lewis Before Record 35,265," *Chicago Tribune*, September 21, 1934.

33. Wilfrid Smith, "Lewis, Londos Agree on Rules for Title Bout," *Chicago Tribune*, September 19, 1934.

34. "Chicago Bans 'Horse Play' In Mat Game," *Huntsville Times*, January 5, 1933; "Illinois Bans Wrestling After Savoldi-Londos Row," *Marshall News Messenger*, April 11, 1933.

35. Yohe, *Facts Within*, 144. Footage of the match can be seen at https://www.youtube.com/watch?v=IsOZTdEnMBs.

36. "Honest Wrestlers," *Time*, October 1, 1934.

37. Maurice O. Shelvin, "Record 35,265 Crowd Sees Londos Keep Mat Title," *St. Louis Globe-Democrat*, September 21, 1934.

38. "The Wrestling Champs Add a Bit of Clowning to an Ancient Sport," *Washington Post*, April 14, 1935.

39. "Pulitzer Prizes for 1922 Awarded" *New York Times*, May 14, 1923.

40. Johnston, "Cauliflowers."

41. "Wrestling Honest; Curley Testifies," *New York Times*, June 14, 1935; Swanton v. Curley.

42. Johnston, "Cauliflowers."

Chapter 20
The Upset of the Century

1. "Danno Has Crowd Appeal," *Boston Globe*, January 4, 1935; Steve Yohe, "A Study of Danno O'Mahoney" Wrestling Classics, September 23, 2022, http://wrestlingclassics.com/cgi-bin/.ubbcgi/ultimatebb.cgi?ubb=get_topic;f=10;t=001932;p=0. O'Mahony's name was often spelled O'Mahoney in American newspapers.

2. Charles A. Smith, "Did They Double Cross Danno?" *Boxing and Wrestling*, July 1956.

3. Griffin, *Annotated Fall Guys*, 148.

4. "Boxing Moguls Seek Popular O'Mahoney From Wrestling Mat," *Los Angeles Examiner*, April 28, 1935.

5. Schaap, *Cinderella Man*, 224.

6. Smith, "Did They?"

7. James O'Leary, "O'Mahoney Victor Before 40,000," *Boston Globe*, July 31, 1935.

8. Hy Hurwitz, "Danno Takes Title with George's Help," *Boston Globe*, July 31, 1935.

9. "20,000 Cars in Worst Traffic Tie-up for Two Hours After Wrestling Bout," *Boston Herald*, July 31, 1935.

10. Burt Whitman, "40,000 See O'Mahony Beat George—Match Ends in Brawl," *Boston Herald*, July 31, 1935.

11. "O'Mahoney," *New Yorker*, July 20, 1935.

12. Henry McLemore, "Some Doubts About O'Mahoney's Future," *United Press*, October 29, 1935.

13. "O'Mahoney Victor When Shikat Fouls," *Boston Globe*, April 2, 1935; Perry Lewis, "Russian Fouls, Then Pilot Floors Champ," *Philadelphia Inquirer*, September 28, 1935; John Lardner, "Danno Has Trouble with Non-Union Foe," *Buffalo Evening News*, January 10, 1936. Part of the magic of wrestling, or insanity, is that it's hard to know just how scripted some of these events were. In the case of Yvon Robert, at least, it is very possible that his run-in with O'Mahony was staged. It is known that Paul Bowser was considering making Robert champion after O'Mahony, and this match may have been part of that storyline. In the case of Shikat and Kalmikoff, their conflict with O'Mahony was almost certainly genuine.

14. Yohe, *Facts Within*, 155; "O'Mahoney's Purse Held in Houston," *El Paso Herald-Post*, February 8, 1936. To escape the Houston match, O'Mahony resorted to flipping his opponent, a 245-pound wrestler named Whiskers Savage, over his head and out of the ring. Savage was said to have fallen eight feet, landed on his head, been knocked unconscious, and suffered a back injury. It's impossible to know if this is true or part of some post-match press agenting.

15. Sid Mercer, "Mondt Trims Shikat in Private Struggle, But Captures No Title," *New York American*, December 29, 1933.

16. Alvarez v. Shikat and Haft.

17. Alvarez v. Shikat and Haft.

18. Dan Parker, "O'Mahoney's Death Recalls Mat Cross," *Daily Mirror* (New York, NY), November 25, 1950.

19. Jim Jennings, "Shikat Pins Danno to Win Mat Crown," *Daily Mirror* (New York, NY), March 3, 1936; Jon Strickland, email message to author, July 18, 2021; Louis Effrat, "Shikat Regains World Wrestling Crown by Beating O'Mahoney On Garden Mat," *New York Times*, March 3, 1936; "Shikat Beats O'Mahoney To Regain Title," *Chicago Tribune*, March 3, 1936.

20. Dan Parker, "Danno Dealt Out in Double Cross," *Daily Mirror* (New York, NY), March 4, 1936.

21. Parker, "O'Mahoney's Death Recalls."

22. Smith, "Did They?"

23. "Became a Pro in 1924," *New York Times*, March 3, 1936.

24. Parker, "O'Mahoney's Death Recalls."

25. "Danno Loses to Dick Shikat," *Boston Globe*, March 3, 1936.

26. Hy Hurwitz, "'Raw Deal' Shouts Danno's Manager as Title Changes Hands," *Boston Globe*, March 3, 1936.

27. Alvarez v. Shikat and Haft.

28. Griffin, *Annotated Fall Guys*, 159.

29. John Lardner, "Shikat's Ingratitude Pains Mother Trust," *Lincoln Journal Star*, April 28, 1936.

30. Al Haft to Jack Pfefer, October 25, 1934, Jack Pfefer Wrestling Collection, Hesburgh Libraries, University of Notre Dame.

31. Haft to Pfefer, April 10, 1936, Jack Pfefer Wrestling Collection, Hesburgh Libraries, University of Notre Dame.

32. Pfefer to Haft, April 17, 1936, Jack Pfefer Wrestling Collection, Hesburgh Libraries, University of Notre Dame.

Chapter 21
The Game Is on the Level

1. "Rasslin' Crooked? Mr. Curly [sic] Tells Court 'Taint So," *Daily News* (New York, NY), April 24, 1936; "Curley Names Six Big Bosses," *Star Tribune* (Minneapolis), April 24, 1936.

2. Fritz Howell, "Wrestlers Supply Answer to Shakespeare's Gag: What's in a Name?" *Evening Independent* (Massillon, OH), May 1, 1936.

3. Dan Parker, "Mons. Jack Curley Hears No Evil," *Daily Mirror* (New York, NY), April 25, 1936.

4. Dan Parker, "Mr. Shikat Leaves Trust Holding Bag," *Daily Mirror* (New York, NY), undated clipping.

5. Liana Aghajanian, "The Legend of Ali Baba: The Incredible Story of Armenian Genocide Survivor & World Wrestling Champ Harry Ekizian." Ianyanmag.com, April 21, 2014, http://www.ianyanmag.com/the-legend-of-ali-baba-the-incredible-story-of-armenian-genocide-survivor-world-wrestling-champ-harry-ekizian/.

6. Doc Holst, "Baba Grimaces and Foe Loses," *Detroit Free Press*, March 3, 1936.

7. Sam Greene, "Hail to Ali Baba!" *Detroit News*, April 25, 1936.

8. Fritz Howell, "Shikat Back in Court to Learn Who Is His Manager," *Dayton Daily News*, April 27, 1936; "Shikat, Ex-champion Again, Will 'Tell All' About Game Monday, *Star Tribune* (Minneapolis), April 25, 1936.

9. Alvarez v. Shikat and Haft.

10. "Shikat, Ali Baba Wrestle Tonight," *New York Times*, May 5, 1936.

11. Joseph C. Nichols, "Triumph Over Shikat Gains World Mat Championship for Ali Baba," *New York Times*, May 6, 1936.

12. "Funeral On Saturday for Mrs. Ereta Shikat," *Columbus Dispatch*, May 15, 1936; Untitled Article, *Columbus Dispatch*, May 15, 1936; "Wrestler's Wife Burned in Crash," *Columbus Dispatch*, May 5, 1936.

13. "Alvarez and Shikat Parted," *Boston Globe*, May 12, 1936.

14. "Blame 'Natural Causes' for Grappler's Death," *Decatur Daily Review*, June 27, 1936; "Wrestlers Clash!—Death Wins," *Oakland Tribune*, June 26, 1936; "Mike Romano Killed in Wrestling Match," *Miami Herald*, June 26, 1936; "Wrestler Dies During Battle," *Sault Daily Star*, June 26, 1936; "Wrestler Fatally Hurt By Headlock," *Long Island Daily Press*, June 26, 1936; "In This Corner—Ed Contos," *NWA Official Wrestling*, April, 1953; "Fun: Fans Get A Kick Out Of It, Little Realizing That It Is Serious," *Birmingham News*, June 28, 1936; Tom Anderson, "About Doc Burns, Who Died Of Injuries Received In Mat Bout," *Nashville Banner*, September

26, 1932. Romano was one of at least a dozen to die from injuries, infections, and automobile accidents during the 1930s, including the following: Stanley Stasiak, who died from an infection on September 13, 1931, after injuring his arm in a match; Eddie Baker, who died in the ring on May 16, 1937, from a suspected heart attack; Joe Shimkus, who died on May 31, 1934, from a concussion suffered from a fall from the ring; and Doc Burns, who died from complications of an in-ring injury in September 1937. In the days before his death, Burns was visited in his Nashville hospital room by Tom Anderson, a sportswriter from the *Nashville Banner*. When Burns saw him, he smiled weakly and asked, "Well, is this one a frame-up, too?"

Chapter 22
Such a Muddle

1. "Heat Wave Broken, Humid Spell Next," *Philadelphia Inquirer*, July 14, 1937.

2. Curley, "Memoirs," April 1932, 30; Westbrook Pegler, "Fair Enough," *Green Bay Press-Gazette*, October 23, 1936.

3. Teal and Kenyon, *Wrestling*, 105; "A Tin-Eared Cannon? Never!" *New York American*, April 3, 1936.

4. Ed White to Jim Londos, July 12, 1937, Jack Pfefer Wrestling Collection, Hesburgh Libraries, University of Notre Dame.

5. "Wrestling Stakes It All On Nagurski," *Minneapolis Journal*, June 30, 1937.

6. Dan Parker, "Bronko Demanded Dough With Title," *Daily Mirror* (New York), July 9, 1937.

7. Griffin, *Annotated Fall Guys*, 12.

8. Untitled article, *Ironwood Times*, June 4, 1937.

9. Griffin, *Annotated Fall Guys*, 11.

10. Untitled article, *The Evening Independent*, June 14, 1937.

11. Dorothy Dey, "Night and Day," *Miami Tribune*, June 15, 1937.

12. Teal and Kenyon, *Wrestling*, 105.

13. Ed Curley, "Willard to Get $1,000 Per Day with Circus," *San Francisco Examiner*, May 19, 1915.

14. "New York Day by Day," O. O. McIntyre, *Santa Cruz News*, June 7, 1935.

15. "Operate on Jack Curley," *Kansas City Times*, July 7, 1934; "Jack Curley Has Operation," *Daily News* (New York), July 7, 1934.

16. Jack Cuddy, "Dual Upset Rocks Mat," *Los Angeles Times*, June 29, 1935; Bill Henry, "Bill Henry Says," *Los Angeles Times*, June 27, 1935.

17. "At Home with the Jack Curleys," *New York Post*, February 3, 1936.

18. "Storm Halts Heat After 6 Die Here, Delays Trains, Causes $50,000 Fire," *New York Times*, July 13, 1937; "Storm Routs Heat," *Daily Mirror* (New York, NY), July 13, 1937.

19. "Sports World Mourns Death of Jack Curley," *New York American*, undated clipping; "Curley Dies; Sports Promoter"; "Curley's Death Robs Sports of Ace Promoter," *Chicago Daily News*, July 13, 1937.

20. Dan Parker, "Jack Curley's Last Show a Sell-out," *Daily Mirror* (New York), July 15, 1937.

21. Dan Parker, "Curley's Domain Taken by Enemy," *Daily Mirror* (New York), August 14, 1937.

22. Bob Considine, "On the Line," *Daily Mirror* (New York), July 16, 1937.

23. Hornbaker, *Capitol Revolution*, 93; "Curley Estate Small," *New York Times*, July 17, 1937. Curley had famously made and lost several fortunes during his life and the estate he finally left behind was smaller than many had anticipated—less than $10,000 in total value.

24. George Barton, "Sportographs," *Star Tribune* (Minneapolis), August 21, 1939.

25. Johnson and Oliver, *Storytellers*, 31–41.

26. Gallico, *Farewell to Sport*, 312–13.

27. Parker, "Dan Parker Says," *Courier-Post*, December 26, 1940.

28. Riess, "Honesty Is."

Epilogue
Paradigmatically Fake for Real

1. Jeff Leen, *The Queen of the Ring: Sex, Muscles, Diamonds, and the Making of an American Legend* (New York: Atlantic Monthly Press, 2009), 83.

2. Jo Ranson, "Radio Dial Log," *Brooklyn Daily Eagle*, December 2, 1939.

3. Leen, *The Queen*, 155.

4. Thesz and Bauman, *Hooker*, 112–14; John Capouya, *Gorgeous George: The Outrageous Bad-Boy Wrestler Who Created American Pop Culture* (New York: Harper-Collins, 2008), 47–49. Finran was one source of inspiration for George's act. The other was a wrestler from Texas named Sterling "Dizzy" Davis, who threw flowers to the crowd and adopted an effeminate manner. Another possible inspiration, noted by George's biographer John Capouya, was the boastful and eccentric one-time heavyweight boxing champion Max Baer.

5. Capouya, *Gorgeous George*, 117.

6. Capouya, *Gorgeous George*, 260–62, 277–78.

7. Richard Meltzer, *A Whore Just Like the Rest: The Music Writings of Richard Meltzer* (Cambridge: Da Capo Press, 2000), 478.

8. For a full history of the Justice Department's investigation of professional wrestling promoters, see Tim Hornbaker's fine book, *National Wrestling Alliance: The Untold Story of the Monopoly That Strangled Pro Wrestling*.

9. Thesz and Bauman, *Hooker*, 54–55.

10. Scott Beekman, email message to author, September 23, 2022.

11. Theodore Dreiser, *Sister Carrie; Jennie Gerhardt; Twelve Men (Library of America)* (New York: Penguin Books, 1987), 962.

12. Stanley Walker, "Spartacus in Westchester," *New Yorker*, July 16, 1927.

13. W. O. Mcgeehan, "The Menace to American Pugilism," *Vanity Fair*, December 1923.

14. "Dr. B.F. Roller Dead; Retired Surgeon," *New York Times*, April 20, 1933.

15. Jacobs, *Milo*, 192–93.

16. "Wig Waggin," *Omaha Bee-News*, January 10, 1937; "Farmer Burns, King When Rasslin' Was Rasslin', Dies," *Chicago Tribune*, January 10, 1937.

17. "Milestones," *Time*, January 18, 1937.

18. Jan-Christopher Horak, "Cinema Culture in 1920s Berlin," Published March 28, 2014, https://www.cinema.ucla.edu/blogs/archive-blog/2014/03/28/cinema-culture -1920s-berlin; "Fritz Samuel Rachmann," *New York Times,* August 6, 1930; Koegel, 341–45.

19. "Admirers Pay Last Tribute to Wrestler," *Taylor Daily Press*, January 11, 1931.

20. Neal Please, "Mighty Son of Poland: Stanislaus Zbyszko, Polish Americans, and Sport in the Twentieth Century," *Polish American Studies* 74, no. 1 (Spring 2017): 7–26; and Yohe, 188.

21. Zbyszko's co-star in *Night and the City* was Mike Mazurki, the wrestler who most successfully transitioned to Hollywood. Mazurki appeared in well more than 100 films and television episodes, including director Josef von Sternberg's *The Shanghai Gesture* (1941), Cecil B. DeMille's *Unconquered* (1947), and Billy Wilder's *Some Like It Hot* (1959).

22. Marj Heyduck, "Too Many Wives," *Dayton Herald*, January 2,1946.

23. State of California Department of Public Health. Certificate of Death: Kemal Abd-Ur-Rahman, December 29, 1948.

24. Kay Proctor, "'Why, Oh Why Did They Kill Him?' Sobs Widow of Slain Wrestling Fan," *Los Angeles Evening Post-Record*, July 12, 1935; "Lou Daro Gives Widow, Babe, of Slaying Victim, Trust Fund for Support," *Los Angeles Evening Post-Record* July 24, 1935.

25. Lou Daro to Jack Pfefer, October 30, 1936, Jack Pfefer Wrestling Collection, Hesburgh Libraries, University of Notre Dame.

26. "Hearing Before the Special Assembly Committee on Athletic Affairs in California," State of California; "L. A. Rassling Payoff Exposed," *San Francisco Examiner*, April 21, 1939; "Wrestling Promoter's 'Pay-Off' Revealed in California Probe" *St. Louis Star and Times*, May 12, 1939; Tim Hornbaker, "The Daro Era in Los Angeles Ends," Legacy of Wrestling, September 23, 2022, http://www.legacyofwrestling.com/Daro .html.

27. Art Cohn, "Cohn-ing Tower," *Oakland Tribune*, January 15, 1942.

28. "Lou Daro Passes After Long Illness," *Los Angeles Evening Citizen News*, July 12, 1956.

29. "Wrestler Sonnenberg Flattened Again on the Matrimonial Mat," *Minneapolis Star*, April 14, 1940.

30. Thesz and Bauman, *Hooker*, 228.

31. "Sonnnenberg Heard in Suit," *Boston Herald*, April 4, 1933.

32. "Jury Fails to Agree in Case Against Paper," *Berkshire Eagle*, April 13, 1933.

33. Jan Isabelle Fortune, "'Dynamite' Gus on The Morning After," *Dallas Morning News*, May 25, 1930.

34. Billy Sandow to Jack Pfefer, November 7, 1966, Jack Pfefer Wrestling Collection, Hesburgh Libraries, University of Notre Dame.

35. Ralph Friedman, "Billy Sandow, The Jason of Wrestling," *The Sunday Oregonian*, February 12, 1967.

36. "The Final Headlock," *Oakland Tribune*, March 30, 1948.

37. Alan Ward, "On Second Thought," *Oakland Tribune*, December 18, 1946.

38. Thesz and Bauman, *Hooker*, 157.

39. "Ed 'Strangler' Lewis Sees Benefits from Blindness," *Wellsville Daily Reporter*, May 2, 1964.

40. A.J. Liebling, "A Reporter At Large—Pull His Whiskers!" *New Yorker*, July 8, 1939, 57–65.

41. "Wrestlers Wear Strange Costumes for A New Gag," *Life*, April 29, 1940.

42. Jack Miley, "Jake's Juggernauts," *Collier's*, October 22, 1938.

43. Mitchell, *My Ears*, 104–5.

44. A.J. Liebling, "A Reporter."

45. "Mat Promoter at Three New York Clubs Admits His Wrestling a Fake," *New York Enquirer*, November 6, 1938.

46. "Paramount Newsreel—In A Class by Himself!" https://filmlibrary.sherman-grinberg.com/?s=file=39948.

47. Jack Miley, "Jake's Juggernauts," *Collier's*, October 22, 1938.

48. Mitchell, *My Ears*, 108.

49. Jack Pfefer to Sam Muchnick, February 21, 1952, Collection of Tim Hornbaker.

50. "Death of Jack Pfefer Verified, Nobody Else Like Him!" *Ring Wrestling*, undated clipping.

51. "'Wrestling Is Better Today,' says Mondt," *Newark Star-Ledger*, July 8, 1969.

52. "'Wrestling Is Better Today,'" *Newark Star-Ledger*, July 8, 1969.

53. Charley Rose, "Jack Curley in Class by Himself as Promoter," *Ring Wrestling*, February 1965.

Bibliography

Allen, Arly. *Jess Willard: Heavyweight Champion of the World (1915–1919).* Jefferson, NC: McFarland & Company, 2017.

Asinof, Eliot. *Eight Men Out.* New York: Henry Holt & Company, 1987.

Beekman, Scott. *Ringside: A History of Professional Wrestling in America.* Westport: Praeger Publishers, 2006.

Betts, John Rickards. *America's Sporting Heritage, 1850–1950.* Reading: Addison-Wesley Publishing Company, 1974.

Bowser, Eileen. *History of the American Cinema: The Transformation of Cinema, 1907–1915.* Berkeley: University of California Press, 1990.

Brady, William. *Showman.* New York: E. P. Dutton & Company, 1937.

Broun, Heywood. "Sport for Art's Sake." In *Bohemians, Bootleggers, Flappers, & Swells: The Best of Early "Vanity Fair,"* edited by Graydon Carter. New York: Penguin Press, 2014.

Burns, Martin. *The Life Work of "Farmer" Burns.* Omaha: A.J. Kuhlman, 1911.

Byington, Lewis Francis, ed. *The History of San Francisco, Volume I.* Chicago: S.J. Clarke Publishing Company, 1931.

Capouya, John. *Gorgeous George: The Outrageous Bad-Boy Wrestler Who Created American Pop Culture.* New York: HarperCollins, 2008.

Chapman, Mike. *The Life and Legacy of Frank Gotch: King of the Catch-as-Catch-Can Wrestlers.* Boulder, CO: Paladin Press, 2008.

Churchwell, Sarah. *Careless People: Murder, Mayhem, and the Invention of "The Great Gatsby."* New York: Penguin Books, 2013.

Cochran, Charles. *Secrets of a Showman.* London: William Heinemann, Ltd., 1925.

DeArment, Robert K. *Bat Masterson: The Man and the Legend.* Norman: University of Oklahoma Press, 1979.

Dreiser, Theodore. *Sister Carrie; Jennie Gerhardt; Twelve Men (Library of America).* New York: Penguin Books, 1987.

Evensen, Bruce. *When Dempsey Fought Tunney: Heroes, Hokum, and Storytelling in the Jazz Age.* Knoxville: University of Tennessee, 1996.

Fullerton, Hugh. *Two Fisted Jeff.* Chicago: Consolidated Book Publishers, 1929.

Gallico, Paul. *Farewell to Sport.* Lincoln: University of Nebraska Press, 2008.

Glennon, Lorraine, ed. *The 20ᵗʰ Century: An Illustrated History of Our Lives and Times*. North Dighton: JG Press, 2000.

Goldstein, Judith. *Inventing Great Neck: Jewish Identity and the American Dream*. New Brunswick: Rutgers University Press, 2006.

Gorn, Elliot J., and Warren Goldstein. *A Brief History of American Sports*. 2nd ed. Urbana: University of Illinois Press, 1993.

Griffin, Marcus. *Wise Guy: James J. Johnston: A Rhapsody in Fistics*. New York: Vanguard Press, 1933.

———. *The Annotated Fall Guys: The Barnums of Bounce*. Annotated by Steve Yohe and Scott Teal. Gallatin, TN: Crowbar Press, 2019.

Hackenschmidt, George. *The Russian Lion*. Unpublished manuscript in possession of author.

———. *The Way to Live: Health & Physical Fitness*. London: Health & Strength Limited, 1908.

Harris, Neil. *Humbug: The Art of P. T. Barnum*. Boston: Little, Brown, and Company, 1973.

Hauser, Thomas. *The Boxing Scene*. Philadelphia: Temple University Press, 2009.

Hawkins, James J. *Mabray and the Mikes*. Little Rock, AR: Democrat Print and Lithographing, 1910.

Heffelfinger, W. W. *That Was Football*. New York: Barnes, 1954.

Hewitt, Mark S. *Catch Wrestling: A Wild and Wooly Look at the Early Days of Pro Wrestling in America*. Boulder, CO: Paladin Press, 2005.

Hitchcock, Edward, and Richard Nelligan. *Wrestling, Catch-as-Catch-Can Style*. New York: American Sports Publishing Company, 1898.

Hornbaker, Tim. *Capitol Revolution: The Rise of the McMahon Wrestling Empire*. Toronto: ECW Press, 2015.

———. *National Wrestling Alliance: The Untold Story of the Monopoly That Strangled Pro Wrestling*. Toronto: ECW Press, 2007.

Jacobs, Max. *Milo and the Halitosis Kid*. Unpublished manuscript in possession of author.

———. *The Role of the Promoter in Professional Wrestling*. Unpublished manuscript in possession of author.

Jares, Joe. *Whatever Happened to Gorgeous George?* Gallatin, TN: Crowbar Press, 2015.

Johnson, Jack. *Jack Johnson in the Ring and Out*. Detroit: Gale Research Company, 1975.

Johnson, Steven, and Greg Oliver. *The Pro Wrestling Hall of Fame: Heroes & Icons*. Toronto: ECW Press, 2012.

Johnson, Steven, and Greg Oliver. *The Pro Wrestling Hall of Fame: The Storytellers*. Toronto: ECW Press, 2019.

Johnston, Alva. *The Legendary Mizners*. New York: Farrar, Straus & Young, 1953.

Kahn, Roger. *A Flame of Pure Fire: Jack Dempsey and the Roaring '20s*. New York: HarperCollins, 2012.

Keefe, Rose. *The Man Who Got Away: The Bugs Moran Story*. Nashville: Cumberland House, 2005.

Kent, Graeme. *A Pictorial History of Wrestling*. London: Spring Books, 1968.

Koegel, John. *Music in German Immigrant Theatre, New York City, 1840–1940*. Rochester: University of Rochester Press, 2009.

Koszarksi, Richard. *History of the American Cinema: An Evening's Entertainment, 1915–1928*. Berkeley: University of California Press, 1990.

Lang, Arne K. *The Nelson-Wolgast Fight and the San Francisco Boxing Scene*. Jefferson, NC: McFarland & Company, 2012.

Lardner, John. *White Hopes and Other Tigers*. New York: J. B. Lippincott Company, 1947.

Leen, Jeff. *The Queen of the Ring: Sex, Muscles, Diamonds, and the Making of an American Legend*. New York: Atlantic Monthly Press, 2009.

Leider, Emily W. *Dark Lover: The Life and Death of Rudolph Valentino*. New York: Farrar, Straus, and Giroux, 2003.

Lewis, Ed. Unpublished manuscript in possession of author.

Liebling, A. J. *The Telephone Booth Indian*. United States: Crown, 2008.

Lindberg, Richard C. *Gangland Chicago: Criminality and Lawlessness in the Windy City*. Lanham: Rowman & Littlefield, 2016.

Lundin, Hjalmar. *On the Mat and Off: Memoirs of a Wrestler*. New York: Albert Bonnier Publishing House, 1937.

Martin, Carol. *Dance Marathons: Performing American Culture in the 1920s and 1930s*. Jackson, MS: University Press of Mississippi, 1994.

Maurer, David W. *The Big Con: The Story of the Confidence Men*. New York: Anchor Press, 1999.

McCallum, John D. *The World Heavyweight Boxing Championship: A History*. Radnor: Chilton Book Company, 1974.

Meltzer, Richard. *A Whore Just Like the Rest: The Music Writings of Richard Meltzer*. Cambridge: Da Capo Press, 2000.

Meyers, John C. *Wrestling: From Antiquity to Date*. St. Louis: Von Hoffman Press, 1931.

Miller, Donald L. *Supreme City: How Jazz Age Manhattan Gave Birth to Modern America*. New York: Simon & Schuster, 2014.

Mitchell, Joseph. *My Ears Are Bent*. New York: Vintage Books, 2008.

Mitchell, Kevin. *Jacobs Beach: The Mob, the Fight, the Fifties*. New York: Pegasus Books, 2010.

Morton, Charles W. *It Has Its Charms*. Philadelphia: Lippincott, 1966.

Nickell, Joe. *Secrets of the Sideshows*. Lexington, KY: University of Kentucky Press, 2005.

Oliver, Greg, and Steven Johnson. *Pro Wrestling Hall of Fame: The Heels*. Toronto: ECW Press, 2007.

Page, Joseph S. *Nonpareil Jack Dempsey: Boxing's First World Middleweight Champion*. Jefferson, NC: McFarland & Company, Inc., 2019.

Portnoy, Eddy. *Bad Rabbi: And Other Strange but True Stories from the Yiddish Press*. Stanford, CA: Stanford University Press, 2018.

Race, Harley, with Gerry Tritz. *King of the Ring*. New York: Sports Publishing, 2004.

Reading, Amy. *The Mark Inside: A Perfect Swindle, a Cunning Revenge, and a Small History of the Big Con.* New York: Alfred A. Knopf, 2012.

Roberts, Randy. *Papa Jack: Jack Johnson and the Era of White Hopes.* New York: The Free Press, 1983.

Samuels, Charles. *The Magnificent Rube: The Life and Gaudy Times of Tex Rickard.* New York: McGraw-Hill, 1957.

Sante, Luc. *Low Life.* New York: Farrar, Straus, and Giroux, 1991.

Schaap, Jeremy. *Cinderella Man.* New York: Houghton Mifflin, 2005.

Schwartz, David G. *Roll the Bones: The History of Gambling.* Sheridan: Gotham Books, 2006.

Singer, Ben. *Melodrama and Modernity: Early Sensational Cinema and Its Contexts.* New York: Columbia University Press, 2001.

Smith, Gene, and Jayne Barry Smith, eds. *The Police Gazette.* New York: Simon and Schuster, 1972.

Stevens, Dana. *Camera Man: Buster Keaton, The Dawn of Cinema, and the Invention of the Twentieth Century.* New York: Atria Books, 2022.

Stulman Dennett, Andrea. *Weird & Wonderful: The Dime Museum in America.* New York: New York University Press, 1997.

Teal, Scott. *Raising Cain: From Jimmy Ault to Kid McCoy.* Gallatin: Crowbar Press, 2020.

———. *Wrestling Archive Project: Classic 20th Century Mat Memories; Volume 1.* Gallatin: Crowbar Press, 2015.

Teal, Scott, and J Michael Kenyon. *Wrestling in the Garden: The Battle for New York.* Gallatin: Crowbar Press, 2017.

Tennenbaum, Ray. *Sleeperhold.* Unpublished manuscript available at http://www.ray-field.com/wrestly.

Thesz, Lou, with Kit Bauman. *Hooker.* Gallatin: Crowbar Press, 2011.

Ward, Geoffrey C. *Unforgivable Blackness: The Rise and Fall of Jack Johnson.* New York: Vintage Books, 2006.

Wheeler, Jimmy. *The Italian Temper: The Story of How Alphonse "Babe" Bisignano Turned Out All Right.* Eat Sleep Wrestle, 2020.

White, Richard D. *Kingfish: The Reign of Huey P. Long.* United Kingdom: Random House Publishing Group, 2009.

Williams, Thomas Harry. *Huey Long.* New York: Vintage Books, 1981.

Wilson, Charles M. *The Magnificent Scufflers: Revealing the Great Days when America Wrestled the World.* Brattleboro: The Stephen Greene Press, 1959.

Yohe, Steve. *Ed "Strangler" Lewis: Facts Within a Myth.* Vancleave: Ramble House, 2015.

Ziajka, Alan. *Lighting the City, Changing the World: A History of the Sciences at the University of San Francisco.* San Francisco: University of San Francisco, 2014.

Index

Page numbers in italics indicate photographs